My Body Is My Own

A GUIDE For Parents
THE COMPLETE CHILD PROTECTION HANDBOOK

**By
Renowned
Child Protection and Recovery Specialist**

Ty Ritter

Table of Contents

Notes:

DEDICATION

This book is dedicated to my wife Christine and my daughter Laury, for their years of fear and uncertainty, and to all the children lost forever.

Most Special Thank You

James Bruner and Elizabeth Stevens, for their endless support and guidance, and to Bob and Judy Daggs, for without whose deep moral concern for the children and generous support, this book and so much more, would not be possible.

Notes:

I lived at all

In some way, however small and secret, each of us is a little hurt, a little angry. We are all a little lonely, crying to be heard and understood. Never entirely understanding someone else, mattering not how hard we try. Each of us remaining partially a stranger, even to those who love us, mattering not how hard they try. Consequently, an attempt to entirely understand those not close to us is and always will be a fruitless effort.

Why is it that the cruel are weak, forcing their will on the innocent? Why is it that gentleness is found in the strong? I have learned that those who do not know fear are not brave, for courage is the capacity to confront evil.

I am able now to more understand many others, as I see them for what they are by their foul deeds. I have come to realize that which is most important of all, fulfillment, comes only when I push my intellect and heart to the farthermost reaches of which I am capable in this fight against wickedness. For the purpose of life is to matter, to count, to stand for something, to make a difference that I lived at all.

Ty Ritter

Notes:

Forward

The information and facts presented in this book are based, in large part, on the actual experiences of my wife Christine, myself and members of our recovery teams. The "Facts" are going to scare the hell out of you, but at the same time, give you the strength that only knowledge can bring. Between the covers of this book, I have given parents the vital information needed in today's society to protect their children from the atrocities forced every day on someone's child. You will find the pages within this book steeped in solid, accurate and complete information. I am supplying you with the knowledge and guidance needed regarding the two most important subjects to parents today: child kidnap prevention and child sexual abuse prevention. Included is verified information from victims, and others involved. You will discover within these pages a combination of professional advice and a great deal of old fashioned common sense, offered by myself and other child safety experts. Pamphlets, brochures, booklets and some books covering only one or another of these subjects do exist. This is partially the reason I have a driving desire to introduce parents to the one complete parental guidebook to turn to for all the answers.

My objective is not to be politically correct, nor do I intend to be sensitive toward politicians or police agencies. Neither will I dance around, soft shoe, sugar coat or give you any false sense of security. This book has been written in a degree of anger, which, as you read on, you will not only understand, but you yourself will also become angered. My objective is to put before you the most accurate information and tools available. After having read this book, you will know how you can protect your child from predators. You'll also know what to do if something does happen, what to expect from governmental agencies, and whom you can turn to. You're going to learn the facts, and how tragic the facts really are. Most importantly, you're going to learn what you, as an individual parent can do to help yourself.

There will be those who read "My Body Is My Own" and act on it, and there will be those who read, yet take no action. I file them away under possible future statistics, or is it victims?

Notes:

Notes:

Introduction

Over 200 years of American evolution has left many of our values depreciated, and in some cases totally bankrupt. Much of this depreciation has occurred by indirect means. This is called disparagement (taking away, lessening, or lowering in value). Everyone has opinions as to how this has happened. Some say it's the movies and TV, while others lay the blame on modern music. Some will point to greed and fear, or maybe it's the fault of well-meaning politicians. How about all of the above? Even the experts are baffled, or at minimum, can't agree. The particular values I am referring to are those that allow pedophiles to infiltrate our society to the degree that they can now openly and proudly announce their agenda. Values that will free a man, having served only four years behind bars after having kidnapped, raped, sodomized, chopped off the arms of a young girl with an axe, leaving her in the desert for dead. Values that turn a blind eye to kidnapped American children being sold into sexual slavery in foreign countries.

Since disparage is the new, seemingly incurable cancer of the day, it is up to you as parents to protect your children. That's where this book, a guide for parents to your children's safety, can help. Unlike a doctor, I cannot cure a cancer. However, you can protect yourself and lessen the risk of being attacked by the disease. "My Body Is My Own" can help you protect your child and lessen the risk of your child being attacked by something just as terrifying as cancer, a pedophile.

Something of great importance that you will read again later on is: this book is not about being a Republican or a Democrat. Since in my career I have protected both party members, I consider myself a "Republicrat." Nor is this book about being a Hindu, Jew, Christian, Buddhist, Muslim, or even an Atheist, it is a book about protecting all children. If you feel as I do, regarding the safety of all children, you are welcome in my home... always.

I recovered my first kidnapped child over 30 years ago. My wife Christine has been my recovery partner since before our marriage in 1981. Christine is an Australian born redhead who served in Vietnam with the USO, entertaining troops. She has also worked behind and in front of movie cameras doing commercials, television and motion pictures. Christine is currently a member of the Screen Actors Guild. I am a former Marine and have been a bodyguard to presidential candidates, royalty, CEO's and movie stars throughout most of my career.

Together, Christine and I have owned and operated a child kidnap recovery network and anti terrorist and bodyguard school, which trained and assisted private corporations, including law enforcement, in preparation for the Olympics. I have also assisted State and Federal and foreign agencies in a private sector capacity, instructing and technical advising. I formed a nonprofit organization/charity called Project Child Save (PCS) a children's kidnap recovery network. We specialize in the recovery of children who have been kidnapped from the United States and other countries and sold into sexual slavery all over the world. [http://www.projectchildsave.org] In spite of multiple successful recoveries and an adviser to shows such as Geraldo's and having been featured on many radio and television talk shows, including "Dr. Phil", as well as invited guest speakers for several organizations, PCS is struggling to survive, due to a lack of funding.

Normally I do not get involved in parental kidnappings unless absolute proof of child sexual abuse has occurred, and court documents verifying child custody rights are produced to our satisfaction and to that of our attorney's satisfaction.

Most of the work done on behalf of kidnapped children over the years by my recovery teams has been a well-guarded secret, for security and safety reasons. The kidnap and sale of children has become very big business in many countries, in particular, countries in South America and now Europe. When I first became involved in recoveries, a blond haired, blue-eyed girl sold for approximately $15,000 to $20,000. The sale price today has reached $100,000 in some cases. Due to our success and the devastation we have left behind while recovering children, we have made many enemies. My family has had to relocate many times due to threats against us. In 1977, I was the victim of an assassination attempt, shot and wounded by a sniper while walking my dog. There are those in South America and a few other places that would like to see us dead for our efforts to stop child trafficking and child pornography.

Since Christine and I have been involved in the safety and well being of children, and have experienced first hand the devastation to the victims and parents alike, I have been asked for years to write this book. My name does not have the alphabet behind it, however I believe "My Body Is My Own" to be of special interest and invaluable to parents due to my decades of experience in the trenches and the fact that I have worked side by side with police departments and governmental agencies attempting to locate and recover missing children. Hence, I know their strong points and their shortcomings, and I am not going to hold anything back.

Notes:

CHAPTER 1

PREDATOR'S PROFILE

At the precise moment the telephone began ringing, the front door chimes announced a visitor. There I was, caught between the two with that look, you know the look, and we've all been there, just for a second that look of minor panic. At that moment, my wife Christine entered the room moving in the direction of the front door. As she walked, she motioned me toward the ringing telephone, giving me a look of, "Are you deaf", while rolling her eyes. At the front door stood a married couple in their early 30s, both with blonde hair. Christine's first thought was that they looked Scandinavian, and then like so many times before, Christine recognized the intense pain and fear in the woman's eyes. As Christine showed them into the living room, her stomach knotted. Another recovery, Christine thought as she clenched her hands at her sides. After a quick telephone conversation with Huntington Beach police Lt. Dennis Hahn, I entered the living room saying, "You must be the Magnusons, I was just talking on the phone with Lt. Hahn. He told me he had recommended us to you, and that you would be coming by."

The scenario you just read is one true example of how we become involved in the recovery of a kidnapped child. Whether we are recommended by an individual police officer, attorneys, child find organizations, or other parents we have helped in the past, we are usually discovered through word-of-mouth. My wife Christine and I have witnessed many missing children cases that have the earmarks of the victim having been taken out of the United States. By "earmarks" I am referring to the facts surrounding a missing child, such as no one

1

saw anything, the child is simply gone, (missing without a trace) which is often the case when professional kidnappers and/or child traffickers are involved. In addition, another alerting "earmark" that child traffickers may be involved is that certain children are worth more on the market than others. An example would be a female child between the ages of two and six, with blonde hair and blue eyes. She will bring the highest price. It rips our hearts out when a child is missing and many of the signs point to the possibility the child was kidnapped by slave traders. We cannot and will not approach parents, alerting them of the possibility that their child may have been taken out of the country. There are many reasons as to why we cannot make the first contact. It would be considered ambulance chasing and self-serving by many. Also, there is no absolute proof that the child was kidnapped for the purpose of sale into sexual slavery in a foreign country. Another consideration is that there are no guarantees regarding locating and recovering the child. These are some of the reasons I have chosen to write this book. I hope that parents will use this book as a guide, helping to insure the safety and protection of their children against abduction and sexual abuse. The information in this book will be extremely valuable if a child has been abducted, assisting parents in locating and safely returning the child.

I have chosen Predator's Profile as the first chapter for a very good reason: **there are over four million child molesters living in the United States today.** Many experts, including myself, consider that a very conservative number. The average child molester will sexually abuse between 30 and 60 children before being caught, establishing a lifetime record of as many as 380 children. One out of every three girls and one out of every seven boys will be molested at least once before age 18. There is on average one child molester per square mile in the United States and that number grows daily. If you live in a county of 3,000 square miles, it is possible and most probable that you are living among sexual offenders. Three thousand (3,000) child molesters. California alone has convicted an estimated sixty-three thousand (63,000) first time offenders for child molestation, and that number grows daily. Statistics clearly show (prove) that these particular types of offenders are four times more likely than any other violent offenders to recommit their crimes.

I believe that you as parents or guardians need a strong arsenal to fight this war. And it is a war! Your arsenal needs to be made up from knowledge, which means accurate information about the war and the tools available to you to fight it, but it is most important to know and recognize the enemy! In this war, your enemy is the pedophiles who are stalking children in countries all over the world, including the United States. The battlegrounds are parks, shopping malls, beaches, campgrounds and public swimming pools, neighbor's yards, corner stores, our own yards, the Internet, libraries and even our schools and churches. The list does not end there. As a matter of fact, there doesn't seem to be an end to the battlegrounds. I have chosen to label it a war because this worldwide scourge has all the attributes of war, and as in war, in the final analysis even our souls are violated. Pedophilia is a crime against humanity!

Gathering from our own experiences and from those of other experts, I have compiled the most up-to-date predator's profile available to date. However, due to our ever changing society and the inevitable new inventions, predators are and do evolve continuously. Hopefully, responsible adults will seek out new accurate information regularly. **It's your responsibility!**

Who is a pedophile?

Webster's dictionary defines a pedophile as one "affected" with pedophilia. So what is pedophilia? Webster's describes it as "Sexual perversion" in which children are the preferred sexual objects. Now, as I see it, this person would be described as a "Pedophiliac" [My word]. We are all familiar with the "iacs", you know, like necrophiliacs and a few other maniacs, so the question is, how do we know who is and who isn't a "pedophiliac?" Actually, this is a very easy question to answer! Pedophiliacs are doctors, lawyers, priests and everyone in between. Shockingly, sometimes even some parents are pedophiliacs. I guess it isn't such an easy question to answer after all. Is there anyone we can trust? Of course there is! You can totally trust everyone, except maybe… the plumber, teachers, bus drivers, coaches, salesman, and sad to say, even some clergymen and policemen, etc. Is there a specific race of people who are pedophiles more than another race? **Absolutely Not!** Pedophilia is a psychological condition that does not involve racial preference and it does not necessarily necessitate action. There are pedophiles you might consider great neighbors, decent peo-

3

ple, who would never normally harm anyone for any reason. Some of these individuals realize they have a problem and go to great lengths to avoid situations that may lead to sexual contact with children. There are also those pedophiles willing to spend much of their time and money in pursuit of sexual gratification from children. What you cannot depend on is the possibility of the danger in unforeseen situations and a moment of weakness in those pedophiles attempting to fight off their perverted sexual desires. What you can depend on is that under the right circumstances your child could be in jeopardy. Something else you can depend on: pedophiles are like everyone else in that they are connected in one way or another to corporations, religions, special groups, governmental agencies and especially organizations dealing with children. On the other hand, there are many pedophiles you would not consider decent people. They are the ones who do not try to rationalize their motivations, or their actions. They don't care, nor do they seem to be inhibited at all by the possibility that they may seriously harm a child physically or psychologically. They just don't care.

Are you paranoid yet? Maybe just a little bit? I hope so! Just a little bit. That's what you have to be in this day and age "a little paranoid." It is also very important that you teach your children to be "a little paranoid." I call it "protective paranoia." Sure, there are many people you can trust, and while you're trusting them, you must know everything possible about your child's whereabouts and safety at all times. No exceptions, no excuses. Your child's well-being is up to you! For the safety of your children, you may have to modify your lives. Does that sound extreme to you? Actually, it's not as bad as it sounds. We adjusted our lives for our daughter Laury's well-being. Christine and I made the decision to operate our business from our home.

This gave us every opportunity to be there for Laury, wherever "there" was. We were able to drop Laury off and pick her up from school daily and did so with few exceptions until she was finished with high school. Because we were able to take complete control of our work schedule, Christine and I were present at every function and event our daughter was involved with. I am not saying everyone can do what we did. On the other hand, you will probably be very surprised at how much more you can do regarding your child's safety. As you read on, I guarantee you'll find an astonishing amount of informa-

4

tion regarding your children's well being and the answers to all of your questions.

What makes them tick?

This question is not as complicated as it sounds. It's pretty much black and white, although there are some that do definitely try to make it complex. Some of the experts will tell you that pedophiliacs can't help themselves. Some "experts" explain that most sexual offenders were molested as children themselves and a force beyond their control drives them like demons to abuse defenseless children as they were abused. I do not understand that, as I have spoken with many pedophiles and to the number, each and every one of them has claimed that they were in full control of their actions. Again, you see, we do not understand, as they put it. Most pedophiles believe, or claim to believe, that there is absolutely nothing wrong with what they do. "It is perfectly natural." Now, I have but one thing to say about that: "That is beyond the shadow of any doubt, the dumbest thing I've heard all day, and I've been up since 5:00 am." These spewers of wisdom also claim that the children they molest are not hurt, physically or mentally. Of course, they don't consider what they do to children molestation. Again, we do not understand. "Children like, want and are entitled to sex." Ask any pedophiliac.

I have read what seems like tons of literature that keeps pouring out from organized groups of pedophiles. Also, a great deal of my time has been spent reading personal letters from pedophiliacs directed towards advocacy groups and others seeking to stop or at least disrupt the demonic activities of child molesters. Reading their letters allows us to get into their heads a little bit. Not without expert assistance, of course. Our findings are interesting in their simplicity! The problem isn't that these individuals are unable to find mates, or that they were necessarily molested themselves as children. As I gathered the facts, I discovered a great many pedophiles are married, have girlfriends, or are even engaged to be married. It may surprise you as it did me, that most pedophiles we dealt with seem to become offended when asked if they molest children because they themselves were molested. Many interviewees became even more offended when asked if they are unable to relate to sexual partners within their own age group. They also choose not to refer to non-participants of adult child sex as being

5

"Straight", due to the fact that they consider themselves "Straight." Nor do pedophiles like to be categorized along with child molesters. The reasoning behind that could be a whole other book. Their blood seemed to reach a boiling point when while interviewing them I used words like molestation, force, rape or any other descriptions that denoted that the child was not a willing participant. Believe me when I say that they were frequently visually upset. In some of their own words... " She was asking for it." " He said he liked it." " They always tell me they're having fun." "I give them something they don't get at home, **Real Love**." In each of the referenced quotes, none of the children being referred to was over the age of nine years old. The pedophiles are right, you know, we don't understand! We especially don't understand when pedophiliacs tell us that they live for the hunt; relish the control, daydream about the creamy smooth young skin, knowing that they are the first to have this "Unsoiled love partner." Hard to imagine he may be referring to an eleven-year-old girl, or just as probable, a four-year-old boy. Yes it's true: they would vomit out these pearls of wisdom faster than I could ask the questions. Oh, and what seemed to be a favorite: "I'm teaching them the right way to have sex."

Pedophiles can stop if they choose, but why? "There's nothing wrong with what we do, it's perfectly natural." In order to answer the original question, what makes them tick, you have to ask another question: are perversions an illness, or a choice? Many experts choose illness and defense attorneys employ many of those experts. That defense doesn't seem to hold much water! Jurors don't buy it, nor can I think of the time a judge fell for it. Of course there's the exception to every rule. I'm sure it has happened, you know, when those clever defense attorneys twist and turn it until they make it work. There are also those judges that never seem to make the right decisions. For example, the judge who ruled, "A prostitute cannot be raped." Thank God that those judges are few and far between. Ironically, pedophiles will only allow themselves to be labeled sick when they're facing time in prison.

Men are the pedophiliacs I have dealt with the most, simply because they are the most common, and the most willing to gloat. Because of their willingness to brag, men are also more easily enticed into conversation about adult child sex and child porn, specifically their own escapades. It seems to have something to do with conquest, or notches in their belts. Consequently, you'll find most of my references and examples are from men. I believe strongly that pedophiles make choices and many experts agree with me, or maybe it's me agreeing with them. My beliefs are based mainly on my conversations and numerous interviews with pedophiles. In most of my conversations with them, they were led to believe that my team member and I were also pedophiles. This encouraged a sense of security. They had no worry of guilt, or threat of consequence. I found that many of the child molesters I interviewed, or had conversations with, to be highly intelligent individuals. However, it is important that you realize that this perversion covers a wide spectrum of people. Some are of extremely high intellect, while others have the **IQ of an ice cube**. I have dealt with everyone from vagrants to corporate executives, from the poorest of the poor, to the richest of the rich! I find it difficult to believe that pedophilia is an illness when these individuals themselves agree, and will claim vehemently, that their sexual preference is just that: a preference. When they exclaim; "I prefer tits just starting to form" and "What turns me on is a little tiny patch of baby fine pubic hair, just coming in." One pedophile grinned at me defiantly as he announced, "There's nothing tighter in this world or feels better than a seven-year-old's pussy." Each of these quotes comes from what I would describe as middle class individuals, save one, who was definitely upper class, that is, as far as education and money could take him. It is very clear to me that they're making choices. This is my opinion. Because I say it doesn't make it fact, however, it is an educated opinion, an opinion from the trenches, and many experts agree. There are those pedophiles that claim they cannot deal with adult relationships, but they're few and far between. They claim they cannot communicate, nor can they become sexually aroused by another adult. Some experts call that an illness. Other experts say it is simply fear and the lack of self-confidence and/or that their equals intimidate them. Both expert opinions are, of course followed by, "stemming" from etc, etc, etc. My opinion comes from dealing with pedophiles face-to-face, on the streets at their level and in their territory, where they feel safe and comfortable. I believe them to be amoral individuals, "stemming" from a lack of self-discipline, integrity and scruples, completely bankrupt of moral fiber. Also having an overflowing abundance of the attitude "I don't care who I hurt or how many lives I ruin."

Pedophiles believe their acts are "perfectly natural," but breaking the law. A favorite argument of pedophiliacs is: "When their menstrual cycle begins, that's nature saying they're ready." They do acknowledge that they are breaking the law, "Man's Law," as they put it. Most of the predators I have talked with agreed that it is wrong to break the law. So tell me, if they are ill, but admit to breaking the law, are they still not making choices? Predators, who sexually abuse and sometimes kill children, are cowards with ice-cold hearts and a void soul.

What is their MO?

Let's put it in everyday language: How do pedophiles (child molesters) operate? Better yet, how do they pick and choose their victims? That depends on individual circumstance. If a predator has regular access to your child, for example, an uncle, aunt, or maybe a teacher, then there is a situation where the pedophile has no need to prowl the streets. A neighbor, on the other hand, has to take a little more time and be ever more cautious. He will more than likely try to create a situation where he has access to your child. He may invite them to his house for a swim, or be the good neighbor who offers to baby-sit. There are also those pedophiles that have the access and opportunity, yet choose not to operate so close to home. These individuals will prowl the parks, libraries, malls, or kid hangouts in other neighborhoods, often in cities other than where they reside. Adding to the list, there is the pedophile that falls into the right place at the right time. An example might be, your child decides to take a shortcut through an unlighted vacant lot where a vagrant pedophiliac has homesteaded. I know, I know, what is an unsupervised child doing out on the streets after dark? Don't ask me, it's your kid! Problem is, I see it all the time.

Those pedophiles not having regular access to children, cruise areas and establishments frequented by children. They prefer cruising in vehicles rather than on foot, lending to covering larger areas and quick getaways when spotted by an observant adult. Some pedophiles are satisfied temporarily by masturbating while observing children. Others get temporary satisfaction simply by quickly touching, or by being touched by a child. I have dubbed the next pedophile the "NetPed."

This one uses a computer to cruise the Internet chat rooms and blogs. He's looking for that child who wants to engage in communication. The "Net Ped" will often quickly enter risqué conversation trying to determine if he has discovered a plausible target or not. Of course, most of the time the conversation does not start-off risqué, but will turn to sex rather quickly. The pedophile will see to that. He's an expert with plenty of experience and doesn't want to waste any time on a kid that's not willing to talk about sex. Pedophiles have claimed to me that they can jump into a chat room and know within five minutes which child to target. They have also claimed that they have a better than 65 percent chance that the child they chose will eventually meet with them.

Every child loves a puppy or a kitten. Pedophiliacs know that and depend on it. They will use photographs of puppies or kittens and have been known to use real animals to lure children away as well. Usually puppies are the favorite lure, along with promises of money and often a free puppy, or both. "If you will only help me find my lost puppies, you can have one to take home for your very own. I'm so worried, won't you please help me?" Generally, but not always, pedophiliacs will try to coax your child into coming with them willingly, using whatever promises have worked for them in the past. Pedophiles will spend hours in a mall following parents and their children. Stalking, watching, waiting for the moment your eyes are busy elsewhere, or your child has wandered. It only takes a moment!

Christine and I recovered a child that was kidnapped on Christmas day in 1982. The victim was a two and a half-year-old girl, playing with her new toys inside the family's fenced front yard. Her mother kept a close eye on her daughter from the front porch, until her telephone rang. By the time she returned from answering a wrong number call, her daughter was gone. The mother later estimated the time it took to answer the call was approximately 45 seconds. It was later determined that the telephone call was more than likely a ploy to distract the mother. In this particular case the child was kidnapped by professionals, then sold into sexual slavery in South America. My wife and I specialize in recovering kidnapped children that are forced or sold into sexual slavery, which includes child pornography in foreign countries.

Children are kidnapped every day from the United States. Your first line of defense is **YOU!** It is unwise ... allow me to re-phrase that, it is downright stupid, to leave the security and well being of your child to anyone else, including the police. You must always keep in mind: anyone else could be the enemy. Pedophiles have been known to seek out employment that purposely puts them in direct contact with children. One example would be driving a school bus, another would be the lifeguard at your neighborhood pool. Predators will also commonly travel great distances, thinking nothing of driving to other cities and counties searching for new hunting grounds, and new victims, or as pedophiles like to say "Fresh meat."

Do I sound angry, agitated, or just plain pissed? You would have to put yourselves in my place. I guess I've seen it all. I have definitely seen too much! If you were to delve into the deepest, darkest corner of your mind, you could not begin to imagine what some predators have done and are doing to children. At the hands of sexual predators, one child will suffer more than any child should suffer in five thousand lifetimes. Not all pedophiliacs are satisfied with merely raping their victims!

I think it's necessary to share with you an example of what I meant by my last statement. During a child kidnap recovery, which took place in the early 1980's in Brazil, several recovery team members including myself, entered one of four buildings located on the property of a ranchero. The ranchero was nestled in the jungle approximately thirty miles outside Sao Paulo. Upon entering the first room we discovered film equipment that included cameras, lighting, makeshift staging and two Latin men. One man in his underwear, the other naked and clumsily trying to conceal a rapidly retreating erection. While three team members took charge of the two undressed men, I initiated a room- to-room search accompanied by other team members. We were looking for our primary recovery subject: a three-year-old girl we'll now call by her code name, Trinket. The adjacent room from where the two Latin men were was an oblong bathroom with all the fixtures and utilities on one side of the room. The opposite side was completely bare and unfinished raw wood. Approximately in the middle of the room and against the wall was a toilet that appeared to have never been cleaned. It bore the scars and filth stains verifying years of use. Beyond the toilet was the sink. In front of the sink was a tiny wooden crate the little girl must have used to climb up on the sink, where she sat, forced to washout her blood-stained sheets. Trinket looked at me and held out her arms. Somehow she knew that she was going home. We deposited Trinket in our padded bulletproof carry cylinder and did just that, brought her home.

I know what it is that some of you want to know, but don't bother asking about what happened to the two Latin men. I will share with you this: we fondly refer to them as Null and Void.

The child-for-sale sex market has grown into a multi-billion dollar worldwide monster. In South America, which is where most of our work is, a 3x5 black and white pornographic photograph of a child will sell on the black market for between $10.00 and $40.00. The sale price depends on a variety of things, such as, the photograph's action and the subjects involved. If a photograph depicts actual sexual acts involving the child's participation, not simply nudity, and the child is of light complexion, the value is higher. But if the child is American, or European, with blonde hair, that's top dollar stuff. The same rules apply for videos, except the value is way up there. We recovered a child that had literally thousands of pornographic photos taken of her and three movies shot on VHS video that we know of. She was three years old.

Who is their target?

Pedophiles are always on the lookout for the ideal situation, a child that they can have regular access to, and of course, the unattended child. They will take their time studying a situation, observing which child is being walked to school, or to the bus stop; which children have someone to meet them and walk them home. They are watching for the situation when a child regularly waits to be met, or the one where the parent or guardian is often late or irregular. Like most predators, pedophiles seem to have the patience of Job. Some predators know where they are going to take their victim before they have committed the abduction. Most do not and leave it to chance. They simply grab the child and try to put as much distance between them and the point of the abduction as fast as they can.

If you will think back a few pages, I talked about the predators who may have regular access to your children. The relatives, or close friends and neighbors you trust, or at minimum, should be able to trust. Many pedophiles take a different approach; they call it "Shopping." As they have explained it to me, that is exactly what they're doing, "Shopping." With the trust you have placed in their lap, so too, have you placed your child. Pedophiles are specifically looking for something we see all the time. They're "Shopping" for that certain child, the one that can't seem to get enough. Enough what? Enough attention. You know the ones: the children that keep hanging on. Sure, you've seen it too! After arriving at a relative or friend's home, and all the hugs, kisses and gift giving is done. There it is, the kid that won't go away, hanging, clawing and climbing all over you, or simply clinging to your side. Sometimes the child just silently holds on to your arm, clinging tightly against you as if she belongs to you, or wants to. Sounds funny, no? NO, it's not funny! What you are witnessing is a child desperately seeking attention. That child is a victim, waiting to be found by a predator!

Pedophiles are always on the prowl for children with too much time on their hands and no place to go. You've seen them too, just hanging out, or wandering aimlessly, hanging out with obviously nothing better to do with their time. I can hear some of you now: "So, that's what kids do today, and just because my kid's hanging out doesn't mean they're going to hop into just anybody's car." What you are missing here is the other ingredient: you're putting all of your money on your kid to make all the right decisions. When was the last time you witnessed that? The kid has already made a wrong decision: he or she is out and about wandering aimlessly and there is a chance she's already attracted the attention of a predator. What you have not allowed for is the pedophile's cunning! Predators carry a bag full of tricks and some of their conversations and tactics border on genius. Remember, most pedophiliacs have been doing it for a very long time. Some pedophiliacs belong to groups that share information, stories, photos and tactics. In plain English, many children do not stand a chance, especially if the pedophile has all the time he needs. Depending on the child, it could mean as little time as an hour, or even less time. If we're talking about abduction, it only takes a second. If the predator feels it will take more time, he will make arrangements for a rendezvous the next evening, or as soon as possible. Free drugs and alcohol are often used as an inducement for young teens. Pedophiles are generally willing to spend plenty of time and money on children, as it helps win a child's favor and may cause the child to feel indebted.

I want to break here for a moment because I need to fill you in on some other important information. Pedophiles are beginning to be recognized and are gaining support from what might be described as people of higher learning. Can you believe, especially after everything I've been telling you about pedophiles, that an Associate Professor of Sociology at Temple University is trying to assist these predators? Believe it or not, she is calling for more tolerance and understanding of pedophiles, even claiming the word pedophile is too harsh and judgmental. She prefers it be called "Child adult sex." Well I don't mind calling it child adult sex, but they're still pedophiles! The "lady" also questions research results regarding long term effects of child sexual molestation. This particular supporter and protector [I'd name her, but I believe she's been in print too much already] of child predators believes the punishments inflicted on pedophiliacs for "Child adult sex" are much too severe, adding that they need social acceptance. Pedophiles are seeking legitimate status, social acceptance and political protection. Well, guess what folks? As long as learned individuals continue to support these creatures that stalk your children, and you continue to do nothing, the pedophiliacs are going to get all that, and more.

Sorry, I digress. Another favorite target of pedophiles is a child alone in a public restroom. Anywhere and any type of public restroom, absolutely no exceptions. Now a special word or two for some special people. This volley is aimed at you fathers. That's right, I'm talking to you, Dad, Daddy, Poppa, Pop, Pappy, or as your better half may sometimes refer to you, "Stud Muffin." I don't care who's on what base, what inning it is or how many outs there are. Gather up your beer, your hot dogs and air horn and escort your kid to the bathroom when he or she has to go. It is your responsibility. It is your job! And if you think about it, you don't want to leave the well being of your child to a security guard that is probably paying more attention to the game than you were. Mom, here it comes. I am aware that this is your moment of relaxation in a heavily scheduled day and God knows you deserve it. You're face down on the beach. It took ten minutes of struggling to get that top off without exposing yourself to the world. You're about three minutes into a book you've been trying to get at for over a week. What do you do? You're going to do what any good mother would do. If you can find it, you're going to go through hell putting your top back on. You're probably going to walk somewhere in the neighborhood of a quarter of a mile, escorting your child to the bathroom. About now is when you discover that the polish you put on your toenails this morning for tonight's formal has all but been ground off by the sand. But if you think about it, you don't want to leave the well being of your child to anyone else. Not even a lifeguard who was probably paying more attention to you struggling with your top than you were. I don't worry about moms nearly as much as I do dads. Most of the great protectors don't do half the job they should. The plain truth of it is fathers are not nearly as watchful as mothers are. I know that there was a time once when parents didn't have to watch their children every moment of the day and night. I am also aware that there once was a time when doctors made house calls. Those times are gone! You fathers need to start giving more time and attention to your children, and maybe be a little more protective, like Mom. I know that some fathers couldn't do a better job. I'm talking to all of the others fathers that know they could.

It would be impossible to count the times my wife and I have had to listen to fathers saying "It's my fault." and "I should've been there", or "I'll kill the Son of a bitch." I implore all parents, especially fathers, to take more responsibility for your children's well being. It is up to you as one half of the partnership, or co-chairman if you will, to make sure you have done everything possible to prevent your children from becoming victims and not leave it all up to Mom. Every phase of your families' security is up to you. It's your responsibility. It's your job! You will learn more about how best to do your job in the chapters ahead.

Organizations

I regret to have to inform you that there are many established pedophiliac organizations, some private and secret, others relatively visible. By relatively visible, I mean self-delegated members, or appointed spokespersons of sorts staying busy making themselves and their organizations known. One group that has stepped forward in a big way is NAMBLA, and their attitude seems to be one of "in your face." N.A.M.B.L.A. stands for North American Man / Boy Love Association. Some time ago they held a convention in Texas. News was, over three thousand (3,000) showed up. That is somewhere in the neighborhood of "a lot of pedophiliacs" who don't care if their identities are known. I can only imagine how many there are who prefer to remain anonymous. A short time after that, Christine and I were surprised and shocked to see them marching in a gay rights parade. We were surprised that the homosexual community was willing to march side-by-side with the pedophiliacs. We were shocked that pedophiles were willing to show their faces, on parade no less. As much as I hate to admit it, Christine predicted that pedophiles would eventually push for open acceptance, including political recognition and protection. She actually said, "The day will come when they will show their faces proudly and defiantly in public." I hate it when she's right. Christine's prediction was made approximately ten years before it actually happened. Although Christine knew that some day it was going to happen, she was as disappointed in some of the gay community as I was. Before anyone goes ballistic on us, we want you to know that neither Christine nor I believe that all gays support pedophiles. We know it is a very small percentage. In fact, this is as good a time as any to thank the gay community for their enormous past support of our kidnap recovery efforts. Their genuine emotional and moral concern has been proven by their physical efforts and monetary generosity.

N.A.M.B.L.A. members refer to themselves as "Boy Lovers." However, if given the chance they can also be little "Girl Lovers" and many are. I know this to be true because I personally have had conversations with N.A.M.B.L.A. members, and they have admitted to me that they have had sex with adolescent girls when the opportunity arose and still would.

They are pedophiliacs and by their nature these individuals seek out others who share their predilections. Each of the organizations I investigated seemed to spend a great deal of their time discussing and swapping the best ways to ingratiate themselves with children. Most often when pedophiles get together, eventually they get around to sharing details of past and most recent conquests. Some will pass around photographs of their victims, much like proud husbands and fathers showing off pictures of their children around the office.

I have discussed my findings regarding these groups and their meetings, including their activities, with both State and Federal Law Enforcement. I generally leave these discussions extremely frustrated, as are most of the law enforcement officers I deal with. The most common argument I come up against is, "These groups are shielded in the United States by the First Amendment, freedom of speech, and as long as they operate within the law, they are protected." Now, what warrants my skepticism about that is, I know that in many, if not all, states it is against the law, a felony as a matter of fact, to deceive a minor child for personal gain. It is also a felony in most, if not all, states to be involved in a conspiracy to commit a crime. What is a conspiracy? Webster says, "the act of conspiring together/an agreement among conspirators." So where's the crime? Well, we don't have all the ingredients yet, so what's missing? Let's see what we have so far, we have two or more people talking about breaking the law, but that's still not enough. It takes at least two people and one overt act, attempting to break the law. Now, you have a felony in every state! I have personal knowledge of FBI infiltration into these organizations. By the FBI's own admission, agents have witnessed these conversations and numerous overt acts. I cannot understand why the arrest of these group members for conspiracy to commit a crime (a felony) has not occurred. There is always the possibility that massive arrests are forthcoming. I, being the eternal optimist, plan to hold my breath for as long as it takes!

Allow me to tell you what a member of a child-love group that I was investigating said at a meeting. I listened intensely to a spokesperson for a group of pedophiles at one of their meetings. He completely confused and baffled me. Allow me to paraphrase: the man stated that he and many other child lovers oppose adult child sexual relationships, only because of the propensity for a sexual bond to damage children psychologically. He contended that ours is a society that creates guilt over adult and pre-teen sexual activity, making the children feel exploited, used and guilt-ridden. I find it incredulous that these individuals claim society places guilt on a child victimized by an adult. When in reality, a common tactic of child molesters is to frighten and convince through threats and intimidation that the child has done something very bad. A pedophile will continue his assault on the child by adding, "Your mother and father will be mad at you, and no one will like you ever again." Did I mention that I was also offended and insulted by the speaker's explanation?

Here we are again: it is you and I who do not understand. It is the majority that is wrong. It is our fault that a child is made to feel dirty and used. (Pedophiles contend that it is not their actions, or responsibility to the children, claiming that it is our problem.) You see it's our problem because pedophiles believe that society has created this "taboo" because of our outdated Puritan views.   Considering that pedophiles obviously possess a distorted mindset, we must be ever vigilant to their intentions and watchful of their activities.   It is our responsibility to take whatever action necessary to thwart the efforts of organizations such as N.A.M.B.L.A.

As of this writing, there are pedophiles posting information on the Internet informing other pedophiles on how to infiltrate children's organizations. You may be familiar with the targeted groups: your child may even belong to one. The groups that are being infiltrated are the Boy Scouts of America, Cub Scouts, Sea Scouts, Big Brothers, Big Sisters, Brownies and the Girl Scouts of America.

Through the Internet, pedophiles have set up a worldwide network of people who share the same sexual desires. Along with sharing their feelings, they share information, but most important, they constantly confirm to each other the legitimacy of their acts. They have told me, and I quote, "We have a special understanding of children that parents do not possess." They consider, that what they do is "Helping children." Helping them by introducing children to sex sooner and the real love that only they can give. With great pride, a pedophile exclaimed to me, "An added benefit that the children receive is the enjoyment of a longer sex life." He smiled as he turned and walked away, a smile that seemed to say what a great thing I'm doing. Of course, the reality of their acts is at best self-deception and at worst, lies and most definitely self-gratification.

There are pedophile groups encouraging their members to adopt children, often children from third world countries. They are also instrumental in providing the instructions as to how to proceed. Don't you find it alarming that individuals would go to the extreme of adoption to satisfy their sexual desires? I do! I am amazed at how one tenth of one percent of a population can dictate what is right and what's wrong, and gain protection and power. Pedophiles believe if they say and do something long enough, it will become acceptable, the norm.

Good police work
Both Christine and I feel privileged to know some of the police of-

ficers assigned to child protection units. We have witnessed unbelievable dedication and unparalleled sacrifice. A particular officer always comes to mind. He worked for the city of Orange in Southern California. Being a police officer was all he knew and ever wanted to be. Eventually, he ended up working the child abuse unit. He was good at his job. It's a job not wanted by the many. The powers that be decided to leave him there for 11 years. He didn't allow low lack of finances to hamper an investigation; he simply dug into his own pockets. When overtime was not approved, he simply dug into his own time. Everyone noticed his work. You could tell by the awards he was presented. However, no one noticed he was slowly being eaten away by the atrocities he witnessed against children. He proved to me that it is truly amazing what a difference one person can make. He showed me what one single caring individual could accomplish. Here's to you, Skipper, wherever you are. God bless you!

Everyone knows there are some great cops out there! Literally thousands have given their lives trying to save someone else's life. Documented cases of police officers rushing into blazing infernos, when they could have easily said to their superiors, "the fire was too intense, there was nothing I could do." Attempting to save a drowning victim, an officer jumped into freezing water. He managed to push the victim toward sheets of floating ice. The victim was able to hold onto the ice until help arrived. The police officer that saved the drowning person was terrified of water and had never learned to swim. He drowned saving another.

I'm not going to be talking about those police officers. I am going to be talking about some of the higher-ranking officers, the officers responsible for public relations that are completely wrapped up in bureaucratic red tape. Many of these high-ranking officers find themselves in the middle of a squeeze; they are actually caught between City Hall and the Federal Government. The fact that many of these officers like the idea of playing politics adds to the problem. The problem is that states, counties and cities all count on federal funding. This means your local government has to conform to federal government politics and policies if they wish to continue receiving federal funding. In short, the federal government says, if you want us to help you, you must do what we say. The problem is our federal government says some pretty terrible things, and sometimes worse is what they won't say. Even though our President did recently say that we are at war with child molesters etc., our government won't admit that crimes against children in the United States of America have reached epidemic proportions. Neither will they admit some children are kidnapped from the United States and sold into sexual slavery in foreign countries. I can only liken it to Ma Bell admitting your telephone can be tapped. They would never admit that they couldn't keep your sensitive conversation private. No government agency, not the Justice Department nor the FBI will even admit to the possibility that a child kidnapped from some small town in South Dakota could have ended up in Argentina or Bolivia.

According to the Los Angeles police department's 1996, 1997 and 1998 statistic reports of missing children due to unknown circumstances in California number 16, 534. Out of these, 195 were stranger abductions, which may mean the kidnapping was witnessed and the kidnapper was a non-family member. Obviously, there are no statistics regarding non-witnessed kidnappings as to the kidnapper being a family member or not. Now we come to children missing under suspicious circumstances, (including without a trace) which generally is an indication that it was a stranger abduction. They total 2,682. Remember that these numbers refer to California children only. I recently received statistics stating that over 400 children are kidnapped annually by non-family members from the greater Los Angeles area alone, never to be seen again. These statistics were later denied. Going by these statistics and judging from past experience of child molesters who kill their victims, backpackers, fishermen, hunters, forest rangers and people simply enjoying a Sunday afternoon walk should be stumbling onto shallow graves quite regularly. Is it possible that we are not stumbling onto grave after grave because some, possibly many, of the children are in fact still alive in a foreign country? I believe that our recoveries do indicate, if not prove, that this is a distinct possibility. Our information and the reporting of sightings to the Justice Department and the FBI have ironically been ignored.

The U.S. government does not wish to admit that it cannot protect our children from what seems to be the perfect crime. If a child is kidnapped from Anaheim, California, who is going to be looking for that child in Brazil or Colombia? I am embarrassed to say that I receive more cooperation and official support from foreign agencies. By far, the most truthful entity and the most willing to assist in recoveries has been Interpol.

I spoke with a former FBI agent regarding the rape and murder of a little boy, whose name shall remain anonymous in order to avoid further pain for the family and embarrassment to the ex-FBI agent. He said, "The killer of this child is no pedophile, because pedophiles love kids." Excuse me! The child was raped and then murdered, that's a pedophiliac! Pedophiles, it has been proven, are builders. Like most other criminals, they start small and work their way up to increasingly more violent and horrific acts. Many pedophiles advance in their fantasies, which they act out for gratification, sometimes ending in murder. I am sick and tired of the distinction some individuals constantly try to make between pedophiles and child molesters. A pedophile prefers sex with children, which by law and all reasoning is child molestation. While a child molester's sexual activity is self explanatory, it does employ the same illegal and unreasonable sexual activity, child molestation. Now, if someone, anyone, can prove to me that a pedophile is not capable of child abduction, I would then be willing to admit to a difference between a child molester and a pedophile. If it were possible to prove that to me, then I would be willing to admit that pedophiles are not often child abductors. I would then be forced to admit that pedophiles are smart enough to molest your children without having to kidnap them...EVER!

A London journalist here in the U.S. was interviewing me regarding children kidnapped and sold into sexual slavery. She had been covering a story involving the discovery of children locked in crates aboard a ship in the English Channel destined for South America. After spending two days interviewing me, she ended up at the Federal Building in Los Angeles interviewing an FBI agent. The journalist asked the agent about the kidnappings and the sale of children in foreign countries. The agent responded with "I have been an agent for over 21 years and there has never been a child kidnapped and taken to a another country for sale, trade or any other reason." Surprised, the journalist asked, "Are you sure you want to answer that off the top of your head? Maybe you could check your records." To which the agent replied, "We don't keep records on that. I mean if we did, where would it end." At the time of those interviews, I had copies of four federal warrants for that exact crime in my possession, which the journalist was shown.

Another example of cooperation and good police work happened in 1988. Universal Studios and Champion Productions hired me to technical advise and head up security on pre-production work on a Robert DeNiro film in South America. The movie's working title was "Stolen Flower." It was a fictitious story from a book of the same title, about a child kidnapped and taken out of country. With Mr. DeNiro's blessing, I was allowed to search for American children in South America, as time would allow. Posing as a dealer in pornography, I was able to view a film still in the editing stages. The pornographer was informed prior to my arrival that I was interested in the purchase of films using Scandinavian or American girls. As I watched the film being spliced together, the editor bragged continuously of its star being an American. It was a horrifying film involving many Latin children forced to do horrific things. Then, as an adult on screen motioned to someone off camera to enter, a blonde-haired girl approximately 10 to 12 years old came into view. She was naked and obviously very frightened, holding a T-shirt positioned to cover as much of her as possible. The T-shirt was yanked to the floor as she was ordered to kneel down in Portuguese. It was obvious she did not understand the command. As the little girl was being sexually abused, she began to cry. Eventually, the abuser became frustrated and angry, ordering her away with hand signals. The little girl stood up and while facing the camera, put her T-shirt on, turned her back and walked directly away from the camera allowing the viewer to read the back of her T-shirt. In block print, possibly using a felt pen was "Oakland A's."

I tried desperately to find out more about the little girl and to purchase the film. Mr. DeNiro offered whatever money was necessary to try to buy the child, if possible. For many reasons, we were unable to locate the child, or purchase the film. Upon returning to the United States, I immediately contacted the Oakland police department and told them of what I had witnessed. Approximately one week later I was contacted by the San Jose Police Department. The detective asked more questions regarding the identification of the child. He also asked me what I considered a strange question: "Why did you contact the Oakland Police Department rather than the FBI?" I thought the answer was rather obvious, but bothered to explain. I also asked if any child had been taken from the Oakland A's Stadium, possibly during a game. The detective did not answer, but told me that the FBI would contact me.

After two weeks and not a word from anyone, I again contacted the detective at the San Jose Police Department. I asked what was going on and told him the FBI had not yet contacted me. The detective informed me that

The FBI told him that they had tried to contact me via the telephone and I was not at that number. Nor was I at the address I had given the detective, adding that I had never lived at that address. After I recovered from the initial shock, I informed the detective that I had been living at that address for six years. I asked the detective if he had the original telephone number I had given him weeks earlier, and that he had passed on to the FBI. He replied that he did. I asked the officer to hang up the telephone and call me collect, which he did immediately. The detective had no answers and wasn't really interested in discussing it further. I tried numerous times to contact the FBI regarding this incident, to no avail. Some of the most frustrating events in my life have involved Federal agencies.

The only explanation I can think of is that the federal government does not want to admit that a crime of this caliber is being successfully perpetrated against American families. The reasoning behind our government's choice not to recognize this problem may be complicated. You have to think the way they think, and they are generally thinking unsolved crimes on their books and expenditure. To coordinate an operation involving foreign countries and their agencies could be very expensive. And which of our agencies would handle it? The question our government would be first to ask would be, "How many children that are kidnapped end up in foreign countries?" There are many that would eagerly answer that question: 5,000, 10,000, or maybe 50,000. The truth is, no one knows. In a funny sort of way, it is the truth that lets our government off the hook. The truth is if there aren't too many kids abducted to foreign countries, it's cost prohibitive. However, if there are many children ending up in places like South America, they don't want to admit that it's happening. On top of that it's easy for abductors to take children out of the country. Generally no one is looking at who is crossing the border heading out of America.

In June of 1988, a report was presented to the West European Justice Ministers and to the Council of Europe. The report stated that

22

more than one million children are bought, sold, traded and kidnapped into sexual slavery each year as part of a multi-billion dollar International sex trafficking racket. That was a conservative number, even then. The trafficking of children is growing worldwide and has become a serious problem in Europe and in the United States as well. The report continued, "Those responsible have enormous financial resources and the trafficking of children brings them billions of dollars each year." Actually, sex trafficking and child pornography is second only to drug trafficking in most countries.

Much of Europe is trying to coordinate efforts with other countries. With the help of Interpol, more than a decade later, they are starting to see some minor results. That's good police work, which could be a whole lot better if governments would truly recognize and fund this war against child atrocities.

How do they get caught?

Often by accident, but to be completely honest, many are apprehended due to quality police work. However, some are accidentally stumbled onto and some are never caught, especially the ones that kill. In New York City, the police were not aware of a string of serial killings until a man on the way to a landfill was stopped for a malfunctioning taillight. Upon inspection of the vehicle, a body was discovered in the trunk.

Unlike some criminals who boast of their crimes, pedophiliacs that kill are more secretive and often go unpunished. Pedophiles also do not fall into the category of those criminals discovered through stupidity or carelessness. Since many pedophiles have obtained positions of trust, it is especially difficult to catch them. We have to be patient considering that the bureaucrats have only recently begun unraveling their red tape. When documented crimes, even crimes well-known to the general population, are denied to exist by law enforcement, you have to realize we have a long way to go.

One such popular denial by law enforcement is snuff films. Sad, considering I can document case after case. Snuff films were confiscated in 1983 in Anaheim Ca., 1985 in Sacramento Ca., Seattle Wash., New Bedford, Ma., San Jose, Ca., New York City, NY.. I can continue, but I believe you've gotten the point. By the way, there are also all the snuff films that have been filtering into the United States from

South America since the mid-1970's.

We don't need denial; we need qualified officers skilled in child sexual exploitation. The officers need complete departmental support including all the tools and funding necessary to do their job properly. One of the most valued tools available to police today is the informant, as they are referred to in the courtrooms, or snitch, as referred to in the squad rooms. Unfortunately, they too are for the most part ineffective in the world of pedophiles. If only pedophiles were as easily identified as the dirty old man in a long overcoat offering a kid a piece of candy, as depicted on TV.

The fact of the matter is that kids catch pedophiles best! Yes it's true. Kids that have been properly instructed as to what to do when they are touched, or made to feel uncomfortable, by an adult. The "Tell an Adult Program" has been reasonably successful. Tell an adult and if that adult won't listen, tell another adult and keep telling adults until you find one that will listen. The "Tell an Adult Program" would be much more successful if parents would open the more delicate lines of communication with their children. By delicate, I mean your child should feel comfortable talking to you about anything. To be able to communicate with a child successfully one must refine the art of listening. That's right, close the mouth, open the ears. When your child is confident that you will listen, they will almost always tell you their problems. Keeping strong lines of communication open can be difficult, considering your role as parent and disciplinarian. Most children will eventually talk to their friends, because they know their friends won't judge them, or get angry toward them. Therefore, along with being a parent and disciplinarian, you have to establish a balance as a friend, a friend willing to listen. It will be tedious, difficult and seemingly never-ending. Some parents will find it necessary to seek professional assistance. Since parents cannot be with their children one hundred percent of the time, you must develop great communication. It's your job. Do it! Remember this, children with big problems will eventually confide in someone because they need to. Why not make it you that they choose to trust?

Many pedophiles will try to develop a relationship of sorts with their tentative victims. Through the course of their endeavors, pedophiles will say many things over that period of time, which will amaze, intrigue and astonish most children. If you are listening to your child, you will be forewarned, generally more than once. Children will test parents. It's an amazing technique if you think about it. The child will just chatter on and on. How many times have you witnessed a parent paying absolutely no attention to their child and telling the child, "Stop your rambling." Quite often, your children are repeating what they have heard recently that amazed, intrigued and astonished them. Children seldom know exactly how to handle things that intrigue them, or things they think might make you angry. So rather than be direct, they will often throw things out of their mouths at inconvenient times or mix them in with everything else they're saying. Parents call it rambling. I call it testing, testing to see if anyone will pick up on it. If you aren't listening, your child may consider it to be all right, not a bad thing. Of course, if it were a bad thing you would have gotten angry. After all, in a child's mind, you were told all about it.

Since pedophiles frequent areas where children gather such as parks, playgrounds, schoolyards, arcades etc., they are often spotted and frightened away by attentive adults. Sometimes a description and even a license plate number are turned over to police. This action generally does not lead to an arrest because the perpetrator was caught short, before he was able to commit his crime. However, it does allow police to gather information regarding predators in the area, and if something does happen, it gives the police a place to start.

This may come as a surprise to you, but many pedophiles are discovered by the Post Office through suspicious packaging and other situations that alert postal officials. The Post Office and other agencies have multiple procedures and techniques they employ against pedophiles and child pornography traffickers. As I consider myself a responsible citizen, I choose not to divulge any agency's investigative and arrest procedures or techniques. When the United States Post Office is involved, almost inevitably the culprits end up facing charges. However, since the widespread use of computers and video cameras, mailing much of their material is considered passe. This is especially true when it comes to pedophiles sharing ideas and material (child porn) they know to be deemed illegal. The Federal government and other agencies including private groups, are finally putting together a formidable force to combat child pornography and pedophiles on the Internet. The major problem is the enormous growth in the child porn industry. When I first investigated the world of child porn by computer, six to eight sites existed. Now there are tens of thousands. We will be discussing with you further the mixed blessings of the computer and the Internet later in the book.

In many cases it is difficult, and in some cases impossible, to get convictions against pedophiles. The difficulty is primarily due to the age and maturity of the main witness, the victim. Without the victim's testimony, it can be impossible to achieve a conviction. Most parents understandably do not wish to put their child through a police questioning and the trauma of a courtroom trial. This is inevitably the case, especially when the crime involves the actual rape of their child. Prosecuting attorneys have a difficult, let me rephrase that, an impossible, task ahead of them when evidence is weak and a child's testimony is necessary for conviction. The prosecutor knows that if he or she uses a child's testimony the defense attorney will be allowed to cross-examine the child. Since we have observed adult witnesses nearly self-combust under the stress of cross-examination, a child doesn't stand much of a chance. Sure, they make special allowances for children, and everyone seems to step lightly. Defense attorneys aren't stupid. They know they don't have to be loud or hard on a child to make it appear that a child is mistaken and confused. A favorite tactic of defense attorney's dealing in child abuse cases is to demonstrate to the jury that the child could easily be mistaken. They go about this in the simplest way, by asking the child basic questions such as, "What is the difference between boys and girls?" If a child cannot answer that question satisfactorily to a jury, it casts doubt on all of the child's testimony. Your child must be capable of identifying the basic anatomy of boys and girls.

Have you gotten the message yet? It is extremely difficult to arrest, much less get a conviction against, a pedophile. With few exceptions, pedophiles have to be caught during the act of a kidnapping and/or the actual molestation in order to guarantee a conviction. Of course, many are caught after the fact, but that's too late, isn't it, and still doesn't promise a conviction. In case you don't get it yet, here's one more example. I went to work on a case involving a wife and mother taking her three-year-old girl and running away from her husband with her boyfriend. The reason I was involved was the boyfriend had multiple convictions of child molestation. The three-month search took me through four separate states and Mexico, culminating back into the

United States, in Arizona. The FBI and innumerable police departments were involved. With the assistance of the Douglas City Police Department, the mother and boyfriend were arrested and the child was turned over to my custody. I immediately had several medical evaluations performed by separate specialists in regard to the little girl's health and well-being. The evaluations were unanimous. All doctors involved agreed that the three-year-old had been a victim of vaginal and anal intercourse and that semen specimens had been discovered and removed. The medical reports separately described severe lacerations and bruising inside the vaginal vault and also surrounding the vagina. The medical reports included trauma to the anus and surrounding the anal opening. The reports alerted me of the presence of nonprescription drugs in her system. The child had also contracted gonorrhea.

Now, the prosecuting attorney marched all of the evidence before a magistrate. I had proven beyond the shadow of any doubt that this three-year-old little girl had been sexually abused beyond belief. The mother had even confessed to witnessing her boyfriend having intercourse with her daughter at least seven times. However, since jurisdiction could not be established, both the mother and her boyfriend walked away free. The established fact of these atrocities committed against this little girl was not enough. Because I did not have knowledge as to exactly where the crimes occurred, the courts could not determine which state could or would prosecute. I hope you get it now! Your best defense is an open and honest communication with your children. You must also teach them how not to become victims. Keep reading and later in the book, I'll tell you how!

Remorse

As the radical secularists trample our society's Judeo-Christian heritage and values, I hear more and more examples of people plummeting to new depths of inhumanity. A case that comes to mind happened not long ago in the state of Washington. Predators were arrested and charged with plotting to kidnap a child. The plan was to sexually exploit the child for weeks while sexually gratifying themselves as they pleased. Finally, the arrangement was to actually kill the child during the making of a "Snuff" film.

I find it extremely difficult to consider the slightest compassion, or find any forgiveness, after having personally witnessed the abominations committed against children I have recovered. To consider compassion, forgiveness or to believe for a moment that pedophiliacs are capable of remorse is as I said, extremely difficult to consider. In addition, I feel I can speak for most parents of sexually abused and/or murdered children by adding the murderers should receive the same consideration that was shown to the child they tortured. You have to understand, for one to feel remorse, one must acknowledge wrongdoing.

Pedophiles do not consider sex with children wrong. As pedophiles see it, to demand that they never have sex with a child again is the equivalent to demanding a heterosexual man never to have sex with a woman again. Which explains why sexual child molesters hold the record for being repeat offenders. Pedophiles claim their sexual desires are healthy and normal. If child predator's actions are so healthy and normal, why do so many feel it necessary to kill their victims in an attempt to hide what they've done? What pedophiles really want is for you to keep your nose out of their business. Never mind that their business is stalking, raping and sometimes murdering your children. As it was put to me by one of them not long ago, "I do not appreciate your self-righteous attitude, which probably stems from sexual frustration. Stop interfering with my private life." He continued "Maybe if you'd get off your high horse and put your face in some preteen pussy you'd change your mind." I'm going to let you guess as to which one of us hit the other one as hard as humanly possible, turning the recipient's jaw into sawdust. Although I realize many consider it wrong to extract justice or personal satisfaction in this manner, I on the other hand, realized some satisfaction, but not nearly enough justice.

Child molesters constantly use the same excuses "In parts of Europe, Like in France, it's not illegal." and crude statements such as "If they're old enough to bleed they're old enough to butcher." Well, many, many and more years ago, that last crude statement may have applied. However, in those days, a wife was expected to have children, cook the meals and sometimes she pulled the plow when the horse was sick. Back then the young lady expected to have a husband that would be sticking around and providing for her. Back then; it was not only customary, it was often necessary. Back then it was legal for a man to choose a young wife as long as she had started her menstrual period.

However, as Bob Dylan once said, "Times they are a changing." and along with the times and laws changing, morals have changed too. When men or boys who thought they were men, began losing sight of the important stuff like morals, scruples, integrity and honor, laws had to be changed. You know, back when both men and boys began jumping from bed to bed without any intentions other than a good time. Adding to that, I have never heard a pedophile say he would never touch a child before she had her period. Oh, and by the way, this ain't Paris!

Know this about child molesters: the general rule is there are only three instances when pedophiles act remorseful. And take notice, I didn't say have remorse, I said, act remorseful. The first time is when they are arrested; the second time is just before sentencing and the third, when trying to make parole. Like most rules, there are the exceptions. There is another time that they act remorseful: in the case of child molesters, the exception is when they're caught more than once. Then they start to act all over again.

I believe I have clearly demonstrated to you that these individuals are intent on sexually gratifying themselves with your children. My experience with pedophiliacs has proven to me that they do not know the meaning of remorse! This is not a Democrat or Republican issue, nor is it any of the previously mentioned; as a matter of fact it isn't political or religious at all! It is about the children and their families suffering a childhood lost, or a child lost...forever.

The Constitution of the United States of America, as magnificent as it is, has its shortcomings. I believe our forefathers left some things up to integrity, morals and common decency, not to mention common sense. While the Constitution guarantees the people of the United States of America freedom of speech and numerous other freedoms, it should be clear to everyone that one man's rights cannot infringe on or exclude another's choice. Does the above statement refer to people who have reached the age of reason only? Does the Constitution exclude our children? From its inception, America ideally has stood for fairness and equality for all of its citizens. We have the glorious freedom to make our own choices and take our own chances. Now, having taken all of that into consideration, please tell me, what possible choice or chance does a four-year-old, or seven, or nine, or even a fourteen-year-old, have against an experienced pedophiliac? For that matter, any adult bent on convincing and deceiving any age child?

You do not have to be a Constitutional scholar to know when individuals are using our declaration of freedom and justice as their personal gauntlet. Pedophiliacs have publicly claimed their sexual freedom preference to children using religion, psychological medicine, art etc. Oh, and of course the constitution. There are those constantly busy testing our country's moral fiber while shielding themselves from prosecution by applying their personal interpretation to our Bill of Rights. The democratic way has always been, majority rules, so why do we allow the minority thinkers to push us around? Particularly allowing that one tenth of one percent that commit crimes against America's children and humanity.

We as parents need to draw the line, and that line must say, **leave our children alone!**

Medical cure?

There are both doctors and scientists claiming medical breakthroughs regarding adults that sexually assault children. However, I have not witnessed any results involving a medical cure and neither have any of the experts I have talked with. Nor have I been allowed to examine documented evidence of a breakthrough of any kind. I also cannot buy into the experts who claim that most predators do what they do because they themselves were abused children. There are uncountable individuals who have suffered the torments of childhood abuse leading normal, moral and quality lives. Many are first-class parents. Consequently, I choose not to put my hopes in a medical cure at this time. Nor will I acknowledge excuses for those reasons, and one other reason. The other reason is, I have met and talked with many self-admitted pedophiles that claim, they have never had sex with a child. They also claimed that they had never attempted to have sex with an adolescent. When asked why, most replied, "Because I know its wrong." Yes, I too was skeptical, so skeptical that I arranged, with their cooperation, several polygraph tests. God Bless them, they were telling the truth. Which helped confirm what I have always believed: pedophiles, like most everyone else, make choices. If an individual truly believes that their sexual conduct is natural and innocent of wrong-doing, there is no cure.

I can expose case after case, nationwide, of convicted sexual offenders receiving early releases from prison because parole boards deemed them "Safe" to re-enter society. Now, call me crazy, but when state or Federal government entities declare an individual eligible for another chance, what they are saying is, they believe the individual to be "Safe" and ready to re-enter society. Is it wrong to assume that by "Safe" the parole board experts mean they consider the individual "Cured?" It's difficult to understand that, even though our parole boards have access to the same statistics as the rest of us, they do not seem to be aware of the recidivism by sexual child molesters. In case you didn't know, child molesters rank at the top of the list of criminal repeat offenders. Many experts believe castration is the only true cure. It is not a cure at all! I will talk with you in depth about castration and why it is not the answer later in the book.

The only true "cure" is a pedophile who chooses to refuse his sexual urges because he knows it's wrong and ruins lives, which makes it the right choice.

CHAPTER 2

CHILD SEXUAL ABUSE

Definition of child abuse

In recent past history, you have read or heard in the news of parents being charged with child abuse for taking hand to butt of their little angel and forcing said victim to sit quietly. More than likely the unruly squirt also received a few verbal threats. These incidents of brutality have been reported everywhere, in airline terminals, restaurants, churches, on airplanes... everywhere. These reports can only mean one thing, that there are some people who actually consider this type of discipline to be child abuse. However, having followed up on many of the cases I have found most to be dismissed. It is good to have caring watchful eyes out there, except it would be more beneficial to have <u>knowledgeable</u>, caring watchful eyes out there. Remember that knowledge is our most important weapon in this war.

It is most important that you also understand what constitutes child sexual abuse. Child sexual abuse occurs when any person, adult or juvenile, forces, tricks, threatens or coerces a minor child into having any kind of sexual contact with him or her. Showing children pornographic pictures or films, or telling them explicitly sexual stories can be a form of sexual abuse. Touching children inappropriately is sexual abuse. Some children are forced, or encouraged, to have sexual intercourse with parents, uncles, grandparents or friends of the family. This also includes the obvious: children who are forced to partake in sexual activity with strangers. Child abuse laws exist because what I have described to you not only happens, but also happens frequently. These laws are meant to provide protection for children who obviously cannot protect themselves.

As you were previously informed, this book is a guide for parents and complete child protection handbook. Consequently, there may be areas of reading some find difficult due to the sensitivity of the subject matter. Please keep in mind that this information is invaluable to parents when something has happened to your child or, if you observe something suspicious pertaining to someone else's child. You may have also noticed, when I am referring to a child, I generally use (she) as my example. This is done purposely, as most victims of sexual child abuse are girls, although it is important to know that the same violence inflicted on girls is also forced onto boys, just not as frequently.

The section you're about to read contains state and federal public law regarding the definitions of child abuse according to code. Here's the guidelines used by our courts to define child abuse.

Child abuse is defined in both federal and state legislation. The federal legislation provides a foundation for states by identifying a minimum set of acts or behaviors that characterize maltreatment. This legislation also defines what acts are considered physical abuse, neglect, and sexual abuse. The Child Abuse Prevention and Treatment Act (CAPTA), as amended and re-authorized in October 1996 (Public Law 104 -235, Section 111; 4 2 U.S.C. 5106g), defines child abuse as, at a minimum, any recent act or failure to act: Resulting in imminent risk of serious harm, death, serious physical or emotional harm, sexual abuse, or exploitation of a child (a person under the age of 18 years, unless the child protection law of the state in which the child resides specifies a younger age for cases not involving sexual abuse) By a parent or caretaker (including any employee of a residential facility or any staff person providing out-of-home care) who is responsible for the child's welfare.

CAPTA defines sexual abuse as:

Employment, use, persuasion, inducement, enticement, or coercion of any child to engage in, or assist any other person to engage in, any sexually explicit conduct or any simulation of such conduct for the purpose of producing any visual depiction of such conduct; or rape, and in cases of caretaker or inter-familial relationships, statutory rape, molestation, prostitution, or other form of sexual exploitation of children, or incest with children.

With the reauthorization of CAPTA, withholding of medically indicated treatment has been defined as failure to respond to an infant's life-threatening conditions by denial of treatment, (including appropriate nutrition, hydration, and medication) that would most likely be effective in ameliorating or correcting all life-threatening conditions. This definition does not refer to situations where treatment of an infant, in the treating physician's reasonable medical judgment, would prolong dying, be ineffective in ameliorating or correcting all the infant's life-threatening conditions. In addition and including: if it would be futile in helping the infant to survive, adding, this definition does not include situations where the infant is chronically or irreversibly comatose.

Each state is responsible for providing definitions of child abuse and neglect within the civil and criminal context. Civil laws, or statutes, describe the circumstances and conditions that obligate mandated reporters to report known or suspected cases of abuse. They also provide definitions necessary for juvenile/family courts to take custody of a child alleged to have been maltreated, which includes sexual abuse. Criminal statutes specify the forms of maltreatment that are criminally punishable. (The state statutes series from the National Clearinghouse on Child Abuse and Neglected Information summarizes over 30 civil and criminal state statutes pertaining to child maltreatment.)

Recognizing child abuse

There are four major types of child maltreatment: physical abuse, child neglect, sexual abuse and emotional abuse. They can be broken down even further: mental suffering, corporal punishment, cruel and unusual punishment and so on. We're dealing primarily with child sexual abuse, which goes hand in hand with emotional and psychological abuse. However, child sexual abuse will often manifest the same symptoms as other forms of maltreatment. Consequently, I feel it is necessary that you be informed of symptoms most often attributed to non-sexual abuse also.

Sexual child abuse includes fondling a child's genitals, intercourse, incest, rape, sodomy, exhibitionism, and commercial exploitation through prostitution or the production of pornographic materials. Many experts believe that child sexual abuse is the least reported form of child maltreatment because of the secrecy or **"Conspiracy of silence"** that so often characterizes these cases. I agree!

During the course of sexual abuse, the child is automatically exposed to other categories of abuse. Those abuses are emotional abuse, psychological abuse, and verbal abuse. Together, they culminate into one form or another of mental injury, sometimes-severe mental injury. Emotional abuse includes acts of omissions by the parents or the caregivers that have caused, or could cause, serious behavioral, cognitive, emotional, or mental disorders. In some cases of emotional abuse, the acts of parents or other caregivers alone, without any harm evident in the child's behavior or condition, are sufficient to warrant child protective services (CPS) intervention. For example, the parents or caregivers may use extreme or bizarre forms of punishments, such as confinement of a child in a dark closet. Less severe acts, such as habitual scapegoating, belittling, or rejecting treatment are often difficult to prove and therefore CPS may not be able to intervene due to a lack of visual evidence of harm to the child.

Although any of the forms of child maltreatment may be found separately, they often occur in combinations. Emotional abuse is almost always present when other forms of abuse are identified. However, I have continuously found in cases involving child sexual abuse that it is inevitably accompanied by emotional and psychological abuse.

So how do we as lay people recognize child abuse? The only avenues available to the average person are attending seminars conducted by qualified lecturers, quality literature and learning to be alert to warning signs. The signs can be glaring alarms, such as constant bruises, burns, and even broken limbs, although often hidden under clothing. The presence of visual irritation including rashes or rawness of the penis or bleeding in the child's external genitalia, vaginal, or anal area. In some cases, telltale signs are not always so obvious. Often sexual child abuse manifests itself in the form of malnutrition. Depending on the type of maltreatment the child is being subjected to, he or she may complain that it hurts (down there) when walking or sitting. Complaints of itching or pain may also be a sign of sexual abuse, but keep in mind that children are often subject to rashes that can be caused by other activities or situations.

Young children who have been sexually abused may also exhibit behavioral signs of their abuse. They may show excessive curiosity about sexual activities, or touch adults on the breast or genitals. Excessively is the key word here. Remember that there is the natural curiosity factor. Common sense should play a big part in your judgment. It is important to be able to identify different behavioral signs and different injury signs.

Let's discuss what is an accidental injury to a child and what isn't, and how you can determine which is which. Normal, acceptable injuries by accident are almost always to the child's knees, elbows, chin, nose, and forehead. You know, all the body parts kids seem to lead with. When bruises or any suspicious marks such as cuts, bites, and burns appear on soft tissue areas such as the buttocks, back, neck or thighs, you need to pay particular attention to that child. These are the most common signs that would indicate that you are most likely witness to the aftermath of child abuse, especially if it is repetitive. Another indicator of child abuse is bruises and other injuries in different stages of healing. The age of bruises can be detected by the following consecutive colors: red, blue, black/purple and green tint, dark to pale green to yellow. This is a biochemical process, which happens in all children. It must be noted that it is more difficult to detect the color of bruises in children of color, particularly black children. When in doubt, turn it over to the professionals. A doctor is capable of recognizing bruises and distinguishing the age of bruises in any child regardless of skin color.

Non-visible injuries to the abdomen can be detected by swelling and/or tenderness and, in severe or progressive cases, vomiting. These symptoms generally mean there are internal injuries. The leading cause of death in physically abused children is by head injuries. Head injuries can be detected by swelling, dizziness, vomiting, retinal detachment, blackouts and bilateral black eyes, which generally are an indication of bleeding in the brain. Keep an eye on your child's playmates. Adding to the possibility of child abuse is a child that is reluctant to discuss how the injuries occurred. Quite often, abused children have a vocabulary that pales in comparison to other children of the same age.

Due to the thin line between punishment and abuse, parents sometimes unintentionally lose sight of their objective and don't always think clearly. An example is that mothers and women in general frequently diet. Some will deny themselves food for a long time, frequently for days on end. Some women consider it a self-imposed punishment for being overweight. It becomes reasonable to some mothers to punish their children in the same manner as they punish themselves, by denying their child food. So obviously, another warning sign is a child that seems to constantly be overly hungry. In addition, you need to be attentive to any grown-up that is verbally attacking or ridiculing their children, including negative comments and indifference towards their child. While you're at it, keep an eye open for the child that prefers to spend most of their time alone in fantasy play, especially when there are other children to play with close by.

Child sexual abuse is not as easily detected, although sexual abuse does not come without it's own warning signs. Some children become aggressive and even violent and the physical violence can often be aimed at their younger siblings. The anger inside the child can manifest itself in many forms and take many directions. Often times the anger shows up as aggressive violence toward stuffed animals or dolls. It's only natural because the child has been hurt and is striking back in the only way it knows how. In very young children, quite often a sign of sexual abuse is the child will sit by itself in a corner or some other out of the way places, stroking a safety blanket or other personal item.

Frequently it is common for children between the age of infancy and three years to be affected with non-organic failure to thrive. Failure to thrive is the diagnosis if the child's height, weight, or head circumference is less than the third percentile. Typically, the child's weight will be below the third percentile with the child's head circumference and height above the third percentile. Organic failure to thrive is caused by a child's psychological problems, whereas non-organic failure to thrive is due to environmental problems related to nurturing and/or feeding. Normally, non-organic failure to thrive is caused by emotional deprivation or physical neglect. However, recent studies indicate that non-organic failure to thrive is present in some sexually abused children as well. Other symptoms exhibited in children suffering from non-organic failure-to-thrive syndrome are vomiting and/or diarrhea, anemia, rashes, urinary tract infections, fevers, weakness, or extreme tiredness. Children are blessed in that they possess highly functional alert systems. It is up to us as the adults and parents to monitor children's alert systems. All children's alert systems, not just our own children's. Adolescent communicative skills may not be the best, but their alert systems are fantastic, especially when adults are paying attention (watch and listen).

Here are some more examples of signs that should alert an observant adult or parent. Sexual behaviors in children, which indicate sexual knowledge not ordinarily possessed by young children. For example, sexual aggression toward other children or a child that continually talks to other children about their private parts may also be an indicator. Remember what we talked about earlier? Eventually, a sexually abused child will talk about it in some manner to another child. Pay attention to your children and their friends' conversations, especially if they think they are alone or that you cannot hear.

Often, signs take the form of the child being withdrawn and depressed, but not always. Sometimes the child seems to be outgoing and gregarious. That is one example of why detecting child abuse can be very difficult. If you suspect a child is being maltreated, you must notify the proper authorities immediately so the child can be protected and receive qualified professional help as soon as possible. Now, what we are going to talk about next is very important in determining actual sexual child abuse. It is important to know that child sexual abuse, or any other maltreatment of children, must be based on the detection of a **cluster of indicators**, rather than the observation of one or two clues. I will be discussing clusters of evidence with you further on.

Listening to your children

This section is dedicated to helping you better communicate, listen to, and inevitably understand your children better then ever. Previously, I advised you to listen to conversations your children are having with you and between children under your supervision, even if that means without the children's knowledge. It is imperative for you to know as much as possible regarding the children your children play with. Your best chance of discovering if a child is being sexually abused will come from the abused child. Pay attention! If it doesn't come in the form of the child's words, it will definitely manifest itself in their demeanor and actions.

Encourage conversations with your children as often as possible. Listen to what they don't or won't say as carefully as you listen to what they do say. Recognize when your child is uncomfortable or dancing around a subject. Depending on your upbringing, personality and existing relationships, you may find it difficult or even awkward engaging in what you consider to be sensitive topics. If this is the case, you may wish to consider books on the subject, or professional help. When seeking professional help with a child or family psychologist, you will discover that most will tell you that they are qualified to help you. Most psychologists, it seems, feel qualified to assist anyone, regarding any subject. You need to know, that like any other profession, each field has its own specialists. Psychologists also specialize. Find a psychologist that specializes in adult-child relations and communication.

Sexual abuse may take place within the child's immediate family referred to as incest. By immediate family, I am referring to the individual family unit (mother, father and children,) although some experts include close relatives, (aunts, uncles, cousins and grandparents) as incest. The step-parent ranks the highest in reported sexual child abuse within the home. Some experts also consider a sexual relationship between the step-parent and child without bloodline ties a form of incest. Exactly how they come to that conclusion, I'm not sure, however that does lead us into the next subject, which is alertness.

Please be especially interested and attentive to your children's actions and conversations immediately after they have spent time with relatives. If your child talks about a stepparent, especially if the child has initiated the conversation, you must listen carefully. Does this mean we should constantly be leery of relatives and step-parents? Absolutely not. The bond between families is, or should be, the strongest and most caring unity one experiences in life. Good step-parents, as I choose to believe, are very, very, very special people. What I mean is that you as parents must be constantly alert to abuse and completely attentive to your children. If you are alert and constantly vigilant, protecting your child against all possible predators, you may discover one in your own family. Believe me, you wouldn't be the first.

Boys as well as girls are vulnerable to sexual abuse, although statistically boys are not as likely to tell as girls are. I believe boys are not apt to tell due to the socialization of boys, which teaches them that they should not acknowledge vulnerability. Thus, they consider themselves the aggressors, not the victims. That leaves us with the question.... Are girls sexually abused more than boys, or is the sexual molestation of girls merely more likely to be reported? No one really knows, except I do know that it is much more difficult to discover the sexual abuse of a boy child.

I also know that pedophiles commonly threaten children with harm, and quite often tell the child if she does not keep their secret, he will kill her mommy and daddy. It is also common for pedophiles to frighten a child by claiming monsters and other creatures, that children are typically afraid of, will come to get them. As you can see, that's a whole lot of baggage for a child to carry. The good news is that no child is willing to carry that much baggage indefinitely. Some children don't say anything, believing that they are protecting their parents. If you suspect that this is a possibility and know something is wrong, you must convince your child that nothing is going to harm her or you. You must also convince her that you can help. Obviously, the very best way to achieve all of this is to have open, quality, communication with your children before something happens. I cannot repeat this enough, because it is the most important single thing you can do for your children.

Common behavioral

You should have noticed by now that many of the signs and behavioral actions attributed to child maltreatment seem to apply to most, if not all areas of child abuse. Nothing is for sure; there are no guarantees and that's why the experts ask the experts. Since maltreatment of children covers such a wide spectrum, and a child's mind is so complicated in its escapes, it is impossible for anyone to know exactly where it begins and where it ends with each child. Only a medical doctor is qualified to determine if a child has been sexually molested or not.

Different types of child abuses do often overlap. An example is a young boy accidentally witnesses an overly rambunctious act of love-making by his parents. The child also has been emotionally maltreated to a small degree in the past, and this treatment continues sporadically. The child is frustrated, confused, and angry. In his frustration and confused anger, a young girl he is playing with triggers his temper over whatever it is kids fight about. They start fighting and rolling around on the ground. The boy begins mimicking the rambunctious sex act he had once witnessed. Which symptoms of what type of child abuse do you <u>think</u> you are witnessing? It's difficult to tell, especially when interpreting the forces and reasoning behind a child's behavior.

Some children who have been sexually abused are very afraid of specific places or things. Commonly, they are the bathroom, bedroom or a certain piece of furniture such as a bed or sofa. There are a multitude of signs that may indicate a child is being or has been sexually abused. Here are some more examples. A child displays precocious sexual behavior such as masturbation, in front of other children. Often, an abused child will ask other children to show their penis or vagina. Another child may alert you to the possibility of abuse by playing with dolls, one on top of the other. Generally, when an abused child is playing with dolls, the play is accompanied by a conversation between the child and the dolls. The conversation may contain words that were spoken to the child during the abusive act, such as "This won't hurt, I promise." Sometimes an indicator can be put to you in the form of a game: "I have a secret, but I can't tell you what it is." This may be a child sworn to secrecy through threats trying to let you know without breaking the promise of secrecy.

When children are in pain, it is impossible for them to contain it. The child may not be able to sit still, constantly leaning from cheek to cheek and wiggling as though she has to go to the bathroom.

Do you have to go to the bathroom Susie?

No, Susie replies, my bottom hurts.

Did you fall down?

No, it hurts where Bobby touched me.

Bobby is the next-door neighbor's 19-year-old son. It is at this moment that you should stop asking questions and seek professional help. As I said, different types of child abuse can manifest in many ways. Emotional maltreatment can show up as speech disorders, rocking motions and facial tics, or they may not materialize in any form for many years. Emotional maltreatment signs are rarely physical. However, the scarring can go deeper than actual lacerations. Emotional abuse most often manifests in physical development and speech disorders. Emotional maltreatment is often accompanied by physical and/or sexual abuse. Emotionally maltreated children are not always physically abused, but physically abused children, especially sexually abused children, are emotionally maltreated as well.

You must keep in mind at all times that you cannot conclude that a child is suffering from any type of abuse from one or two acts. You must witness repetitive action from a child (a cluster of acts) before considering alerting the authorities. You must also realize cultural differences. Are any of your child's classmates or friends' immigrants from Nicaragua, Cambodia, Afghanistan, Mexico, Cuba, Thailand, and Russia etc.? A minor difference between cultures would be that some cultures teach their children to avoid eye contact with adults, while others insist on it: "Look at me when I'm talking to you." In the United States, a girl is considered a minor until she reaches the age of 18 years, although there are a few archaic state laws still in existence that differ from the majority of states. In many other parts of the world, a girl is no longer considered a minor when she starts her menstrual period and is also considered ready for marriage.

What I am getting at is that if your child plays with a child from another culture, there is no need to press the panic button because your child's friend may not be embarrassed or concerned about nudity or relieving himself in front of you. Those acts and others that we may find embarrassing or offensive may be commonplace in other cultures. Many people from other countries consider us extravagant for offering male and female public restrooms. In addition, nude or topless beaches are commonplace in many countries around the world. If you allow your child to associate with children from other cultures, you need to be prepared to encounter different values and customs. Here in the United States, we teach our children to be independent, believing this will help them develop positive self-esteem. Yet many cultures encourage children to be dependent. Surely, there is more than one right way to raise a child.

However, it is important to remember that in the United States of America the legal definitions of child abuse and child neglect are not flexible. If an abusive practice is considered a cultural practice, it is still considered child abuse in the United States, and we are obligated by our morals and our laws to report it.

It is extremely difficult, if not impossible, to describe every symptom and behavior regarding child sexual abuse, especially considering that the symptoms and behaviors are constantly evolving with time and society. It is equally difficult to use scenarios as examples, for they are never ending. One must also take into consideration that a publishing company does not exist that would publish a book containing every word on the subject. A book such as that would be larger than the largest telephone book in the world. It is my intent, however, to supply you with more than sufficient information to safeguard your children.

While you're processing everything you now know regarding child sexual abuse behaviors, you need to know and begin processing common natural behaviors. In other words, the stuff your kids will naturally start doing sooner or later. I refer to it as "Limited natural interest." The word limited is very important. <u>Limited</u> natural interest means your child's interest should not be excessive, nor should it be constant. I am going to categorize for you the approximate age groups and their activities. Keep in mind, as you read on that there are exceptions to every rule and to children as well. I am supplying you with approximate age groups beginning with two and three-year-old's even though forms of masturbation can and often do begin before the age of two, and it's perfectly natural and normal. About now, you should be asking, what is the purpose of Ty telling me all this? My reasoning is to contribute to your existing knowledge in order to complete the connection between you and your child. In addition, helping you recognize abuse of another's child.

- 2 to 3-year-olds may begin to show interest in the different-postures used by boys and girls while urinating and may even begin becoming interested in the physical differences between boys and girls.
- 3 to 4-year-olds become extremely conscious of their navels and often begin verbally expressing interest in physical differences between boys and girls. Also, verbalizing about the different postures used by other children while urinating. Girls at this age will often attempt to urinate standing up. Overwhelmed with curiosity, both boys and girls may attempt to quickly touch a parent's vagina, breast, or penis. Boys begin to notice their own erections, often bending the penis com-

pletely to one side before releasing it, allowing it to spring back and forth, and may subconsciously repeat this several times. Some experts consider this a mild form of masturbation. Between three and four years of age is when your child's curiosity may include the family pet's private parts. (Usually male canine pets.) This is not an unusual curiosity.

- 4 to 5-year-olds are still interested in their belly buttons. Under social stress they will commonly grasp their genitals, and may suddenly need to urinate. This is also the show and tell age for both boys and girls. "I'll show you mine, if you show me yours." This is the age both sexes begin verbally expressing their thoughts and ideas about elimination (human waste). They also become more interested in other people's bathrooms than your average interior decorator. They may also demand privacy for themselves, but are extremely interested in the bathroom activities of others.

- 5 to 6-year-olds are familiar with, but not too much interested in the physical differences between sexes. They are usually not as interested in sexual play or the "You show me yours, I'll show you mine" games. They are less apt to expose themselves and less interested in bathroom play. They also seem to have lost all interest in unfamiliar bathrooms.

- 6 to 7-year-olds have a marked awareness of, and a born-again interest in the differences between the sexes, particularly in body structure. A mutual investigation of each other by both sexes is commonplace. This mutual investigation most often reveals practical answers to questions about sex differences. Mild sex play and exhibitionism will occur during play. The game of "You show me yours, I'll show you mine" has made a comeback. This age group often plays "Hospital" and some children have even gone so far as to take rectal temperatures. Giggling and the calling of names, or remarks involving words dealing with elimination functions often accompany this play. Older children subject some children to sex play. The age and power differences between the children are critical in defining this as normal sex play or a form of exploitation.

- 7 to 8-year-olds sometimes act as if they are bored with sex, definitely showing less interest in it. There is still some mu-

44

tual exploration with some experimentation including sex play, but usually less than between the ages of 6 and 7. It seems to be a time of reflection, or possibly they are simply regrouping in preparation for their next phase.

- 8 to 9-year-olds have a rather high interest in sex, with some sex exploration and play, but less than it was between 6 and 7. With others, it can be the opposite. This is the age when "peeping" often begins, smutty jokes are funny and provocative giggling seems to be intertwined with their conversations. Cursing with their peers along with writing and spelling aloud "sex" words, is the thing to do. Touching themselves is still done, although, generally unconsciously.

- 9 to 10-year-olds will often talk about sex information with their friends, usually same-sex friends. They have by now become very interested in the details of their own organs and their functions. They have taken to sex swearing, sex poems, rhymes, and riddles; also, the search for pictures in books has begun. Masturbation without reaching orgasm is not uncommon at this age.

- 10 to 11-year-olds may have started occasional masturbation. Their interest at this age is with not only themselves and their friends. They now have become very interested in the difference between themselves and grown-ups. Many children, generally boys, will go to great lengths, taking risks to "Peep" on grown-ups. Often considered a safer target for "Peeps" is an older sibling. Pubic hair seems to have their interest when parents do not allow their children to see them disrobed (totally naked).

- 11 to 12-year-olds in some cases have started masturbating regularly. Generally boys more than girls. This is the age where sex slowly begins to occupy a great percentage of their thoughts. This is also the age when boys spend a great deal of their time trying to figure out how they can touch a girl's breast or any other special place, and make it look like an accident. Generally, they don't work up the nerve.

- After age 12, most everything kids do falls into the category of hormones run amok. It is common behavior for boys to masturbate daily, some, multiple times daily. This _may_ be the only exception to "Limited" and "Excessive" natural behavior.

Studies have shown boys who are kept very busy do not masturbate excessively. Hard-working students involved in extra school programs and sports, combined with homework, chores and/or a part-time job, rarely have time or the energy for masturbation, much less excessive masturbation.

Ninety-nine point nine percent of the behavior you just read about is natural activities, so don't panic.
Habitual masturbation is more difficult to diagnose in boys than it is with girls. It is more difficult to determine with boys, due to the stage of adolescence when most boys masturbate excessively. On the other hand (no pun intended), most experts agree that if a girl is masturbating excessively (multiple times daily), it could be habitual. Some experts believe this activity may lead to a form of nymphomania as an adult.

Detecting sexual abuse
The history of sexual child abuse is the history of mankind itself. Pedophilia has been well documented by the Romans, Greeks, Egyptians, and even in the Bible. It is today as it was then, an act of barbarians. There is no difference today. Our society is full of these degenerates. However, today's society is also full of wonderful, caring, self-giving and in some cases, very well trained individuals on the lookout for pedophiliacs. Qualified caregivers are constantly observing children and their parents.

Interaction between child and parent can supply a trained observer with invaluable information that could save a child's life. A qualified caregiver can learn a great deal by simply watching a child being dropped off for the day.

Along with the problem-solving attention given to child molestation intended to provide a safer environment for children today, a climate of fear has been created between children and male adults. It is normal for an adult to want to pick up, hug, kiss and even tickle a child. Children need nurturing and physical comforting. It is important to their mental health. It can be an uncomfortable situation, especially for men. Men have to be conscious of the fact that someone may consider it improper for a grown man to tickle a child and it could be reported. Consequently, many men of good moral character have become standoffish towards children, not wanting to take the risk. Once again, the child is victimized, a form of emotional maltreatment imposed by society. Society trying to protect its children. We can; however, take satisfaction in knowing that society's cure is far better for children then the alternatives. Still, the cure itself is not without its own long-term effects on children. So, does anyone have a better idea? We will further investigate what might be better ideas in "SOLUTIONS" and how other countries handle the same problems and their results. Until someone with a better idea comes along, we will continue to monitor behavioral indicators of child sexual abuse and remain suspect of every hug and tickle.

Detecting sexual abuse in your own child should not be difficult to attentive caring parents. After all, you know your child better than anyone else. You know when something is different, when something isn't right, or when your child is off. You know, don't you? Studies have shown, including my own studies, that many parents do not know their children well enough to pick up on erratic behaviors when they first occur. It is generally not because the parents are not attentive and caring, rather because their lives are going a hundred and eighty two miles per hour in order to survive in this dog-eat-dog world. Sad to say, there is also the exception to this rule. There are parents who just don't care enough to pay attention to their children. Nevertheless, I'm not talking to those parents; I'm talking to you. Because you're an attentive parent, you're going to notice anything wrong or different about your child's physical appearance or behavior. Obviously, you will immediately detect cuts, bruises, bleeding and take heed of any complaints. Especially, pay attention to unusual or strange complaints. Complaints involving their private parts and of course, it goes without saying, you are going to pay particular attention to conversations your child is having, right? Right! Especially conversations involving older people. For example, the man next-door, or the teenage boys that live directly behind you. If nothing else, you'll hear some pretty juicy gossip from a five-year-old. Hey, it's cheap entertainment.

On a more serious note, our children are totally dependent on us. Quite often predators target the very young, so young it is difficult for them to express themselves, and predators count on that. Consequently, we have to remain vigilant and we must educate our children from an early age. I will discuss educating your child in the section of this book designated "Early childhood education." I have already introduced you to many indicators of child sexual abuse, but I feel it necessary to point out more indicators and behavioral patterns. It is necessary and important because an observant parent may well become aware of a situation before the child is actually injured. I know you all agree with me when I say that's really important.

In an abnormal family setting, a female child may be receiving special consideration, unreasonable amounts of attention, and an overall unfair favoritism over her siblings. When a father or a stepfather makes unreasonable or outrageous excuses for their princess, it may be a warning and flags should go up. I am referring to a father whose actions are out of character when it comes to his daughter. Of course, there is again the exception, a family of six boys and one girl for instance. It doesn't take a rocket scientist to know who's going to get the preferential treatment in that family. I'm talking about a father who seems to be allowing his daughter to get away with murder. A father who is sexually abusing his daughter will make excuses and allowances for her that he hasn't made in the past and would normally never consider **(Acting out of character)**. He may feel he has no choice, considering he has a secret to protect. A definite indicator of the possibility of sexual abuse is out-of-character favoritism. Mothers, I want you to especially be alert to the signs that something may be wrong. If it turns out that your husband or boyfriend is sexually molesting your child (boy or girl child) you sure as to hell had better do something about it! I'm counting on you not to be concerned about how you will get by without him. Oh, and by the way, your child is counting on you too. Believe me, you'll survive. The alternative is, if you don't do something about it, your child may not survive. That kind of selfishness will do nothing but earn you a place in jail... and in hell, I hope.

I have talked with mothers who admitted to me that they were aware of the out-of-character treatment their daughters were receiving. However, most claim ignorance. Some mothers did however admit a jealousy toward their daughters. Adding to that, some chose to blame their daughters, while others blame themselves for not having been more sexually cooperative or active with their husbands. In addition to the atrocities committed against the children, some of the mothers I interviewed became accessories to the abuse by remaining silent, allowing it to continue. I was neither shocked, nor even surprised, when I learned that some of the mothers interviewed, while their children are grown-up and long gone, are still living with the pedophiles.

Evidently, some mothers, possibly many mothers, are willing to allow their children to endure heinous torture rather then possibly jeopardize their lifestyles.

There have been many explanations and excuses, written by some pretty impressive experts, as to why mothers will live in silence, allowing their children to suffer in such a way. Because a mother is weak and insecure is no excuse! Because she is fearing for her own security and future, or afraid of physical violence, cannot be accepted as an excuse for allowing her child to be mentally and sexually tortured. Mothers have no excuse, short of complete and total imprisonment, making it impossible to leave or get help. Most studies have shown that in the final analysis, it is the mother's selfishness. "What will **I** do?" "Where will **I** go?" "How will **I** survive?" "What will happen to **me**?" A mother abandoning her child for herself is making a choice! Children of abusive parents may choose to forgive a mother who made selfish choices. However, it remains true that there is no excuse. Especially in today's society where there is a multitude of resources and help available.

Other indicators of child sexual abuse may be when a child becomes obviously afraid and even cries when that certain friend or uncle comes to visit. When your child is normally excited about visiting family or friends with children near her own age, but suddenly resists violently, a flag should go up. Something may have happened. If your child begins exhibiting a continuous interest in private parts, including wanting to touch your vagina, breasts or penis, something may be wrong. Begin investigating any possibilities. I cannot express strongly enough that you never, but never accuse or make accusations without proof, proof positive. If you feel something is seriously wrong, **seek professional help immediately**.

There have been cases where children did not exhibit any indicators of sexual abuse. Generally, those children are not suffering from any physical pain. Your next question should be "How are we supposed to find out if our child is being molested if they're not exhibiting any indicators?" What a great question. I can tell you're staying on top of this. You should be able to detect if your child is being sexually abused by having opened great lines of communication with your child. Nevertheless, predators will often supply the indicators, especially pedophiles close to your family. If someone within, or close to your family is constantly or overly insistent on taking your children off your hands, it could be a signal and definitely should alert you to the possibility. Another red flag alert would be the same situation, only the individual is interested in watching only one of your children, especially when it's always the same child. Predators close to a family, believing they are beyond suspicion, will go to unusual lengths to assist you with your children. An example: you have to take off work to get a child to soccer practice, but your <u>friend</u> insists on doing it for you. Sounds reasonable and even very considerate, unless your <u>friend</u> must also take off work to do you this favor. **Bright red flags should go up!**

Physical indicators of child sexual abuse

To determine if physical indicators are actually signs of sexual abuse, a medical doctor must examine the child. There is no exception to this rule! If you suspect the slightest possibility of sexual abuse, immediately make an appointment with an expert! Because your little girl has swelling, bruising and even bleeding in the vaginal or anal areas does not necessarily mean it's a positive indicator of sexual abuse. Your little girl may simply be the victim of a fence climbing or bicycling accident. You must allow a professional to evaluate and determine exactly what the situation is, especially before considering or taking any other action.

The list of physical indicators that may signal child sexual abuse is a long one. The problems with some indicators of sexual abuses are that they may also be indicators of things not related to sexual abuse. Bed wetting, uncontrollable spot wetting, rashes and burning sensation while urinating, or vaginal infection and anal irritation, even hemorrhoids in a young child are not necessarily positive signs of sexual abuse. Yet each and every one of these symptoms and more can be attributed and usually are attributed to sexual abuse. Adding to the sexual abuse list is a child having difficulty in walking and/or sitting, a child suffering from pain and/or itching in the genital area and torn, stained or bloody underclothing. To be included are the aforesaid bruises, bleeding, swelling or lacerations on the external genitalia, vaginal or anal openings and obviously vaginal and/or anal tears. Some of the more common physical complaints are a child who suffers from recurring stomachaches, backaches and headaches with no apparent basis for such as condition. Other telltale possibilities of sexual abuse are bruises and/or lacerations of the penis or perineum and difficulty with urination. The even more obvious signs of child sexual abuse are venereal diseases, or venereal sores, ulcers and vaginal discharge.

The next is an indicator I find so distressful; it is difficult for me to alert you to it. New mothers, be watchful for bruising around the mouth of your infant. As hard as it may be to comprehend, much less believe, there are many documented cases of pedophiliacs committing vaginal, anal, and oral atrocities to infants still in the crib. I personally am familiar with two cases involving vaginal intercourse with infants, one a three-month old, the other a four-month old. Both infants succumbed to their injuries. (Neither adult was charged with murder.)

I find it ironic that some people question my right regarding the recovery of kidnapped children when I say, "Once we have a child in our custody we do whatever is necessary to see to it that no more harm comes to that child."

In the deepest and darkest corner of your mind, you are incapable of conceiving of anything that someone, somewhere hasn't done or isn't doing to someone. This is especially true regarding children. Over the course of years of recoveries, I have witnessed heinous atrocities that could have only been inspired and choreographed by Satan himself.

Behavioral indicators of child sexual abuse

As with the above topic, physical indicators of child sexual abuse, I believe behavioral indicators are also important enough to risk repeating myself. At the same time I'll supply you with more signs of child sexual abuse.

Indicators can be as subtle as overly compliant behavior, or as obvious as a child acting out aggressive behavior. Sexual abuse can also manifest itself in pseudo-mature behavior or role reversal. A female victim will sometimes assume maternal responsibility, which is obviously inappropriate for her age and family circumstances. A child

51

may also give you verbal hints about possible sexual activity. For instance, while looking at her father's penis as he exits the shower, four-year-old Cindy blurted, "I know what that's for." A young child that is able to give you a reasonably detailed understanding of sexual behavior can be exposing a definite indicator of sexual abuse. A child displaying a positive lack of trust, particularly with significant others, or a child who is having poor peer relationships and possibly an inability to make friends, may also be indicators of child sexual abuse. Although I must stress that they are, not proof positive of child sexual abuse. Remember, you need more than one or two indicators before you consider taking action. As part of your weaponry in this war, it is essential for you to gather as much information as possible. Here is a list of more possible behavioral indicators you need to remember:

- Sudden drop in school or play performance
- Nonparticipation in school and social activities
- Inability to concentrate in school
- Withdrawal symptoms
- Withdrawal or infantile behavior or fantasies
- Recent sexual promiscuity including frequent or excessive masturbation
- Clinical depression
- Sudden excessive weight gain or loss
- Brothers or sisters that complain of sexual mistreatment
- Regressive behavior
- Running away from home
- Seductive behavior with males (I have witnessed seductive behavior in girls as young as six.)
- Persistent and inappropriate sexual play with peers, toys, or with themselves
- Persistent, aggressive and inappropriate sexual play with others
- Extraordinary fear of males
- Unnecessary and inappropriate sexual modesty
- Suicidal feelings or tendencies

It is your responsibility not to react in an irresponsible manner by assuming any one or two of these indicators mean your child has been sexually abused. Remember that you have to witness a cluster of indicators before you can even consider acting. This does not mean you should wait until you observe a cluster of indicators before having your child examined by a medical doctor if you feel the need, or if a physical indicator is present. When I tell you that there must be a cluster of at least three indicators, this means before you get authorities involved. Even if there are more than three indicators, you should never accuse anyone. Personally, I would rather be accused of murder than wrongly accused of sexually molesting a child! But that's me.

What to do if your child is sexually molested

First and foremost, if you have followed the guidelines that I have laid out, you will know beyond the shadow of any doubt that your child was sexually molested. The reason you know beyond the shadow of any doubt is that you observed a cluster of positive indicators, or you witnessed something so obvious that you <u>immediately had your child examined by an expert a medical doctor</u>. By the way, you know that you have the right to be present during an examination of your child. You should insist on it! Your child has already been traumatized enough. She needs you with her, not close by. You can assist in your child's healing from the very moment you discover she has been molested. To do this, you must remain calm, cool, and collected, mainly for your child's sake, but yours also. When the doctor has completed the examination, and the findings are positive that your child has been sexually molested, **STOP EVERYTHING**. You must not ask your child any more questions regarding the molestation, and you must not allow anyone else to question or discuss what happened with her. Non-experts may unknowingly misdirect and confuse or possibly plant seeds in the already traumatized child's mind. This also includes the doctor, who more than likely is not qualified to question the child. Immediately contact the police department of the city in which the child was assaulted. Police jurisdiction is where the assault took place, not necessarily where the child lives. Early reporting is vital! The examining doctor, by law, must report his findings to the local authorities. Your next step is to contact your husband or wife, if not yet notified. The only exception to that rule is if <u>you know or suspect with good reason</u> your mate to be the perpetrator of your child's molestation.

When the authorities arrive, you have the right to question any police officer or agent's qualifications before allowing that official to question your child. If you're uncomfortable or not satisfied with the official's credentials, insist on having a child molestation expert question your child. Remember that your child has already suffered enough. A non-professional may traumatize the child further and/or possibly disturb or destroy vital suspicious evidence, hence breaking the chain of evidence. If videotaping is not available, you must insist on it being made available. It can protect you and your child. Again, your child has already been extremely traumatized. With videotaping, he or she will not have to recall the story a number of times to different people, causing further trauma. Recounting the assault may also cause the child to become desensitized, due to repetition. It is also wise to videotape your child's questioning by police to prevent the possibility of things being twisted later and possibly being used against you. **You have rights!** Enforce them if necessary.

All of this is based of course, on the premise that you are innocent. On the other hand, if you are the guilty party, I hope upon your reading of this chapter that these particular pages are stuck together, causing you to miss this good advice that is meant to aid the innocent.

As soon as possible, you must gather your thoughts and put things in order. You'll need to supply the police or any other respective agencies involved with the information you have. You should first have ready:

- Your relationship to the victim;
- Your full name, date of birth, age;
- Your address and telephone number;
- Your child's (the victim) full name, date of birth, age;
- Your child's (the victim) present location;
- Names and ages of the victims siblings and their present location;
- Nature of the victim's injury;
- Names and any information you may have knowledge of regarding possible witnesses;
- Names and any information you may have knowledge of regarding the perpetrator(s);

The knowledge you have regarding your child's molestation should be presented to authorities in chronological order. This is important for many reasons. First, they cannot do their work properly without as much accurate information as possible. Second, presenting your information in chronological order aids you in assuring that the authorities receive all the information you have to offer. Third, there is less chance of confusion on the part of the authorities. Fourth, it aids in the healing of the parents when they can feel that they contributed to catching and punishing the perpetrator. Do you see why it is so important that the information is in chronological order? It is important that law enforcement obtains accurate information as fast as possible, enabling them to execute an expedient arrest of the perpetrator or locate a missing child. In either case, time is of the essence.

It is important to know that the reporting of child molestation crimes can be long and tedious. Especially considering that there may be more than one or two agencies involved. In addition, an agency may have special reporting requirements. This may add to your frustrations. Bear with it. It's necessary. The only thing that parents know for sure at this time is that they want the perpetrator caught, as do the police. However, the police know that they not only have to catch the perpetrator, but that they also have to build a good solid case. It must be a case that will withstand the scrutiny of the District Attorney's office. Consequently, there is good reasoning behind spending extra time following any special reporting requirements.

All states, including the District of Columbia and the territories have a reporting statute for child abuse and neglect. While each of the state laws may differ from the others in one or more ways, all share a common framework. In general, reporting statutes defining child abuse and child neglect specify reporting procedures. Some states do not include specific definitions of child abuse. However, most states do include their own definition of non-accidental physical abuse, which does include sexual abuse. Investigate the statutes that apply in your state.

Agencies that may become involved are the Department of Social Services, the Department of Human Resources, or the Division of Family and Children Services. Child Protective Services (CPS) may also be notified, depending on circumstances. You must understand that in order for agencies to do a complete and thorough investigation, unofficially anyone and everyone may be suspect until authorities have

55

had the time to narrow the field. Due to good police work, multiple perpetrators have been discovered, when there was only thought to be one. You may be asked questions you feel should only be asked of a suspect. Again bear with it. If you want the most complete and thorough investigation possible, cooperate! As soon as the authorities are satisfied that you have nothing to hide, they will continue their investigation elsewhere. You may consider it a waste of time, but the authorities have excellent reasoning behind the avenues and techniques they employ. (A report of child sexual abuse is not investigated in terms of accusations made against a possible perpetrator, rather in terms of the child's condition and evidence.) The investigating agency must leave no stone unturned while investigating every possibility. For example, it is not uncommon that the individual reporting the child sexual abuse is actually the perpetrator. In fairness and support to law enforcement agencies, we have to understand that they have heard and seen it all. Most importantly, the authorities know they have an obligation to protect the child. This obligation may include determining if a parent is responsible in any way for the sexual abuse or possible neglect of the child that may have led to or contributed to the sexual abuse.

In fairness to you, the parent, I am obligated to inform you that some of the child protective agencies and agents are so overloaded with cases that their efforts can be no more than superficial exercises. Which, in case you didn't know, is most prevalent in large cities. I am not attacking the deep, strong, personal commitment to the welfare of children of the individual agent. I am attacking the government for allowing such a lack of manpower and funding to exist in what we all should consider one of the most important areas of civic responsibility, if not the most important. Consequently, you must be ever observant of activities conducted by Child Protective Service agencies regarding the welfare of your children. You must be prepared, if necessary, to enlist the aid of an attorney. Almost without exception, I believe that Child Protective Services have only the child's best interest in mind. However, that does not stop them from occasionally acting prematurely, or without all the facts, causing them to make the wrong decision. Past case histories have proven that some agencies have literally trampled the civil rights of parents. It needs to be added that for some unexplained reason it seems to take these agencies forever to right their wrongs. One agency in particular seems to keep making the same mistakes. Allow me to explain. They have removed children from their homes and not returned them for months, and in some cases, years. They had done so without the slightest bit of evidence that anything wrong has happened, simply acting on unsubstantiated information.

If you feel that the actions of a child services agency or the conduct of an agent is questionable, you may consider contacting the Ethics Commission of the National Association for the Education of Young Children. The NAEYC has developed a Code of Ethical Conduct for professionals. Be alert and prepared for that possibility.

I feel it very important and necessary to let you know at this point, if you are a parent that has abused, or is abusing, a child in any way, contact the National Association for the Education of Young Children. They will guide you toward help such as an early childhood program that can be a respite for a child in a troubled family. They believe most parents have the capacity to change their abusive behavior. They also believe they have an ethical responsibility to respond to your needs in a non-punitive, non-critical, and least intrusive manner possible. They are nonjudgmental and have the resources to help you and your child. If you fit into this category, contacting these folks for help is probably the most important thing you will ever do. I promise that if you will trust these people to help you, you will receive from them respect for your decision and the help you need. For the sake of your children, please do it.

If you are attempting to discover the possibility of your child having been molested through conversation with the child, do so in a private place where you will not be disturbed. You must listen carefully, while looking for behavior indications or changes in the child's normal mannerisms such as hesitancy on your child's part to discuss the day's activities. Ask your child to tell you what happened in her own words. Remember that children, particularly young ones, will not normally fabricate stories of sexual abuse, unless you lead them, or should I say, mislead them. During this conversation be supportive, sympathetic, give her praise and let her know you believe her. It is also very important to let her know that she is not to blame, she did nothing wrong. Make sure she understands that she must not feel shame. It was not her fault! You must also assure her that you will

57

protect her and that it will not happen again.

Sometimes the child will show little or no emotional reaction to the disclosure of sexual abuse. This does not mean that she has not been molested, or that she is not affected by the molestation. Many young victims hide their feelings, and are often very frightened. Some children exhibit the effects of having been sexually abused through disturbed behavior. They become hostile, destructive and even self-destructive, while others may strive to be the perfect child in order to keep attention away from them, enabling them to keep their secret. Most sexual abuse is not discovered unless the child is willing to tell someone. Keep a good line of communication open and don't be afraid to talk to your children. Don't be afraid to ask questions, personal questions. When a good rapport exists between parents and their children, the sky's the limit. If parents don't open that line of communication, neither will their children and you can count on it.

After your child has confided in you and you have <u>good reason to suspect</u>, or <u>reasonable cause to believe</u>, that your child has been sexually abused, you must immediately report it. Waiting for more proof may put your child at grave risk. More proof may be a long time coming and witnesses to child sexual abuse are rare.

Your children have to understand that they can tell you anything. They must be instructed from a young age to come to you immediately if something has happened. If your child expresses feelings or has questions about her molestation, be calm, have a matter-of-fact attitude, and try to answer all of her questions honestly. If you do not know the answer to a question, let her know that you will ask the experts, and you will have the answer for her very soon. **Do Not Forget!** It is important never to pressure your child into conversation regarding her molestation or any type of abuse. You should always start the conversation with a question and the question should be, "Would you like to talk about it?"

Adding to that, it is as equally important not to try to silence your child. A silent child doesn't forget and often carries the burden of another's act for a lifetime. It is important for you to understand that children often feel and are lead to believe that they are to blame for bringing trouble to the family. Therefore, it is imperative to reassure the child that they are not at fault. You also have to respect the privacy of your child. This is done by not confiding in many, if any, people regarding the molestation. If your child even suspects that you're telling people, it may very well be the last personal and private conversation your child shares with you.

If there are siblings in the home, depending on their ages, you may want to tell them that something has happened to their sister/brother. Generally they know something is up. You need to also tell them that the child is safe and will be okay. You have to tell the molested child that her brothers and sisters need to know that something has happened and that you are all right. Tell them only as much as they are able to assimilate, or as much as you feel they need to know. You must explain to her that they will not be told everything, although she also needs to understand that it is important for them to know, so they don't worry and also so they can learn and be protected. Let her know she is helping to protect her brothers and sisters. **Thank her for helping.**

If the molestation is pursued in criminal court, make certain your child understands what is happening to the best of his/her knowledge and ability to comprehend. As I have explained, it is important that your child is familiar with identifying basic anatomy. Putting it simply, your child needs to know the difference between boys and girls. Make sure an advocate or guardian ad litem is appointed to protect your child. These people are knowledgeable regarding the criminal justice system and can help you protect your child. If you feel for one reason or another unable to handle this situation by yourself, get help. If you are wise, you will seek counseling services for the molested child and consider counseling for the entire family. You can obtain help including counseling through a sexual assault center or a child protection team, which can be found in most major cities. It is important that this be done quickly, since not all children demonstrate immediate effects after being sexually assaulted. Help given by a qualified psychologist may mean a relatively normal, unaffected life for your child.

Early childhood education

Some experts, and maybe even most, believe four years is the age to begin teaching children about strangers, kidnapping, molestation etc. I however, believe it should start at two years of age and my reasoning is I believe in common sense. You should start educating your child at the age of two because I choose to allow for the possibility of the exceptional child. I agree that by normal standards the education should begin at age four. The problem I have with that is threefold. First, what about those special children? Should we just allow them to fall through the cracks? Second, sometimes parents don't realize they have a gifted child that could be learning and is capable of learning about strangers at the early age of two. Third, a child will absorb what he or she can or wants to, and the rest just goes away. A tiny bit of education is better than none at all. Sure, it can be a little more time-consuming and difficult. However, since I believe that parents are the primary educators of their own children, I am confident you will find the way. You will have to be creative, but it can be fun by using music, creating songs and makeup games. I believe many parents will be pleasantly surprised. Also available are early childhood education programs, which offer a direct service to parents. Usually, they can be located through your local schools, but for sure they can be located on the Internet. It has now been proven that infants' and one year olds cry much of the time due to being frustrated by not being able to communicate. Parents that choose to teach the very, very young sign language will raise a much more contented child.

You should begin with the basic stuff. As I have mentioned earlier, your child needs to be able to identify basic anatomy. (Know and understand the difference between the sexes.) You can't get much more basic than that. Your children should learn as soon as possible the areas of the body no one should touch. That sounds like it could get complicated. Not at all, as a matter-of-fact, it's one of the easier things to teach a child. Simply, point out to your children that <u>places covered by your swimsuit</u> are the places no one should touch. You may consider using drawings and include bright colors for the swimsuits. If you were really good, you would be able to make up a song to go along with your pictures. Sounds like great fun, I can hardly wait for you to get started!

Have you noticed that I start many of my informational directives with "You must?" That is done because there are things you have to do. Important things, <u>you must do!</u> Insuring the well being of your children isn't an easy job and it should be a constant and ongoing practice. As time goes on, it becomes second nature; you'll find yourself doing it automatically. In today's society, it is necessary for survival,

60

sad to say. If you handle it subtly and intelligently, over a period of time your child will become just a little bit paranoid and in today's society that's a good thing.

*You must arm your children with the courage and knowledge to recognize danger and the confidence to make intelligent decisions regarding their own safety.

Children need to learn to look around occasionally while playing to see if someone they don't know is watching or has come nearby. Your child needs to know that bad people usually look the same as good people and that bad people do not look or dress in any special way. Your child should be aware that bad people are men, women or older children. Children need also learn that if anyone makes them feel frightened or uncomfortable, they should run away and tell an adult they know and trust. All children should know that sometimes it's okay to say **"No!"** Even to an adult. Especially when a person of any age touches them, frightens them or simply makes them feel uncomfortable. Even if that person is an adult that they know. Your child ought to be taught to understand that it's okay to scream **"no"**, and run away. If someone, anyone, touches them in the swimsuit area, they should know to **Scream No!** run away and tell an adult. I can't emphasize this enough. Children have a right to feel and to be safe and it is your responsibility to help ensure their safety. One major step forward ensuring their safety is to teach them to help themselves.

There are many things a young child is capable of learning. You will be amazed, I guarantee it. Teach your child their first and, most importantly, their last name. Make sure they learn how to use a telephone to call for "Help", **911**. This is easy stuff, even for the average two-year-old. I call it channeling the terrible twos. A two-year-old is capable of learning complete telephone numbers and much, much more. Allow them to practice on a real telephone. If you feel your child is too young to learn a combination of numbers, make sure they know how to dial "O" for the operator. Explain how the operator can help them by connecting them to home or the police in an emergency. Let them know they do not have to put money in a pay phone in order to talk to the operator. Make sure your child understands what an emergency is. Help your children to learn their address, including city and state. You may consider labeling what you teach your child. For example, your child's defense yell label might be **"Secret Weapon"**

61

and the defense yell is **"No."** Children seem to like and remember **"Secret Weapon"**. Practice with your child so they become comfortable using what they've learned. Be sure your children understand that there are no such things as "Monsters." Let your children know that you believe in their ability to keep safe and that you will always be there to help them. If you don't realize it yet, here's what you are doing that is so very important. You are helping your children through knowledge to build the courage to be **"Proactive not Reactive"** when situations develop. If you follow my instructions, your kid will be very busy learning to be safe, too busy to be your typical two-year-old, and the terrible twos will fly by quite unnoticed. Well, I'll keep my fingers crossed for you.

These are positive steps toward building your child's courage. Remember to use labels for different things you teach your child. Supply your child with a "Code word", which will identify individuals your child can go with. Keep it simple so your child will remember. **Practice** using the "Code word" with your children. You should share your child's "Code word" with authorized individuals such as administrative personnel and teachers where your child attends school. This allows caregivers to know who you have authorized that your child can go with. Make sure your child's "code word" is entered into their file at day care, school, church and any organizations they may be involved with, such as scouts. It is not always wise to take someone's word that something this important has been done. Quality caregivers will not object to you witnessing the **"Code word"** being entered into your child's file. Children have natural rights they are not consciously aware of, rights that they automatically and naturally assume. For example, your children have the right to expect that you are doing everything within your power to see that they are safe. Subconsciously, your children assume and expect it of you. It is just one of many natural parental obligations.

Instructing your children regarding personal safety should not give them the impression that they are solely responsible for their own safety. Instead, it should help them understand that they have rights, and with their new knowledge, they will be able to help you help themselves. Through your teaching, your children will be given a reasonable ability to help themselves, and to seek help from other caring adults if necessary.

As parents you should realize **you are the power!** The material does not exist now, nor will it ever, that can be as effective as you are with your own children. Take the knowledge I am giving you and do whatever it takes to get between your child and the odious crimes that have taken so many children.

Caring for abused children

Sexually abused children need the same things all children need, but more of it. They need you to be more thoughtful, more consistent, more patient, more nurturing. Consequently, you need to spend more quality time with them. Oh, and one more thing, they need professional help! Parents must realize that if their child has been sexually molested, their child's ability to develop cognitively, socially, physically and emotionally may have been delayed. Sexually abused children are funny that way; they need a new foundation of stability built for them. They need to learn to trust adults again. In addition, they need all of their questions answered correctly. The innocent mistake of a nonprofessional may cause irreversible damage, or at minimum, a major setback.

There are adults, of course, who seem well adjusted after having been sexually abused as children and who did not receive special care. But, I'm guessing that since each child is as different as each case, many adults are being tortured by a secret childhood and hiding it well. The point is, we don't always know what's going on in an adult's mind after having suffered from a sexually abused childhood. I am familiar with an individual who was kidnapped and raped at age eleven. Fortunately, she survived and grew up to be a productive citizen. She didn't receive any special help or care, and as I said, he did however, develop what some people might consider an unusual defense. She wears no makeup, keeps no hairstyle, and over the years she has managed to stay 50 to 100 pounds overweight. You see, in her mind, thin and pretty are dangerous. It is obvious to me, and should be obvious to you, that with proper professional caring help, a child has a much better chance at a normal life. Yes, fortunately she survived and did turn out to be a productive citizen. But totally intact, I don't think so.

Early professional intervention can be a respite for a sexually abused child by giving the child positive, safe experiences. These children need a consistent, thoughtful, and developmentally appropriate care program. Because sexually abused children suffer from many forms of developmental damage, they require special techniques that are most effective in helping children to heal. You may be of the opinion that time will heal all wounds. Sorry, but that's not good enough. Experts have developed a series of stages through which young children pass as they learn to trust the world again and become independent. Most sexually abused children never get the opportunity to pass through these stages. That is what is meant when the phrase "she lost her childhood" is applied. It is imperative for sexually abused children to gain a sense of control over their own lives. It is crucial to their ability to make choices and decisions later in life.

When a child has learned from infancy to trust their world because their needs are cared for and consistently met, they also learn, as they grow older, to trust change. They become confident that consistencies will return. This trust allows children to explore their environment, trying new activities so they are able to develop their skills. Sexually abused children have constant lingering fears of abandonment, allowing for little trust in their environment. Many children cope with their lack of trust by relentlessly seeking attention, or the opposite, trying to appear independent, hence completely detaching themselves from others.

It takes time and a great deal of patience on your part, to help an abused child rebuild their lost foundation of trust. You will begin seeing progress as the child begins to learn to trust adults again, and no sooner. As a positive relationship develops, so will the child develop! Even with the help of professionals, you should not become discouraged if the child appears hostile and aggressive. They're simply confused and frightened, trying to fight back. I believe that a show of hostility and even very aggressive behavior to be a good sign of the child not to have given up. When you are faced with a hostile and aggressive child, you can be sure that their spirit has not been broken, as is the case in too many instances. Sexually abused children have a tendency to withdraw, avoiding interaction with others. The child may even put you to the test, purposely trying to provoke hostilities in you. By test, I mean the child may push the envelope to see if you become sexually abusive toward them. A child does this in an attempt to evaluate if all adults exhibit this behavior. If you are consistent and maintain an appropriate level of control, the child will begin to feel safe, and you have begun to build a foundation.

A qualified psychologist should help you in all facets of this healing process. The psychologist should help you prepare a consistent but reasonable schedule for both you and your child. You must always remember that consistency is the cement holding the new foundation together.

During the period when the child is adjusting to your consistency, you must make the child aware of any changes in scheduling ahead of time. It is also necessary to reassure the child that his or her regular schedule will resume promptly. It is important to be exact about that. If regular scheduling will resume in an hour, three hours, or the next day, let the child know. Eventually, you will be able to become spontaneous with schedule changes. With a little extra attention and because you have built a strong foundation, the child will learn to trust you. Spontaneity can also become a part of your consistency. Do you see where we're going here? Simply keep the child informed and as far as any changes occurring, they'll go smoothly. You may want to consider discussing the possibility of minor schedule changes with the child even before you begin. The reasoning behind that is twofold. First, it gives you a chance to explain why the change might be necessary (using possible examples) before it happens, without possibly unduly frightening the child. Second, the child will not feel a sense of betrayal since you had already discussed the possibility of a minor schedule change.

A child has only one way to build trust and that is to slowly start trusting. Now maybe you can understand a little bit better as to why it takes time and a whole lot of patience on your behalf. I have been discussing with you some of the different ways and techniques to regain a child's trust. Have you ever wondered how a child gauges trust in you? I already told you how they might push the envelope, to determine if you will act in an abusive way. It is actually the same thing as the confidence you built in them from the beginning. Like when a child begins to trust in you, when he or she eventually realizes you won't spin them too fast on the merry-go-round. When the child is sure you won't push them higher than they want to go on the swings, or allow them to fall. Knowing you'll be there to hold their hand when they need balance in order to feel safe. It is important to respond immediately to a sexually abused child's crying, even if the child is crying to get attention.

If the child is crying to get attention, it is a feeling of need, and it is very important for the child to know you will consistently be there for them. A very important part of a psychologist's participation in the healing process is, as a professional they will notice small signs in a child's progress that may go unnoticed by a nonprofessional. A psychologist will also know if progress is being made when you're not sure. The psychologist should also instruct you not to involve the child too soon in activities where failure is a possibility. With a young child, it is important for the involvement to be limited to games where there is no right or wrong outcome, games the child can jump in and out of. It is extremely important to encourage the child to make her own decisions and choices. If she chooses wrong, show her other choices and explain to her why the other choices could be better. Then ask her if she would like to choose again, allowing her to believe it is still her choice. As the child becomes more skilled in making decisions, she will become more confident in herself. Molested children are more likely to resist attempts to provide them with guidance. However, as they learn to trust you and become more secure knowing you are truly looking out for them, they will slowly gravitate toward being guided.

I have found one of the most helpful ways to build self-confidence in an abused child is to supply the child with real tools, such as a hammer, screwdriver, saw etc. Under your supervision, allow them to saw and hammer away. With your guidance, build something together, maybe a bird's nesting box or a wind chime. Be sure that the child is allowed to do most of the work. Whatever you decide to build together, it should be something that is visible and a constant reminder of her accomplishment. Doing something involving real tools is important: it allows the child to know you have confidence in her. It allows her to hammer, poke and cut with little chance of breaking a tool, which a child under any circumstances may consider failure. This is important because a broken tool can relate in a child's mind to something she did wrong. In addition, when using real tools, you have the ability to reward the child's good work and progress by allowing her to use even bigger tools. Eventually introducing the child to electric power tools (always under your supervision) is a wonderful way to exhibit your confidence in your child. It is truly amazing what a power drill, a hole in a board, and a smile from a loving parent can do for a child's confidence. If the age of the child allows for the use of real tools, you should encourage it. This will help the child to establish a sense of control and accomplishment, a sense of worth.

If the child is too young for real tools, there are a variety of play tools and other things such as clay and building blocks that she can poke, pound and be physical with. When making something with a child it is not necessary to follow instructions, what's more important is allowing the child to make the decisions regarding her project. A good example is for the child to decide how many openings her bird nest box will have. How many perches will be built into the nest and the color it will be painted should all be the child's choices. Eventually, the child will need to be challenged with problem solving tasks. In the beginning, the problems need to be small and easily solved. This aids children in learning to trust their own feelings and instincts. As you know, the best learning processes employ audio and visual techniques. It would be wise to incorporate them into your child's wellness program.

When a child has been sexually abused, it leaves them with a feeling of abandonment. In order to overcome your child's negative feelings, you must constantly reinforce positive behaviors and accomplishments. You might be faced with arguments and power struggles. It is most important that you do not give in. The child should not be allowed to win. Of course, the child will be angry with you. However, deep inside, the child will feel good that you're in control. Remember, if possible make choices available for your child, and allow her to make her own choices. You can avoid struggles and arguments by simply supplying the child with good choices. While rebuilding your child's foundation you must be so consistent that your child will completely understand your expectations of her behavior. Eventually your child will be able to predict your behavior, and that's a real comfort zone for an abused child.

If you think about it, what you are doing is sharing your direction and strength with your child so that she can eventually mobilize on her own. These are very delicate times, when you should be receiving a great deal of instruction and direction from a qualified psychologist. For example, anyone touching a sexually abused victim may cause flashbacks. This is overcome gradually, by asking the child, can I hold your hand while we walk, and so on. It takes time for a sexually abused child to get use to experiencing **appropriate intimacies**. Sometimes, introducing a special communication such as a special handshake can speed up the process. Something the child considers fun or funny is generally accepted quicker. Humor is a kindness that draws people in, kids too. Humor is especially important when your child has made a mistake or done something wrong, because the child will relate your humor to a form of understanding.

All sexually abused children need special attention. They need constant reinforcement, especially when they do something wrong. When other people are present, the abused child needs to hear things from you that instill self-confidence. Here's a couple of ideas, "Wow, people really seem to like you" and "You really make friends easy." It is important to their self-esteem that they be liked.

Minimizing the risk in child care programs

Most parents know to check out a day-care center before leaving their child. However, most parents are not aware of all that should be checked out, nor are most parents aware of their rights regarding childcare centers and the people who run them. Neither are most parents aware of city, county and state agencies that may possess information regarding the childcare center they are considering. These agencies could have important information that may concern the welfare and safety of children. This information is available to the general public upon request. Some agencies charge a nominal fee. Most do not. Ideally, these agencies exist to serve and protect the public. Some do a pretty good job of it. Some don't. The beauty of bureaucratic authorities is that, you will generally discover any inadequacies quickly. However, in their defense, any problems you may incur will almost always be caused by one individual and not represent the policy of the agency. We've all been there; we know what some government employees can be like. If you are the unfortunate parents ending up face-to-face with one of them, don't be discouraged. Seek help from another. Ask to speak to a supervisor if necessary. Seriously, most government employees are hard-working, dedicated, conscientious workers. You should have no trouble acquiring the information you seek.

I am going to give you a checklist of things you need to do that will assist you in deciding on the right childcare facility. Hopefully, you will be able to begin the process with a referral from a friend. It's always nice to know someone who is pleased with a day-care service, and recommends it. Although a good recommendation from a friend does not mean you should not conduct your own investigation. You owe it to yourself and your child to follow these steps:

- Check with the state licensing board for current licensing and ask about any allegations, complaints, or charges filed against the childcare center. Also, ask how long the center has been licensed. Check the licensed owners name against information supplied to you by the center. Determine whether the owner is also the operator and compare information. I have found the more efficiently run childcare centers seem to be the ones where the owner is also the operator and is present. However, the Owner/Operator's presence may not always mean a better-run facility.
- Check city licensing, asking all the same questions as you did of the state.
- You should contact the Better Business Bureau to find out if any allegations, complaints, lawsuits or charges have been filed with them against the childcare center or any of its employees.
- Find out if the center and its employees are bonded, and if so, how large the bond is. Check with the bonding company regarding any claims against the childcare center or its employees. If they are not bonded, **find another childcare center**.
- You also need to find out if the center is adequately insured. Talk to the insurance company regarding any claims or lawsuits against the childcare center or any of its employees. If the center refuses to give you the name of their insurance company, **find another childcare center**.
- Go to the local police department and inquire as to any allegations, complaints, charges or investigations ongoing or in the past involving the childcare center or any of its employees. Do not be satisfied with an officer standing on the other side of the counter, shaking his head saying, "No, I haven't heard about anything." Insist on speaking with

someone in the child protection unit.

- Contact Child Protective Services (CPS) for any information they may have regarding the childcare center you're interested in.

- Tour the facility looking for unsafe situations or conditions and equipment in need of replacement or maintenance. You want to be satisfied that the center meets legal standards for reasonable efforts to reduce risk to children. All classrooms and play areas should be visible from hallways. Curtains or artwork should not block windows.

- Excluded from this is any state requiring special window coverage in case of earthquakes, which may cause splintering and flying glass.

- Inquire as to policies and practices implemented to protect the children while they are at the center.

- Question their employee selection process, to determine if a comprehensive system for recruiting, screening, and selecting staff members exist. Ask to see their employment application form. Many application forms are designed to screen individuals with prior criminal histories. If their application form does not, ask what their screening procedure is.

- A complete application form should include criminal history, and should ask if the individual has ever been dismissed or fired, and why. In addition, it should ask the applicant if he or she has ever been the subject of a report to Child Protective Services (CPS). It should also ask the individual if their military record includes a court martial, medical disability, or bad conduct discharge.

- Ask if all employees, including substitute workers and volunteers are photographed and finger printed. If not **find another childcare center**.

- You also need to find out the requirements and hiring procedures for substitutes, assistants, and volunteers. A comprehensive screening will supply the employer with a wide range of background information including signs of emotional problems, substance abuse, poor judgment, and insensitivity. Ask if the center accepts reference letters

70

from potential employees. Reference letters are not sufficient; personal conversations with references are a must! Personal conversations give you a chance to detect any apprehension in the person's answers. Letters of recommendation can be written by anyone, and quite often are.

- Ask your tour guide (Owner/Operator) to explain how their program policies and procedures are designed to prevent child maltreatment. Have them explain what makes it difficult, if not impossible, for a child molester to abuse a child at their center.

- Some states require a check of all available public child protection and criminal records, regarding evidence of child abuse or neglect by an applicant. Check with your state. If the state in which you reside does not require this investigation, ask the center if they do it anyway. If they do not, **find another childcare center**.

- Ask if they photograph and fingerprint their staff. Many state (CPS) agencies have centralized registries that can be checked for reports of child maltreatment against staff members. It is important to know that police record checks identify only a small fraction of abusers. If you wish to check on the center or an individual, go to your local child protective service agency.

- Ask the supervisor at the center who does their criminal background checks. Ask for a list of all names of the employees including substitutes and volunteers.

- Ask for a complete list of staff and volunteer names and check them out on the Internet sexual offenders site to make sure all of the employees check out to your satisfaction. You should keep and maintain an updated employee list.

- Periodically, you need to drop-in unannounced at the center. Unexpected visits will give you an opportunity to observe staff and children unprepared for your visit. If center rules state you are to check in at the office and pick up a visitors pass, you should occasionally, conveniently, forget their policy. This will not only enable you to observe

71

staff interacting with the children, it will also allow you first-hand knowledge as to how the center deals with intruders. Of course, apologize when you are discovered, if you are discovered. If you're able to roam freely, **find a new childcare center**.

- If the center is situated in such a way that it allows you to observe staff and children from a distance, I highly recommend you take advantage. One of the things you're watching for is constant staff supervision during outdoor activities. Keep in mind, there is absolutely no excuse for children to be left unattended, not even for 30 seconds. As you well know, in time, that 30 seconds will turn into 30 minutes. If you witness children unsupervised for as little as 30 seconds, your complaint should be verbal and in writing. You should tear strips off them, putting it mildly.

- Inquire with your tour guide as to the center's knowledge of any convicted sex offenders living in the approximate area. Personally check the Internet for convicted sex offenders living in the area of the childcare center, because we're not stupid and we're taking nobody's word at face value. If any are located in a close proximity to the childcare facility, notify the staff and compare information immediately. I will explain more about locating convicted sex offenders in the section of this book titled, "Pedophiles on the Internet."

- Inquire about the center's policy regarding a probationary period for newly hired staff. A probationary period should last a minimum of three months, involving constant observation. All background investigations should be completed before hiring. Allowing a new employee access to children before a background investigation is completed is totally unacceptable.

- Scrutinize the center's curriculum. When you are satisfied the center's standards are acceptable, keep investigating. Now if I sound paranoid, the truth is I could write a whole other book just on cases involving child abuse at daycare centers.

- Completely examine the center's policies regarding discipline and the techniques employed by the staff. Leave no rock unturned. The childcare center should have a written policy. Ask to see it, better yet, ask for a copy. I feel it is important that you have a clear understanding of the purpose of discipline, enabling you to assess the center's disciplinary goals. Disciplinary action should be used to guide and direct children toward an acceptable behavior, enabling the child to eventually develop self-discipline. <u>Corporal punishment and isolation of your child should be forbidden!</u> No one should be allowed to discipline your child except a trained and certified staff member. Discipline should only occur with your permission and only after you have a complete explanation and understanding regarding the techniques employed. The childcare center's disciplinary techniques should be neither physically nor emotionally harmful to a child.

- Question how many certified (Child Development Associates) are staffed compared to the non- certified employees. There should exist a balance where a trained associate is present during all activities.

- Discuss the center's policies regarding touching children and scrutinize their toilet procedures. I am aware of a facility that does not allow any staff member to pick up or hug a child for any reason. Many facilities do not allow staff members to assist a child with toilet duties without another staff member being present and that's an excellent procedure. Most child molestations at day-care centers take place in the restrooms.

- Question the center's policies regarding staff members or volunteers taking children from the center. Without your explicit written permission, they should be forbidden to do so!

- Find out what the center's policy is regarding the presence of friends and family members of the staff at the center. A properly run center will not permit anyone hanging around. The center should have an established set of rules, which help control access to the center by individuals who are not staff members or parents.

- The childcare center should notify you immediately if your child is involved in an accident, regardless of how severe the child's injury.
- Compare this information to the center's policy.
- A quality childcare center will conduct daily visual health inspections as the children arrive in the morning. A morning health inspection protects your child, yourself and the childcare center. Records of these inspections should be kept by the center. The staff should be looking for bruises, burns, and any unusual marks. The children should also be inspected for lice and possible contagious and/or serious illnesses.
- Go over the center's disaster program, policy, plans and alternatives. Inquire as to the children's practicing (Drill) in case of an emergency.
- Ask about the center's procedure if a staff member is accused of child abuse. What you're looking for here is the center's first concern, which should be the child and the future welfare of the other children and, of course, gathering the facts, rather then defending the accused staff member, or the center's program. You need also ask about the center's policy regarding a mere suspicion of child abuse by a staff member. Upon answering this question, you should hear, "A report would be filed with Child Protective Services and licensing authorities immediately." You should hear this because it's the law. As a precautionary measure, you should also hear that the staff member involved has been suspended of all duties that put him or her in contact with children until resolution is achieved.
- Close to the end of your interview, ask to speak with one of the staff. There is absolutely nothing wrong with double-checking some of the information you already received. Ask questions of the employee such as; is a certified associate always present when you're working with the children? Are you allowed to assist a child in the restroom by yourself? Have emergency and disaster plans and policies been explained to you, and so on. If for any reason during your initial visit you're not satisfied with your first

impression, **find another childcare center**.

- At any time, whether it is your initial visit or long into your relationship with the childcare center, if you have an unexplained, nagging doubt, **find another childcare center**.

Women do not have the muscles men have, but God blessed them with a balance called intuition, which generally keeps them out of all the trouble that men need all that muscle for. Ladies, when it comes to placing your child in the care of strangers, I suggest you muscle up all the intuition at your disposal. If you follow my guidelines and pay attention to your intuition, I know your child will be safe.

What to do if you witness actual child abuse outside your family

If you follow my guidelines as to what constitutes "<u>Real</u>" child abuse, keeping in mind you must witness not only one or two, but a (Cluster) of indicators, you will have no trouble making the right decision to report what you have observed. Of course, I hope that you would report any form of child abuse you discover or witness.

The latest statistics on who does the reporting of child abuse is a pretty sad commentary of friends and family. Only nine percent (9 %) of annual child abuse reports are made by friends and neighbors. Worse yet, only eighteen percent (18 %) are annually reported by family and relatives. Law-enforcement, teachers and doctors report most instances of child abuse. We cannot have the attitude of **"I don't want to get involved"** when it comes to children. By turning your back on any form of child abuse, you are personally assisting in condemning a child to a life not worth living. Many abused children end up committing suicide.

By reporting what you believe is child abuse does not necessarily mean it is child abuse. Give the trained authorities the information you have and allow them to make the decision. Remaining anonymous if you choose should not be a problem. While reporting, simply request that you remain anonymous. Child abuse is a community problem. No single individual or single agency should be expected to do it all. If you see or suspect a child is in trouble, report it.

I am going to assume for the moment, that you were raised without abuse. Do you remember how difficult and confusing things were? Do you remember the fear that seized your body when you did something wrong, and your mother said, "Wait until your father gets home?" Do you remember when you didn't complete a school assignment and your teacher said she was going to notify your parents? Stop and think for a moment. Think about growing up in a great family with good parents and how difficult and confusing it was at times. When you got in trouble, you knew you were in for it. Let me ask you a few questions. When your Mom yelled those infamous words "Wait until your father gets home" were you afraid because you knew Pop was going to beat you with his fist, or choke you until you passed out? When you knew your teacher was going to call and tell your parents that you hadn't been completing your assignments, were you afraid because your parents were going to lock you in the closet for the weekend? When you put too much makeup on, did your father order you into the bathroom saying, "Scrub that face, young lady" or did he grab you by the arm pulling you toward the bedroom screaming "If you want to act like an adult, I'll treat you like an adult." Some parent's ideas regarding discipline are unbelievable and unforgivable. Those are the parents that need help and so do their children. Think about your childhood. Now think about theirs. If you witness, or suspect with good reason that a child is being abused, report it.

The reporting procedures in some states do vary slightly. However, Child Protective Services is nationwide. You're obligated to report your findings or well-founded suspicions to   (CPS) and your local police department's childcare unit. Never trust a nonprofessional to handle the situation. For example, if you were to discover within your church or club a child abuse situation, it is not okay to go to your minister or club president in order to turn the problem over to them. Telling your minister, club president or any other nonprofessionals is not reporting it. You must contact the proper authorities immediately! Remember that you can make an anonymous report upon request.

I have heard all of the excuses and complications people can come up with. There are no excuses for not reporting child abuse. It is as complicated as black and white! I am sick and tired of hearing relatives, friends and neighbors after the fact, saying, "Oh yes, I knew something was wrong, I told my husband something was wrong." You have to get involved and you must report it. A child is waiting for someone to do the right thing. The only thing you need to consider before reporting is to ask yourself this; do I feel in my heart of hearts that something terrible is happening to that child? If the answer is yes and you consider yourself a reasonable person, then you have no choice, you must **report it**.

Most frequently asked questions

Many people ask me about our out-of-country child recoveries and we have given lectures at group functions, colleges and a multitude of organizations. However, nothing gives us more pleasure than answering a question from a concerned parent regarding the everyday safety of their children. It pleases us because we get the distinct impression that parents will follow the advice and their children will be a little safer tomorrow than they were today.

Parents in general want their children to be safe, of course. The problem is, most parents have no idea how unsafe it is out there. Nor does the average parent know what to do about it. I know this to be a fact due to the most often asked questions. The information I share with you, answering these most-asked questions, is formed from my personal experiences and also collected from several other expert sources.

1. How many children are reported abused each year?

The latest study is from the year 1996. Approximately three million reports that involved alleged child abuse were reported. Many experts believe more than three million additional cases go unreported and I agree.

2. How many children are actually victims of abuse?

In 1996 Child Protective Service agencies were able to investigate approximately two million of the three million reported cases. Of the approximate two million investigated, approximately one million child abuse reports were substantiated. By "substantiated" I mean that the allegations of abuse were confirmed according to the level of evidence required by state law and state policy. Several studies suggest, and I believe, that more children suffer from abuse than are evident in official statistics from state agencies.

3. Is the number of abused children increasing?

The last national study of substantiated child abuse indicated an increase of approximately 18 percent over a five-year period, and a decline was announced that year. However, another study over a seven-year period concluded an increase of 67 percent. The two studies overlapped three years. Both studies were conducted by federally supported sources.

(We will discuss statistics later in the book and I can make it fun.)

It is important to remember when dealing with statistical studies involving crime that all forms of child abuse are the most under-reported of crimes. Maybe our government will pay a little more attention to the accuracy of their studies and actually do something about the problem. Are you going to hold your breath? I'm not! I believe this surge in governmental attention is due to the recent popularity regarding missing youngsters, human trafficking and television talk show ratings.

(It makes one wonder how long it will last.)

4. What are the most common types of abuse?

Neglect is the most common form of child maltreatment, followed by physical abuse sexual abuse and medical neglect. All culminate in emotional maltreatment. If it were possible to know the non-reported numbers, I am confident that sexual child abuse would be the number one offense. Keep in mind that sexual child abuse is a crime more easily hidden.

5. What age group is victimized most?

Child abuse is inflicted upon children of all ages. However, more than half of abused children are seven years and younger. One quarter of the abused children are younger then four years.

6. Who are abused more, girls or boys?

One study shows 52 percent girls, 48 percent boys. Our experts disagree with those numbers and so do I. Other studies show girls to be way ahead in that particular race. Approximately 69 percent of girls are sexually molested versus 31 percent of boys. Another study shows 77 percent of sexually abused children are girls. I believe the 77 percent figure of girls is more accurate.

7. Who is more apt to abuse their children?

Statistics show children of families in all income levels suffer abuse. Research suggests that family income is strongly related to incidence rates. Children from families with annual incomes below $15,000 per year are more than 25 times more likely to be abused than children from families with annual incomes above $30,000. In this particular study more than half (53 percent) of all abused victims were white, while 27 percent were African-American. Hispanic children were at approximately 11 percent and American Indians, which included native Alaskans (Eskimos), were responsible for 2 percent. All Asian and Pacific Islanders combined account for a whopping 1 percent. The majority of perpetrators of child abuse are parents at 77 percent. Another 11 percent are other relatives of the victims.

Two percent of abuse is handed down by childcare providers and foster parents. There are no reliable (credible) statistics regarding babysitters. In an estimated 81 percent of all child abuse, the perpetrators are under the age of 40. All forms of child abuse included, approximately 61 percent of the perpetrators are female. The perpetrator's gender differs by type of abuse. Neglect and medical neglect are most often attributed to female perpetrators, while sexual abuse is most often attribute to male perpetrators. However, in many states, perpetrators of child neglect, abuse, or any form of maltreatment
by definition must be in a care-taking role. Consequently, statistics from many states are totally inaccurate. Although no single profile fits every case, researchers have identified several factors that seem to characterize many abusive parents. They have found that frequently the abusive parents are:

- A young adult generally in his mid '20s
- Lives near or below poverty level
- Has not finished high school
- Is depressed and unable to cope with stress
- Has experienced violence first hand

8. How many children die from abuse?

Based on data recorded by Child Protective Service agencies in 1996, it is estimated that nationwide, 1,077 children died from a result of abuse or neglect. Children three years of age and younger accounted for approximately three-quarters of these fatalities. Many experts consider these numbers extremely low, considering not all deaths are reported or known to CPS. These particular numbers are not reliable due to a lack of clear documentation by reporting agencies.

As I write, Child Deaths Review Teams, which are compiled of CPS workers, law enforcement officials, medical examiners, coroners, health care professionals, prosecutors etc. who review child deaths to determine cause, are attempting to correct inconsistencies and identify all such deaths. In my opinion, this can only be accomplished when all child deaths and autopsy findings are compiled in a central information bank.

9. Are victims of child abuse more likely to become criminals?

According to a study sponsored by the National Institute of Justice (NIJ), maltreatment of any form during childhood increases the likelihood of arrest as a juvenile by 53 percent. The same study confirmed, by the time they reach adulthood the rate drops to 38 percent and for violent crimes, the same 38 percent. Being abused during childhood increases the likelihood of arrest for females by 77 percent. A related (NIJ) study indicated that children who are sexually abused are twenty-eight times more likely to be arrested for prostitution than children who were not sexually molested during childhood. (I believe these numbers are extremely conservative or flat wrong.)

10. Is there any evidence linking substance abuse to child abuse?

A study by the U.S. Department of Health and Human Services found those children in alcohol-abusing families were nearly four times more likely to be abused overall, almost five times more likely to be physically neglected, and ten times more likely to be emotionally neglected than children in non-alcoholic abusing families. Other studies suggest that an estimated 50 to 80 percent of child abuse cases substantiated by CPS involved some degree of substance abuse by the child's parents.

11. What injuries most commonly cause child fatalities?

- Severe head trauma
- Shaken baby syndrome
- Trauma to the abdomen and or the thorax
- Scalding
- Drowning
- Suffocation
- Poisoning

Many of the above injuries are purposely inflicted. However, many of these same injuries leading to a child's death have been ruled accidental.

12. What differentiates abuse from neglect fatalities?

Listen to what some of the experts say about that. "Data has demonstrated that abuse and neglect fatalities are two distinct categories, which require dramatically different prevention and treatment strategies. Neither category however, is fully understood." In addition, research has recently begun an attempt to distinguish among different types of neglect deaths. For example, supervision neglect includes deaths that involve critical moments in which the parent or caretaker is absent and the child is killed by a suddenly arising danger. (e.g., leaving a child unattended in a bathtub.) Chronic neglect includes deaths caused by slowly building problems. (e.g., persistent malnutrition). The first example appears to be an accident and the parent or caretaker is definitely being neglectful. However, in Webster's dictionary, one of the definitions of abuse is "to use so as to injure or damage; maltreat." Another definition is, "physically injurious treatment: characterized by wrong or improper use or action."

So let me ask you, is a parent or caretaker not being abusive by leaving a child unattended in a bathtub, where the child could easily drown? Is it not considered abusive behavior to starve a child to death? Some experts appear to be trying to complicate and twist crimes of neglect and abuse for the use of defense attorneys and their plea-bargaining. If you are one of the experts working so diligently to separate neglect from abuse, not realizing the tool you are molding helps defense attorneys, let me be the first to enlighten you. If you are a parent whose child was injured or died while left unattended in the bathtub, in your heart of hearts, you know you did a stupid thing, committing a form of child abuse. My heart goes out to you because, of course, it was unintentional and an accident. Neglect according to Webster's dictionary uses definitions quite similar to abuse, such as "to leave undone unattended to esp. through carelessness" and "giving insufficient attention to something that has a claim to one's attention." To willfully neglect a child in a bathtub seems to lend to the possibility of "physically injurious treatment" and "wrong or improper use or action." Child physical abuse deaths are the most baffling, claim the experts. However, some answers are being provided by the research and analysis of data emerging from the Child Deaths Review Teams. Teams in states such as Colorado and Oregon have identified specific "Triggers" that occur just before many fatal parental assaults on infants and young children, including:

- An infant's inconsolable crying
- Feeding difficulty

- A toddler's failed toilet training
- Exaggerated parental perceptions of acts of "Disobedience"

Sometimes rage-based assaults are set off by stimuli other than the child. For example, a father in Chicago became so furious regarding the outcome of a televised ballgame that he beat his five-month-old infant to death. Domestic violence is another factor in child deaths resulting from maltreatment. Preliminary research and early data suggest that children in homes where spousal abuse occurs are at higher risk of being victimized themselves. A person that abuses another within the home may begin with a spouse or partner and then often move onto abusing the children living in the household. As a level of violence escalates, risk of child fatalities increases as well.

13. What is being done about this crisis?

There is an encouraging new development. It is the emergence of multi-agency, multi-disciplinary Child Death Review Teams. This is a phenomenon still so new and evolving that the very existence of the teams is not yet widely known to the public or national media. Already, the Child Death Review Teams have become one of our richest resources for studying and understanding this quiet crisis. Experts from several different agencies and disciplines serve as members of the teams. The teams review cases of child deaths and facilitate appropriate follow-up. Such follow-up includes assuring that services are provided to surviving family members. They also provide information to assist in the prosecution of the perpetrators. They develop recommendations to improve child protection and community support systems. In addition, these teams assist in identifying weaknesses in child protection systems and determine avenues for prevention efforts and improved training. Well designed and properly organized, the Child Death Review Teams appear to offer hope of defining the underlying nature and scope of fatalities due to child abuse and neglect. Some innovative techniques being applied and considered are:

- Universal home visit by trained professionals or paraprofessionals
- Community based programs designed for specific neighborhoods
- Hospital-linked outreach to parents of infants and toddlers
- Effective public education campaigns and innovative ways to reach males

So maybe there's some very special and much needed help on the way. The problem is that rumors of government intervention and a lack of funding have already waylaid the teams' efforts.

Chapter 3

KIDNAP PREVENTION

What parents can do

Before we get into what you can do as parents to protect your children against abduction, I would like to take a moment to give you an idea of what you will be up against. In the United States of America, a child is lost or abducted every 40 seconds. This is not just one of those statistics someone pulled out of the air. This one's a fact! If you remember what I talked about earlier in the book regarding the amount of sex offenders in the U.S. and their numbers per square mile, you should have a good idea of what you're up against. To refresh your memory, there is approximately one child molester per square mile in the United States. The state of California, in which I reside, has the dubious distinction of being, home to more sexual offenders than any other state in the United States.

Here are some truly frightening facts about abductions that end in murder. A study was conducted by the Attorney General for the state of Washington, in cooperation with the U.S. Department of Justice, exploring child abduction murder cases. By the way, Washington State holds the wonderful distinction of the state most active in actually doing something truly positive regarding the protection of its children and the punishment of those that would harm them. My hat is off to the citizens and politicians of the state of Washington and I wish other states would follow their lead. The results of the study are shocking to me and should act as a wake-up call to parents in every state. Their study showed that in 53 percent of kidnappings that ended in murder cases the abductor and victim were not known to each other (stranger abductions). The most common victims were white females, typically an average age of eleven years old, most often described as your normal average kids. Most were from middle-class neighborhoods and had stable family relationships. So if you thought this sort of tragedy only befell problem homes with disjointed families and runaway children, get it out of your head now. Nine percent of the victims were five years of age or younger.

In 53 percent of the cases, the initial contact site between abductor and the victim was within a quarter of a mile from the victim's home. In 33 percent of the cases, first contact was made less than two hundred feet (200') from the victims home. Two hundred feet from their home! **Do you know where your kids are right now?** Typical abductors were white males, an average age of 24 years, unmarried, with prior arrest for violence in 60 percent of the cases. In over half of the cases the abductor had prior arrests and/or convictions for crimes against children. They just keep turning them loose, sometimes without our knowledge, and they locate them next door... "Howdy neighbor!"

Contrary to popular belief, child abductors that kill their victims are not all outsiders or truly loners. Eighty-three percent lived with someone else, and of them thirty-four percent lived with their parents. Almost without exception, the primary motivation behind these murders was sexual assault. As far as murdering their victim, it's called eliminating the possibility of a witness. Of course, there are a few pedophiliacs that don't care whether there are witnesses or not, they just like killing babies. Fifty-seven percent of the raped and murdered children were simply victims of opportunity. The most common elements in these crimes was a motivated offender combined with an opportunity to commit the crime and inattentive guardians at the time of the abduction, which I believe is a crime in itself.

According to the convicted murderers of children that I have interviewed, some feel they have done the family, but mostly the child, a favor by killing them. "You know that by killing them, I'm sparing the kid of having to live with what happened." This thought process is not the norm. However, I have come across similar thinking more than a couple of times. Predators are not always so ruthless-minded, although many will kill a child simply to avoid being identified. Many abductors of children prefer to give a child attention, in the hopes of

85

gaining the child's confidence, rather than creating fear. Many predators actually want the child to like them and will try to convince the child that they won't hurt them. After having raped a child, a convicted offender told me in an interview how he had tried to calm the traumatized ten-year-old. He explained to me that he could tell that she was scared to death, "But I told her, I'm not a bad guy, see how good I made you feel, didn't that feel good? I could tell then that she knew I really wasn't going to really kill her."

There are many predators willing to take the time to develop a relationship with a child, but as I said, it takes time. Quite often these relationships are developing unbeknownst to the child's parents. For a predator to take the risk of developing a relationship over a period of time, it means the predator feels relatively safe in taking such a chance. In the final analysis, it is the parents who are not doing their job as well as they should. Predators on the prowl for a victim are not only looking for a wandering child, they are also looking for a parent not doing their job. For example, a predator watches a woman and her child in a department store. She's going through a table full of handbags. The predator has his eye on the empty stroller beside her, or maybe she is holding something obviously belonging to a child. The predator now knows that there is a pretty good chance that there is an unattended child close by. My point is, whether it takes a predator three weeks at the park next to your house, or just a moment at a department store, predators are counting on you to be a non-attentive and lax parent.

*Timing in reporting a missing child is most critical! In seventy-four percent of cases studied, the child was murdered within two to three hours of the abduction.

I once had a conversation with a pedophile who claimed he could leave at that moment and return with a child within two hours. Since I had witnessed photographs he presented as trophies to his cohorts, I had a tendency to believe him. On a particular occasion, I had not seen him for approximately 45 days, when he finally did show up again he produced twenty-two photographs of himself with 6 different children. The fellow pedophiles he was showing the photographs to, said that they had not seen those particular photographs before. I believe him and them! He told me that his favorite ploy when time allows is to get kids to feel indebted to him. He said he did little things like buy a kid a burger or pay for arcade games. You do that a few times and it's hard for them to say no when you need a favor. Actually, they almost never say no. He also informed me that teenagers are generally easier to get than pre-teens. I quote, "They think nothing can hurt them, ya know invincible, and the girls are always interested in becoming a model or getting in a movie. Just ask them to pose, it makes them feel special I guess." "If you've got a cast on an arm or something, girls are compassionate and always want to help." "Boys fall for challenges, I've got a bad shoulder, do you think you could carry this to my car, it's pretty heavy?" He added, "If they don't believe my line, ya know, suspect somethin, it doesn't matter because they don't want to cause a scene. I just walk away, no big deal." He continued, "Teenagers don't like to be part of a disturbance, they get embarrassed easy." Pedophiles enjoy bragging and will share intimacies if they believe you're one of them and you've gained their trust.

Any offers for photo sessions, modeling, television or movie work, kids should tell their parents and the parents should check it out. When predators use these scams, they often say that they work for, or are affiliated with, a well-known magazine or studio. This is easy to check out.

To think that these "Pedophiliacs" are, as I write, seeking political correctness, hoping for a social acceptance. Their intent is to achieve a politically correct categorization of pedophilia and they are demanding political protection. For individuals who have abandoned their morals and committed aberrant sexual misconduct, that's quite a wish list.

It is important for teens to have their freedom, but parents need to know where they are, whom they are with, and how to get hold of them. By the way, in case you're thinking, "Well that's California for you" the interviews with the bragging pedophile took place in Texas.

I also want to make myself clear: I am not saying teenagers are stupid. The combination of youth, exhilaration, and naiveté often makes for stupid judgment. We've all been there. Here is a common example of mistakes young girls make. Let's call this girl Nancy and let's say Nancy is fourteen years old. Nancy is spending the day hanging with four friends, four of them that happen to be boys. They decide to go to one of the boy's houses, knowing his parents are not home, so they can play his new CD as loud as they wish. Now you tell me, is Nancy being smart, or is she doing a stupid thing? In many cases nothing would happen. Although Nancy is secluded, and with four boys, they are her friends. Most boys under normal circumstances would not take advantage of the situation. Under normal circumstances. Now let's add the possibility of altering the circumstances by adding drugs or alcohol, which could possibly give some boys the courage to do something they would not normally consider doing. Because of Nancy's decision to be in a secluded situation with four boys, she has increased the possibility of something terrible happening to her.

We must all realize that no one is immune from an attack. Sexually related attacks are a big problem that is not synonymous with some states or specific big cities, nor is it most common in overly populated or depressed areas. It's happening every day, everywhere. Remember this, many girls have made poor choices that left them in vulnerable situations that ended in rape and sometimes their deaths. Because you are with friends does not necessarily mean you are safe. Nancy could have chosen to not be alone in a house with four boys who probably did not intentionally lure her to the house with the intention of raping her. One teasing word led to another, someone's taunt seemed to spark another's aggressive action, which started a chain reaction, and before anyone stopped, Nancy was dead. Anyway, that's what one of the boys told me, as to how it happened. Funny, two years after Nancy's death, the boy I interviewed, still didn't really know how it happened. (There were no drugs or alcohol involved in Nancy's rape and murder.)

Is it impossible to totally protect our children from abduction? Allow me to answer this question with a question. Is it your wish that your child leads a relatively normal life? If the answer to the second question is yes, and I hope it is, then the answer to the first question is yes. Due to the sheer numbers of sex offenders polluting our communities with their presence, everyone's children are at risk, every day. If your child walks one, two or three blocks to school, and the same coming home, he or she has more than likely, no scratch that, most probably, has been spotted or even scrutinized and possibly stalked by a Pedophile. If I'm frightening you, I apologize. I apologize for a society that has left me no choice but to frighten you. If you're not frightened for your child, and you do not wish to take steps that will help insure the prevention of a horrendous tragedy from striking your family, then your child may be in serious jeopardy. If you take to heart what you read here, and take action against these monsters stalking our communities and neighborhoods, you will lessen the risk of harm coming to your own child by an enormous percentage. There are, however, no guarantees, although you can greatly lessen the risk to your children by utilizing the information I am providing you with.

This book is designed to help you and your children learn some important rules regarding your responsibility and their safety. Your children's safety is primarily your responsibility. It is foolish to leave it up to someone else, such as your child's teacher or the police. If you will take the time to teach your children what they need to know regarding their own safety, the chance of your child being abducted will be reduced significantly.

Do not be fooled or lulled into a false sense of security by the affluent neighborhood in which you may reside. Abduction knows no social or economic boundaries, and neither do the profiteers and pedophiles.

Therefore, no matter what neighborhood you live in or how affluent it may be, it would be smart on your part to make plans with your children in case of emergency. Something all parents should do is to take some time, possibly on a Saturday or Sunday, to walk with their children in their neighborhood. I say a Saturday or Sunday because are the days that your neighbors are most likely to be home. Consider walking the route your child would take, whether it is from school to home or from the bus pickup and drop-off spot to home. The reason I'm advising you to do this is twofold. First, it gives you a chance to scrutinize the areas your child must travel. It also gives you a chance to alter your child's route if you're not comfortable with a particular street or situation, possibly a run-down area. Second, it gives you and your child a chance to meet some of your neighbors and determine which neighbor you would feel most comfortable sending your child to in an emergency. That's right, you need to go door-to-door talking to your neighbors, and when you've found the lucky ones, talk to them about the possibility of an emergency with your child while walking home from school. Obtain their permission for your child to run to them for help if need be. It is important to establish many locations between your child's destinations. You may get lucky and discover retired folks or a mother that is home the majority of the time in your neighborhood. If possible, try to locate neighbors, preferably females with children of their own. An added benefit is that getting to know your neighbors is always a good thing!

Since there is a great deal for you to teach your children, you need to go at it slow and easy. Do not get angry or even excited while discussing what you have learned with your children. You've got your work cut out for you, so stay calm, collected and be patient. Some experts believe that you should discuss this stuff with your child or children daily, claiming it will empower them with the knowledge to stay out of dangerous situations more quickly. I disagree. I believe you can easily over saturate a child's mind, causing them to begin tuning you out. I'm sure you've witnessed that glazed over look in your child's eyes when you're talking to them and they have become bored. You know the look; the one that says school's in session, but nobody showed up. Although it is important to teach your kids as quickly as possible, to do it daily is much too much. I suggest touching on the subject lightly about once a week initially. When you're satisfied that a good portion has sunk in, then a couple times a month should be sufficient.

Let's be honest, if a predator has targeted your child, he may very well succeed. What the information in this book will do is, **narrow the predator's windows of opportunity**. You can teach your children many things that will keep them much safer in a relatively short time. There is a limited number of "lures" used by child predators. You should be able to familiarize your children with them rather quickly. Candy is still employed as a lure to kidnap the young ones, and beer or drugs are the lure of choice for older children. As I mentioned, predators like to get the older kids feeling obligated. We all know, of course, parents have the right to question any and all gifts their children receive, and that is not only a right but also a real obligation. I hope we also know that it is not normal for adults to bestow gifts on children without occasion or specific reason.

You may want to consider your child's age and level of maturity (each child is different) before informing them of what can and does happen to children who are abducted and/ or molested. I want you to be very careful here, because there is a fine line between frightening and informing children. You may want to consider beginning by asking your children to talk to you about their fears and use this time for gathering and dispensing fact from fantasy. It is important to gather information and just as important to dispense your child's false fears. Keeping that in mind, I believe a child should be informed as to what can happen to them if abducted. You should start discussions with your children by each particular child's age of reasoning. By that I mean when you decide your child can handle it. It's a personal call, and no one knows better than you, when it comes to your own child. Of course, depending on the child's age and maturity, you may want to consider using caution and a great deal of common sense regarding detailed information.

Some experts disagree with me about talking to children regarding what could happen to them if kidnapped and molested. I do believe they should be told, and for a very good reason. At the risk of repeating myself, (considering the child's age and level of maturity) because generally, if you tell a child not to do something without explaining the reason, sooner or later, that child is going to do it. If you tell a child not to do something because they might get hurt, children draw comparisons. Get hurt? Getting hurt will be compared to what they have already experienced, or witnessed, which may not seem too bad, depending on what they have experienced or seen. Telling a child not to do this or that, because there are people who do bad things. Bad things? "My teacher says Jocy picks his nose in class, and that's a bad thing." Children draw comparisons to what they relate to automatically. I believe it is important for you to tell your children as soon as it is reasonably possible. Obviously, if your child is too young to tell, you shouldn't. I am counting on you, and your knowledge regarding your own children. I do not believe that experts can simply lay down certain rules and guidelines for all children of all ages, and I always consider the exceptional child. I am also counting on you, as smart and cautious parents, to be tactful and careful in your explanations and choice of words. **Children in today's society need to be a little paranoid**. If they aren't paranoid just a little bit, then they will not be looking out for their own safety. Even a child with the best intentions, which they all have, you know, will not heed your warnings for very long if they're not a little frightened. It is however, very important not to terrorize your children. I hope we are straight on this. The balance that you're looking for is somewhere between frightened and cautiously concerned. Keeping that in mind, you may consider soliciting the help of a psychologist who specializes in early childhood education and one that agrees with my philosophy.

Being a parent is a scary job, especially considering the world we live in today. Protecting your children from danger should be a constant concern. Although it is a difficult task, I am confident that you are going to follow my advice, applying what you have learned with what you already know, to help safeguard your children. This will help you find comfort in knowing you've done everything you can do to keep your children safe. This is especially true when you have applied the information I have given you about teaching your children to protect themselves. The two most important things your children must have and must apply regarding their own safety are **education and communication**.

I believe that you'll all agree when I say that it certainly is a dangerous world out there for the kids, especially when considering that up to ninety percent of missing person cases involve teenagers and children, according to the FBI. The actual figures, according to the FBI are eight hundred thousand (800,000) cases a year, or two thousand two hundred (2,200) per day. These statistics include missing children, runaways, abducted and other categories such as throwaways. Remember, most experts consider federal statistics extremely conservative, and I couldn't agree more. Many experts believe federal statistics to be off by as much as one half the actual numbers reported to the public.

According to Justice Department statistics and the year doesn't really matter, since the statistics are either wrong or at a minimum, always about the same each year, abductions involving family members were three hundred fifty four thousand one hundred (354,100). One hundred fourteen thousand six hundred (114,600) involved abductors from outside the family. Do I sound a little statistically bitter, you'll understand why when you read about statistics later in the book. If we suppose for a moment that these numbers are correct, it certainly is a dangerous world out there, especially for our children. The above figures, one from the FBI and the other from the Justice Department are taken from the same time period. Which makes me wonder if these agencies are operating on the same planet. No matter, whichever figure is right, if either, it's too damned many. At the risk of being redundant, I will be discussing statistics later in the book and possibly touching on these particular statistics again. You'll have to forgive me, but I find it most difficult to let go when I discover screw-ups of this magnitude by our elite.

I am literally tired of hearing, "Children don't know what to do", or "Children can't be expected to protect themselves" and "Children can not look out for themselves, so we have to look out for them." These words of wisdom are only partially true. Kids can know what to do, kids can protect themselves and kids can look out for themselves. It is up to us to teach them how to do it. However, we also need to continue to look out for them. Although, since we cannot be with our children 100 percent of the time, kids have to take some responsibility in order to help keep themselves safe. Yes, I agree, children should be able to be children. Why should parents be in the terrible position of having to explain to young children about abductions, molestation, pedophiles or even murder and teaching them to help make themselves safe from it all? Worse yet, why should children be in the position of having to learn of these horrible things? Not to mention, actually having to look over their shoulder as they play? Yes it is terrible, but when tragedy strikes, there is no going back and there is no undoing or do over. It's too late. It's as simple as that: **it's just too damned late!**

I wish it were possible for all parents to talk with the parents of missing or murdered children, as I have and do. But since it would be difficult, I'm going to tell you one thing that I know they would tell you, and that is, just like you, we never thought it would happen to us, not to our family, not to our child. The one most important thing that you should remember above all else is, it's happening to someone's child every day; I'm not going to let it happen to mine.

Of course not, no way, absolutely not! It won't happen to you, it won't happen to your family. Well guess what? As I just said, it's happening to somebody's family everyday. Please don't let it happen to your family. Don't let it happen to your child. Don't be a victim! Do not allow any member of your family to be victimized! Do all you can do and pray it was enough.

I forewarned you in the beginning of this book that I was not going to dance around, soft shoe, or sugarcoat the information I am passing on to you. Nor do I have any desire to make attempts at being politically correct. I believe as concerned parents, you want all the best and accurate information as fast as possible regarding the safety of your children. Surely, if something has already happened to your child,

God forbid, you're not interested in sugar-coatings or political correctness; you want the straight stuff without the crap. There's a very good chance nothing will ever happen to your child, but you have to underline chance. We do not have the right to take chances with our children, and our children have the right to expect that we wouldn't. Our children have the right to expect us to protect them. I have had the misfortune of dealing with too many parents who will never see their children again. "Politically correct that."

Now let's talk about what you can do to safeguard your children. First, and most important, as I've already said, you must create an effective communication with your children. Communication is the key to your child's safety. The key to a parent's communication with their children is applying the art of listening. Once you establish good communication with your children, all other things will follow. While you're building communication with your children, begin teaching them their full names, their address, city, state and telephone number, including the area code. Then you should teach your children how to make a telephone call, both local and long distance. Allow your kids to practice making telephone calls. Either by allowing them to make actual calls, or you can hold the telephone's button down while they dial the numbers if your phone is of the older style. They also need to learn dialing or punching "0" for help from the operator and "911." Explain to them that the telephone operator can help them if necessary. They need to know that the operator will connect them to their home or the police department in an emergency. Take your children to a pay phone and allow them to practice. Make sure they understand that they do not need money to make a call from a pay phone to the operator. Inform them that under no circumstances are they to tell anyone on the telephone that they are home alone. Teach your children to respond to the question; "Is your Mommy or your Daddy home?" "My mommy / daddy can't come to the telephone right now, can you call back later or can I take a message?" You should periodically initiate family discussions involving safety issues, but be careful not to over do it. Actually, kids are great; they let you know when they've had enough. They get this glazed look in their eyes that I told you about before. The look that definitely says, I'm not here anymore.

Next, you must inform your child or as to what may be a lurking beyond the front door of your home. [Please, not in those words.] As I mentioned before, use common sense, taking into consideration the age and maturity level of your children. You should consider informing them cautiously as to what can happen. I will be discussing with you later about talking to your children without scaring them. It ain't easy, but it can be done. Now it's time to set up your children's safety rules:

1. With no exceptions, your children must be taught to tell you where they are going, before they go and with whom, when they are returning and what route they plan to use.

2. You are obliged to keep a complete list of your children's friend's names, addresses and telephone numbers. Never allow your children to go to their friend's homes without having that information. Teach your children to help you keep the list up-to-date. (Positively no secret friends.)

3. When your child is visiting a friend, it is up to you to know who is present. (Supervision and older children etc.) You have to teach your children to keep you informed.

4. Your kids need to know that they should walk with a friend whenever possible. Instruct your children to use the (buddy system) whenever possible. Children are less vulnerable in the company of others, and it's more fun to be with friends.

5. They should always tell you which route they're taking to get where they are going and they should not deviate from that route.

6. Your children need to know what to do if someone is following them. Tell them to go to a place where there are other people. They can go to a neighbor's home or into a store, and tell an adult what is going on and ask for help. Explain to your children that there is a difference between asking someone for help and having someone approach them. Let them know it is safest when seeking help to ask a woman, preferably a woman with children.

7. Your children must know that they are never to talk with strangers. Let your kids know that it is not normal for adults to ask children for directions or for help of any kind.

* **Wise adults know better than to ask children for directions.**

8. Children must learn not to be tricked into going anywhere with someone they don't know. Once you believe that you have taught your child not to go anywhere with strangers, test them. Use someone you trust that is not familiar to your children. See if they can be lured away

by this person using candy or the lost puppy trick. Some predators tell children that they have some free puppies or kittens in their car, and coax children into going with them to see or pick out a new pet. You might want to consider trying it out on your child. If your child is tricked into going with this person, do not be angry with your child, but be firm. You have got to convey to your children the importance of what you are teaching them. However, it is important not to scare them. Some kids need more instruction than others and all children need to be reminded periodically. Rome wasn't built in a day, and a kid didn't build it. 9. Warn them that someone might try to lure them into a car by saying that you sent them to pick them up.

10. Pre-establish guidelines as to what your child should do if their bus or regular ride does not show up.

11. Your children need to understand that bad people "Strangers" can be men, women or even older children. They also need to know that bad people do not look or dress a certain way. It is especially important for your children to know that sometimes bad people can look and sound very nice.

12. Let your children know that you believe in their ability to help themselves to keep safe, and that you will always be there to help them.

13. Be sure your children understand what a "stranger" is. Remember that children actually view some strangers as "Friends." A few examples are the mailman, paperboy, or the ice cream man. Sometimes, with very young children it helps to explain what a "Stranger" is by pointing out that if the child doesn't know where he lives, he is a stranger. However, even neighbors, whose residences are known, may still be strangers. Explain to your children that they are people we see sometimes, but don't really know. Teach your kids that it means they are strangers too. Yeah right, it's a tough one, but all-important for your children to understand. Children often ask why their parents talk to strangers, such as people on the street or at the gas station. You should explain that the rules for parents are different from the rules for children, and why they're different.

14. Of course, you have already taught your children not to answer the door when home alone. Teach them to telephone the operator, or punch in/dial "911" if someone is trying to get into the house, or if your child is frightened for one reason or another. Have an arrange-

ment with a neighbor that you trust who is usually home so your child can call them in case of an emergency.

15. Teach them that sometimes it's okay to say no to an adult, especially if they touch, frighten, or make your child feel uncomfortable in a way the child doesn't like.

16. You must teach your child to fight, scream as loud as they can, and run away if someone tries to touch them or take them away. It is important that your children know what to do if they are separated from you while shopping, or in any other situation involving unintentional separation:

- Never leave the store you are in if you are lost.
- Go to the nearest cash register person.
- Look for an employee: someone wearing a uniform, or with a nametag.
- Ask the person if they work in the store and if they say yes, ask for help.
- Explain to your children that they are never to go into the parking lot looking for your car.

17. Your children need to be taught to never go near a car with someone in it. They should know whose cars they can ride in.

18. They must know to never get into a car with anyone without your permission.

19. Make sure your children understand that they are not to go into anyone's house without your permission. Be specific with your child about whose homes they are permitted to enter.

20. Teach your children never to help a stranger look for a lost pet, or anything else for that matter. Nor are they to go with a stranger to look at, or to get, a free puppy and/or kitten. **[Obviously, this includes bunnies or any other pet children love to see and hold.]**

21. Your children should also know never to accept money, or the promise of money, or any other gifts from strangers.

22. As previously mentioned and definitely worth repeating, your children have to learn to yell and scream as loud as they can and to fight hard if someone tries to take them away. **"This is not my daddy, help!"** if it's a man or **"This is not my mommy, help!"** if it's a woman. This wording will alert adults in the area that this is not a child throwing a tantrum, but a child in trouble. (Practice yelling with

your children.) Let your children know that it is okay to break the rules of etiquette when they feel they are in danger. Talk to your kids about that little voice inside them, the little voice that says I shouldn't be doing this, or I'm scared. Teach them to listen to that little voice in their heads.

23. Your children should feel that they could come to you and tell you if someone tries to touch them in a way they don't like. **(Open those lines of communication.)**

24. Your children should know that they should come to you and tell you if someone offers them gifts, including money, or wants to take their picture.

25. Your children must learn not to keep secrets from you, especially about things or people that scare them. If an adult tells them a secret, your children must know to tell you. If your child insists on keeping the secret, explain that the man didn't mean for her to keep the secret from her own family, he meant keeping the secret from everybody else. If the child is persistent and remains silent, do not get angry, get a professional involved. The child may believe she is protecting you because she may have been told that he will hurt, or even kill, Mommy and Daddy if she tells their secret. Police officers that deal with crimes against children are generally very good at getting kids to relax and talk.

*A quick reminder, I am generally referring to the child as a female because crimes against children are generally committed against girls, but not always.

26. Teach your children that no one has the right to touch them or make them feel uncomfortable. Once again, with young children it's helpful to explain that their private parts are those parts of their body covered by their bathing suit. Tell them no one has the right to touch them there. You need also explain to them that sometimes Mommy, or Daddy might touch their private parts if you're helping them take a bath, or checking an injury. A doctor may need to touch this area as part of an examination. Nevertheless, even doctors need a very good reason to touch children there and a parent should be present during any child's examination. You should always be present during any visits with a doctor. If while examining your preteen or teenager, the doctor asks you to leave the examination room, even if only for a moment, your reply should be, absolutely not! There are many reasons

why you should never leave your child alone with a doctor during an examination or any other time, and here are a couple of them. It is possible that your doctor is a pedophile! No, I am not saying doctors are pedophiles. I'm saying there are pedophiles in all occupations and I'm saying why take the chance? Always remember that we can gamble with our own lives, but we have no right to gamble with our children's lives. Another problem regarding leaving your child alone with a doctor is, some doctors feel they have the right to talk to their patient, generally teenagers, about private things such as sex, without a parent being present. They often will take it upon themselves to advise teenagers regarding their private lives. Your child may be the doctor's patient, but you are the parent and the one that is ultimately accountable for your child. If you wish for the doctor to talk to your child that's okay, but in your presence, or not at all.

27. Make sure your children believe you will listen to them and that you will help them if they are troubled.

28. They need to know the three steps to safety if someone threatens or tries to touch them:

1- Say no.

2- Run away.

3- Tell an adult you know and trust.

*If your child is alone at home and something happens that causes your child to wonder if the police should be called, he or she needs to understand that if that thought crosses their mind, they should not hesitate, they should immediately call the police using "911." Have your work number along with the police department, fire department, poison control center and the number of a trusted neighbor posted where your children can see them and/or on your speed dial. Of course, you will have your children check in with you or a trusted neighbor when they get home. Your children checking in upon their arrival at home should fall into the category of things in life that are for sure, like death, taxes... and kids checking in. Oh, and before I forget, never put your children's telephone number or address on their clothing or on anything else. Use an insignia or a code. That goes for their names also. The reasons should be obvious.

Often children are actually acquainted with their abductors even though their parents are unfamiliar with the person. Sometimes describing situations and teaching reactions is easier for children to understand, rather than trying to explain a particular profile of a child molester or "Stranger."

Another difficult thing to explain to a child, or more accurately, to convince a child is what they must do if an abductor threatens them or shows a gun or knife. A predator will show a weapon in an attempt to get the child into a vehicle or simply away from people. Once a predator has accomplished this and the child is in the vehicle and away from people, chances are the child will be harmed and possibly murdered. It is important that your children know that they must not only scream, but they **must also fight**. Teach your children not to go with an abductor, even if the predator has a weapon. Because children that are kidnapped by strangers are most often victims of opportunity, the predator will generally leave quickly when a target begins <u>screaming and fighting</u>. Abductors of children do not want to be caught by a group of people. Some experts believe crimes against children have saturated our society to such a degree that many of us simply shrug when hearing about them. Not so, when it comes to children being raped and murdered. We've all heard people say things like, "The bastard should be killed on the spot" or "They ought to hang him from the nearest lamppost and cut off his penis" after hearing what a pedophiliac did to a child. Those kinds of suggestions become a distinct possibility when a crowd of angry people catches a child molester and child molesters know it. That is a good reason why a child, your child, must know to fight before he or she ends up alone with their abductor.

All parents should keep complete detailed descriptions of their children at the ready. We refer to them as child identification kits. Included in this kit should be an identification information card. (I have included a sample card in this book.) The information cards and kits should include your child's sex, height, weight, blood type and color of hair, color of eyes, date of birth. Whether the child wears glasses or contact lenses, including braces on his or her teeth or having pierced ears, and any other unique or outstanding physical characteristics. The information should also include any scars or deformities. A new color photograph should be taken every six months and added to the child's kit. A videotape of the child should also be added every six months. Videotapes of children have proven extremely valuable for use on television if the child is   missing. It is much easier to recognize a child from videotape than it is from a photograph. If your child is under the age of two, the photograph and videotape procedure should be done every three months. The photograph should be of the child's face, and obviously of good quality. You may wish to consider dental microdots, which are considered positive identifiers. If a child is found and does not know his or her name, or cannot speak, microdots can speak for them. Your dentist can place microdots on your children's teeth. Whether you go with microdots or not, you should have your dentist prepare dental charts of your children for you. You should make certain they are updated each time work is performed. You may consider keeping copies in the child's kit. When I refer to dental charts and records, I am including all x-rays. You can also keep the x-rays in the child's kit. It's up to you, and since you paid for them, they belong to you. If you do not wish to keep copies of dental and medical records in your child's kit, know where they can be located. (Keeping in mind, time is of the essence when a child is missing.) I recommend that you keep copies of your children's dental and medical records, including x-rays in your children's kits.

Dental and medical records, particularly x-rays, can be invaluable in helping to identify a recovered child. Be sure to have all permanent scars, birthmarks, blemishes, and broken bones recorded. If you choose not to keep copies of dental and medical records with your child's kit, then you must find out from your children's doctors where such records are located. Then you'll have to figure out how you can obtain them quickly if the need arises. Next, you must have your children fingerprinted by a qualified individual. Do not attempt to take fingerprints yourself. If fingerprints are to be useful in identifying a child, it is important that they are properly taken. The fingerprint card should also be kept in the child's identification kit.

Your children's identification information cards must also be detailed with such things as skin color, and whether the child has been circumcised or not. Include all available health information, such as regular medication and any existing medical or dental problems. All information subject to change should be updated every six months. Also included in your children's information kits should be their place of birth (city, state, hospital), their passport and social security numbers. Heading your child identification information card should be the parents/guardians' complete names, addresses and telephone numbers. In addition, the child's physicians' names, addresses and telephone numbers. Include the same information regarding the child's dentist.

To give you an idea of what I'm talking about, let's have a little quiz. You've just discovered your child is missing. Without looking, could you describe what your child is wearing right now? Do you observe what clothes your child has on each day before he or she leaves the house?

Do you have a recent photograph of your child?

Do you have recent videotape of your child?

Do you have a set of your child's fingerprints taken by a qualified individual?

Do you have copies of all of your child's health records, or do you know where to obtain them quickly?

Do you and your child have a set plan in case someone who is not a relative/friend approaches him or her, or if your child is separated from you?

Does your child's school call within a reasonable time if your child is absent?

Does your child know whose house he or she may enter in case of an emergency?

Do you have a set plan with your child if he or she misses the bus, or if the usual ride does not show up?

Do you have knowledge of, or are you familiar with any undesirable or suspicious individuals living in your neighborhood, or on the route that your child walks to and from the bus, school or friends houses?

Are you aware of any dangerous street crossings, or residential streets prone to high-speed traffic, which your child has to deal with?

Do you know the full names, addresses, and telephone numbers of your child's friends?

When your child visits friends, are you aware of everyone present at the friend's house?

Do you listen to your child when he or she tells you they do not want to be with someone?

Are you sensitive to changes in your child's behavior?

If you answered as I suspect, you should be very interested in what's coming up.

SAMPLE

CHILD IDENTIFICATION AND INFORMATION CARD

Person w/ legal custody _____#_____
Person child is living w/ _____#_____
Person w/ physical custody_____#_____
Parent/Guardian: Name _____Phone #: _____
Address:_____
Work #: _____
Physician:_____
Phone #: _____
Address:_____
Dentist:_____
Phone #: _____
Adress:_____

Childs
Name_____
   First   Middle   Last
Nickname (_____)
Date of Birth:___ Sex:___ Race:___ Hair Color:___

Eye Color:___Skin
Color:____Circumcision?____Glasses?___Contact Lens? ____
Pierced Ears? _____Body Piercing?____
No __ Yes __ Describe Jewelry and Location:_____

Distinguishing Scars / Marks / Birthmarks / Deformities:
_____

Special Medical Problems:
_____

Special Dental Problems:
_____

Special Medications:
_____

103

Microdot: Yes ___ No ___ [Location]
_____

Location of X-rays:
_____

Special Speech Characteristics: _____
Describe:_____
_____

Hair Samples: at least 50 strands including roots
{Avoid taping over the roots} [Location]
_____

Height Weight
[Up-date Information Every Six {6} Months]
Height~Weight~Date~Height~Weight~Date~Height~Weight~D-
ate

____ ____ ____ ____ ____ ____ ____ ____ ____

____ ____ ____ ____ ____ ____ ____ ____ ____

____ ____ ____ ____ ____ ____ ____ ____ ____

____ ____ ____ ____ ____ ____ ____ ____ ____

____ ____ ____ ____ ____ ____ ____ ____ ____

Fingerprints:[Location]_____
Photograph: [Location]
_____

Videotape:[Location]_____

Passport Number:_____ [Location of Passport]_____
Social Security Number: _____

You may ask, as others have, regarding the purpose of some of the information on the Child Identification and Information Card. Any and all of the information on your child's card may make the difference between locating your child, or never seeing your child again. For example, the section labeled Height and Weight Information may be of great value to law-enforcement, enabling their experts to determine a growth pattern of your child. This will aid the experts who can determine by the growth pattern, as to what the child may look like years after abduction. It is very important to update the applicable information at least every six months. Believe me when I say you cannot possibly supply authorities with too much information. **Do it all, and do it now!** You will feel better knowing you've done everything possible, to safeguard your children. Oh and when new photographs of your children are placed in their kits keep the old ones in the kit in the order they were taken [Make sure they are dated]. This too will aid the experts in determining what the child will look like years later.

If you are not prepared and tragedy strikes, imagine trying to put all of this information together as fast as possible. Ask yourself right now, how long will it take me to round up my children's medical and dental records including x-rays, not to mention the rest of the information that the police will want and desperately need. Now ask yourself, if my child were missing, do I want to waste that kind of time running down documents and photographs? If something happens to your child, time is of the essence. Be prepared. **The first hours your child is missing are the most critical.**

Protecting your own child is, of course, your first priority. However, it is possible for you to help other children who may also be at risk in your community. There are plenty of things that you can do in order to help make your community safer for all of its children.

- Meet with your school officials and local police department. Help them to establish a quality child identification program, if one does not already exist. Identifiers are crucial if the child is found alive or dead. Talk to your child's school Principal and attend PTA meetings. Make sure there is a child safety awareness program in the school. If there isn't a program in place, get involved and help them create one. It is important that children learn about avoiding abduction and molestation from their parents and school programs. **More fathers need to be involved with the PTA!** PTA stands for Parent Teachers Association, not Mothers Teachers Association, that would be MTA and I believe that's already been taken.
- Join with your city management and community organizations to sponsor a child safety day. May 24th or 26th, either day would be an excellent choice, since **May 25th is Missing Children's Day.**
- Help organize through sponsored events, fingerprinting,

105

dental charting, height, weight, and other physical descriptors. Contact local businesses to support the program. Make certain only qualified volunteers are in charge of the fingerprinting.

- If your child's school does not have a call guardian program to telephone parents when children do not arrive at school by a reasonable time, help the school develop one.
- Take part in helping to develop after school programs for children at schools, libraries, or local clubs. Get involved yourself!
- Involve parents who are at home during the afternoon. Have them alternate days each week, watching the neighborhood's children. Make sure the kids know who they are.
- Meet with your neighbors and local police department to form block programs and crime watch programs to encourage neighborhood protection.
- Help educate the "Latchkey" children in your neighborhood on ways to stay safe when home alone. Let them know where they can go or call for help, if needed.
- Find out who your state legislators are. Laws to protect children won't happen unless you take action. Write, call, or meet with your legislators concerning model children protection laws. Express your support for legislators who support child protection legislation, with your actions, not just words.
- Join with organizations to lobby for new laws to protect your children.
- Help organize courtroom monitoring. Enlist the services of your senior citizens and the retirees residing in your community. When judges and juries realize their actions are being scrutinized, stronger sentencing seems to follow. If time allows, you may consider doing some courtroom monitoring yourself. I found courtroom monitoring to be extremely interesting and often entertaining.

[The experience would be complete if they served popcorn.]

If you are truly interested and concerned about your community and your children's safety, you'll want to find out what is being done about the terrible things you read about in the newspaper and see on television news. Our courtrooms will give you those answers. You may be pleasantly surprised or extremely angry, depending on the sentencing habits of the different judges you observe. Some of their rulings will amaze and shock you!

Here are some more things for your consideration:

- *You must be watchful and sensitive concerning your children's apprehension and/or fear of any particular individual. **(Take your child's feelings seriously.)**

- It is also important to be involved in your children's activities. Try to be present at every event possible. Volunteering actually makes you part of their activities and kids love it.

- Allow your children to pick and choose their own routes back and forth to school and friends homes. Do not interfere or alter their choices, unless there is a safety risk involved in their choices. This is very important to their self-confidence and helps them to establish a strong foundation toward their own independence. Be sure to double-check the routes your children have chosen, and confirm that they are using them. Of course, whenever possible, pick your children up and drop them off at school, friends' houses etc.

  This one is a must. It never fails to surprise, shock, and scare the hell out of me when parents leave their children in the hands of strangers that they know absolutely nothing about.
  [You are turning your children's complete well being over to a total stranger.]

- If your children ride on a school bus, **please** check out the school bus drivers! The buses and drivers may be from a privately contracted company. Check them out through the school and the police department. Make sure background checks have been done on the drivers and any temporary or substitute drivers. See if your child's school and the police department are on top of things. Don't take their word for it. Ask to see some proof, especially from the school. The school and police department showing you their standard operating procedure regarding the hiring of school bus drivers can establish proof. Their standard operating procedure should include a criminal background check. After you are satisfied with their procedure, ask them to double check in your presence, making sure their procedure has been followed. Was Raymond (what's his name's) criminal background checked?

Remember, pedophiles and other sexual offenders seek out jobs that put them in close contact with children. I have been made aware of, or personally come across, rapists, armed robbers, kidnappers, murderers, and child molesters employed as crossing guards and school bus drivers. It would behoove you to triple check these individuals on the Internet, no matter what school or law enforcement tells you. Am I scaring you? I hope so, because it sure scares the hell out of me. These criminals manage to slip through background checks fairly regularly, that is when they are checked out at all.

"I only turned my back for second, and she was gone." Never, but never, leave your child unattended anywhere, any time, for any reason. At minimum, keep your child in your peripheral vision. And never take anyone's word that someone has been scrutinized if they are going to be interacting with or in proximity of your children.

As you will remember, we talked about other children possibly at risk in your community. Watch for unattended children exiting the school bus, meet and talk with their parents and try to work something out. Educate them regarding the safety of their children. Recommend they read "My Body Is My Own." Be a good neighbor, be a good friend to the child at risk. While you're at it, you could be my good buddy and buy a few copies of "My Body Is My Own" to pass out to your friends, whadaya say...good buddy?

Always try to keep in mind that no matter what the situation is, if it involves children do not depend on child help agencies 100 percent. Sometimes they take too much time and too often they suffer from bureaucratic breakdowns. If you discover a child you have reason to believe is being abused, neglected, exploited and/or possibly a missing person, which includes runaways or throwaways, call the National

Center for Missing and Exploited Children at: **1-800-843-5678**. In addition, parents can avail themselves to the 24-hour a day hot line at **1-800-THE-LOST**, which is sponsored and operated by the National Center for Missing and Exploited Children.

There are literally numerous things to be done by concerned parents, things that will make the world a little safer for all children. Get busy, but don't worry, I'm not asking you to do it all yourself. Help organize your PTA and other parents in your community. If individual parents would take on just one of the tasks, you will not believe the progress that can be made. Speaking of tasks, here are some more that could be divided equally among the members of the PTA and other parents in your community.

There is so much to be done in so many areas, let's just jump in, starting with advocacy groups and their computer links. Most, if not all, make a wonderful contribution to society and to parents in general. However, they need to be linked, sharing information. Some do, some don't, and they all should. Some are insistent on receiving the total credit for a child find. I feel it is most important to work together for the sake of the missing children, sharing the credit for a job well done when a child is recovered. Some organizations do not share information, hoping that they will be the ones to discover and recover a child, enabling them to receive full credit. These self-centered activities, employed by <u>some</u> organizations appear to be used to help legitimize their particular existence, and draw more attention to themselves, which in turn brings in more donations. Wrong. They couldn't be more wrong. These organizations must unite through computer networking. Computer linkage is the obvious answer. To my amazement, I found that some of these groups were not even aware of the existence of some of the other advocacy group's. They are all good people, doing an extremely difficult job. However, some need to get their acts together a little bit, maybe with your help. I'm talking to you. Maybe you are that one person who has the ability to pull them together. While you're thinking about that, here are some more goals worth reaching for.

Can you imagine the children that could be recovered if every developed roll of film included a picture and statistics of missing children? Now there's a task, convincing corporations such as Kodak, Fuji, etc. to include in every envelope of photographs, a picture and information regarding a missing child. It is a project equal to and possibly surpassing the "Milk Carton Children" project, which was very successful by the way. This is a doable project! What a great way to get the faces of missing children out to the general public, because you know that when folks pick up their photos, they scrutinize their pictures carefully, one at a time.

Possibly one of you reading my book is an executive with a large film company. Your probably thinking "No, we can't do that, families browsing through, and enjoying their vacation photos don't want that special moment ruined by seeing the face of a missing child." Think of the wonderful and positive impact it would have if you were to include photographs of families reunited Get Smart! People are not stupid, nor are they so self centered that they would object to such an honorable, humanitarian effort that your corporation would be doing by helping to bring a kidnapped child home. How dare anyone object to any responsible effort to bring a missing child home? Well folks, guess what, there are individuals out there and some of them are parents, who have the attitude, it's not my kid, don't bother me. However, for every one of them, there are tens of thousands of you. People like you, who are deeply concerned about all missing children and want to do whatever they can.

How about setting up an advocacy group through sponsorships, specializing in families adopting a missing child? Make T-shirts for grown ups and kids, with a quality picture of a missing child on it. Your group could create posters, badges, and bumper stickers and given your varied occupations, I'm sure that you can come up with much, much more. When it comes to getting the job done, there's nothing in this world that matches American ingenuity and that's a fact. All you need is the desire. Simply wanting to isn't good enough; you must have the true desire to do it.

Some of these things may seem like monumental tasks and they may take a great deal of someone's time. However, the more people involved, the less time it takes. Did you know that many major corporations actively look for worthwhile causes and organizations to sponsor each year? With that in mind, we have to think big. In other words, if you were to ask a large corporation for 100,000 bumper stickers, you will probably get them. Had you asked for the machine that makes bumper stickers and a building to put it in, you may even get them. You might be very surprised, as to how far some corporations will go for a good cause. Some corporations will supply corporate materials, knowledgeable and creative employees, and even corporate attorneys to assist you in a good cause. Like I said, you might be pleasantly surprised and amazed at how easy it can be. I have witnessed corporations do all of the above. However, nothing is for nothing, not to belittle what corporate America does for charities. Sponsorships like I have discussed allow corporations monster tax write-offs and provides great public relations, so don't feel you've got your hand out and the corporations get nothing in return. Again, I'm not trying to demean corporate charity. Corporations that sponsor humanitarian causes deserve their tax breaks and any other kudos that may come their way. What I'm saying is, it benefits corporations to support charities and knowing this makes gaining their support a little easier.

Now that we know where the money is coming from, let's get busy in our communities with some worthwhile projects. I think there should be and believe there is a great need for an expertly staffed recovery house for sexually abused children. This house should also act as an adoption and placement center in your community. I also believe a great goal would be to establish one in every major city in the United States.

To some of you, these goals may sound like pie in the sky. Let me ask you, have you heard of a television program called "Americas Most Wanted?" The man who started that show had a son named Adam. Adam had that look that could be on a poster representing the All-American boy. Well, Adam did make it on a poster. He was kidnapped and murdered in a most hideous and grotesque act. Adam's parents wanted to do something, something positive. John Walsh, Adam's father, wanted to do something for Adam and all children, hopefully helping other children and other parents.

The Walsh's had true desire. John is a man on fire. Mr. John Walsh has almost single-handedly accomplished the impossible with a television program that greatly aids law-enforcement agencies in apprehending literally hundreds of robbers, murderers, sexual offenders, etc. John Walsh has made himself very instrumental in the protection of you and your children. He simply had the true desire, and would not take no for an answer. If he can do that, maybe you can do this...

111

[I am proud to have been associated with the Adam Walsh Child Resource Center, searching in their behalf for missing children outside of the United States.]

There's a great need for a center that does nothing but track child pornography in the United States. The center should act as the central distribution center for supplying child find organizations, advocacy groups, police departments, and any other applicable organizations and agencies with detailed information regarding the trafficking of child pornography. Literally tons of child pornography enters the United States annually.

In 1977, we located a kidnapped child in Ribeirao Preto, Brazil, not far from Sao Paulo. The eight-year-old girl had just been sold and moved to a ranchero, which was located on the Rio Claro River at the outer edge of the Goias Providence. (Some people refer to the Goias as rain forest; I like to refer to it as jungle.) The individual who had purchased the little girl was a known, notorious, child pornographer. As we were proceeding with the recovery, things came to a standstill due to the relocation of the child to the ranchero. To make things worse, a lack of funding added to the problem. Gathering intelligence regarding the structure of the ranchero, including the walls around it, how high, how thick etc. and the exact location of the child inside, was coming in slow.

Finally, after two and a half days we proceeded, at 4 a.m. Our standing operating procedure is to enter the target area, locate the child, determine if other children are present, and exit the area undetected. (In our dreams maybe.) Actually, we are almost always able to enter a location undetected, however, with few exceptions, sooner or later someone realizes our presence, making an undetected exit generally impossible. During that particular recovery we were successful in remaining undetected long enough to establish that our principal child was no longer there. While the ranchero was under surveillance, a positive identification of the child's presence there was made. Although she was identified as being there, it was impossible to move at that moment, due to a lack of information regarding the ranchero and her exact location.

While information was being gathered, it was reported to me that numerous vehicles were coming and going frequently. It was impossible to keep track, although we did feel confident that the child was still at the ranchero because reliable information had guaranteed us that this was the location of a major child pornography photography and film making business. The recovery was a failure. However, two good things did come from our efforts. First, I discovered and recovered three South American children, who were turned over to an orphanage that had worked with me in the past. Second, we discovered a building on the property, which was being used as a warehouse. The building was approximately 3,000 square feet and a little less than half full of crates that measured approximately four feet by four feet. Some of the crates were sealed and ready for shipping, while others were still being filled with pornographic photographs, magazines, and videotapes. Seven crates got our particular attention due to their destinations, let alone contents. Each crate had Mercedes Benz automobile engines in them, one of the engines was not completely assembled, nor had it yet been completely filled with child pornography, as the other ones were. One of the crates was destined for Seattle, Washington and another Newport Beach, California. Our procedure, or policy if you will, during a recovery is if we are discovered, once the child or children are removed from the location, and are safe, if time allows, we do our best to ruin each and every piece of equipment possible, including buildings there.

Due to the fact that I take pride in our work, doing the very best we can, all of the crates containing pornography were destroyed plus a few other worthless things. The only words I can use in my defense if necessary would be something someone else once said. George Orwell wrote, "People sleep peacefully in their beds because rough men stand ready to do violence on their behalf." With that said, I believe it is important you know, whenever possible and the situation allows, I and/or team members pose as pornographers in an attempt to buy the principal child. If purchase is a viable avenue, it is safer for the child and my recovery team. I have not been successful in purchasing a child, mainly because the cost of the recovery is less than the pornographers' asking price, which leaves me with no alternative than a forced recovery.

My point in talking to you about that particular recovery is that child pornography is being shipped to locations around the world by the crate loads. The United States' share, as I said, is coming in by the tons annually. A center specifically specializing in tracking child pornography and child pornographers in the United States is greatly needed. Possibly a joint venture, involving multiple corporations is what it would take to make that dream of mine come true.

Let's get back a little closer to home for the folks out there that will have all they can handle doing the necessary and immediate things to keep their own children safe. Let's get started with an area in your home we'll call the emergency center. However, you may call it anything you wish, I don't want to be labeled a control freak. This is the place you keep all of your children's important information. The center is an important place, so as in an emergency you do not find yourself running all over the house trying to locate important information. Your emergency center should be chosen wisely because it should also be the family meeting place during any emergency. You should also consider a secondary center, in case the first is inaccessible for one reason or another. Does this mean you should have a separate or second set of Child Identification Information Kit? It's not a bad idea, but not absolutely necessary. The reasoning behind a second set would be earthquakes, fire or a second set for more than one agency attempting to find your missing child and so on. It's another personal call. Your home emergency center should include, along with your children's Identification Information Kits, a quality first-aid kit, and at least two "ABC" fire extinguishers. A couple of flashlights, a telephone (cellular if possible) at least five gallons of water and anything else you feel comfortable having there. It's a common sense thing. Here are a few more examples, just in case. You'll probably agree that it would be a good idea to keep coats in your center and maybe a pretty good pocket or hunting knife. You may also want to safely store a gun at your emergency center, if, of course, you have been properly instructed in firearm safety and use. (Another personal call.) I do not consider this a survival supply, but rather emergency equipment. Survival supplies such as earthquake readiness kits and supplies might be kept in a separate place. Some folks choose the den, others the kitchen and some folks have chosen the garage as their emergency center. Your choice should depend on the particular layout and structure of your home. No matter what room you choose there are a couple of things to keep in mind.

First, you do not want to locate your center on the second floor of your house: you want it to have at least two [2] avenues of escape.

Windows can also be considered avenues of escape. If you keep a cool head during an emergency, you'll automatically remember where the ID kit and anything else that will aid in the rescue of your missing child is kept, presenting it quickly to authorities. Make sure all-important information gets into the hands of law enforcement rapidly.

If it sounds like I'm getting a little over zealous, you're probably right. I can't help it, I've been in service to people all of my life, and if it's in the realm of lending to family safety, there's no shutting me up. So if it's not really bothering you too much, I'd like to continue a little longer... thanks.

Since we're on the subject, you've probably noticed my repetitiveness regarding certain topics. This is because I believe them to be so important as to bear repeating.

As I was about to say, you should discuss and practice with your entire family what each family member's course of action will be in an emergency. Use different scenarios. It's important to practice. Whether the emergency scenario is a fire, earthquake, or an intruder, practice. Everybody in your family should be taught the proper handling and use of the emergency equipment in your center. For example, your children should know the proper use of a fire extinguisher. Each family member should know to go directly to the emergency center if need be, that is, if it is possible. If it is not possible for one reason or another, then a secondary meeting place should have been established. A good consideration for a secondary meeting place might be the front yard, or at the neighbors house. However, no one is more familiar with your home and property than you are. This means you should have a pretty good idea as to the best and safest primary and secondary locations for your family to congregate in an emergency.

I will be discussing with you periodically more about what parents can do. As you should have noted by now, in each chapter of this book and with each passing paragraph, there is something obvious that caring and concerned parents can do. After you have secured your family, consider extending a helping hand to someone in your neighborhood, possibly an elderly person or single mother you know. How about the latchkey children in your neighborhood? I'm sure they could use a little guidance. Someone needs to take that first step! Is there anything more rewarding then helping a child, especially helping a child to be safe? Will you consider being the adults that take a moment, share a little wisdom, and give a child a little of your time, and possibly save a little one's life? Don't just tell them what they need to do, get in there and help them. Make it happen for the sake of the children. Will you do that?

We have always considered our neighbors our extended family. When we move into a new neighborhood, we make a point of meeting our new neighbors. We do each other favors and when the other is gone, we keep an eye out. Sure, in this day and age it's difficult. Some people consider new neighbors introducing themselves to be aggressive behavior. However, as they get to know you and realize you simply wish to be a good neighbor, they come around. Heck, everybody wants somebody looking out for their place when they are gone. If you're a parent with children that are home alone, nothing is more comforting than to know you have neighbors your child can count on in an emergency, neighbors you can count on.

Talking to your children without scaring them

This section of my book is one of the most important conversations I will be having with you. It is so important that your children understand their role concerning their own safety. It is most important to teach your children without confusing or scaring them. Consequently, it is equally important for you to heed my advice regarding your preparation and handling of this very sensitive subject. You need to follow these instructions to the letter! If you fail to do so, you may cause unnecessary confusion, discomfort and an unreasonable and even unbalanced fear of people and sex, which could follow them into adulthood. You may wish to solicit the aid of a qualified family psychologist who specializes in this area of family service, especially if you wish to expand on my directions. You are probably already aware that children do not always ask for answers to questions they may have, especially when they're confronted with what they perceive to be an awkward or uncomfortable topic and/or situation. If you follow my instructions and answer all of their questions, all will be well. You must also though be intuitive enough to answer some questions they haven't asked and leave the door open for future questions.

Preparation and implementation are task should be handled by both of the parents. The exception to this rule might be one parent's inability to deal with the subject matter due to naïveté, embarrassment etc.

The presence of an uncomfortable parent could do more harm than good. Some adults find themselves unable to discuss sexually related subjects with children. If one parent is unable to handle this task, the other may wish to consider asking a trusted relative of the opposite sex, or an expert, for help. It is very important that the adults, to establish a balance of comfort, represent both sexes. This may also help the child to break any apprehension regarding the opposite sex and sensitive conversations in the future. A child may wish to discuss certain things, or ask particular questions of an adult of the same sex and that's okay. Now here's something that must be considered before you ask a particular relative for help in this matter. The relative that you choose must be someone the child or children know, like, and trust. If you are a single parent, and for some reason, no one is available to help you, not even a trusted friend, it is better that one parent does it. If affordability isn't a problem, remember professional help is always available.

So here we go. First, prepare in advance the subject matter you wish to cover with your children. Try to put yourself in your child's position. In other words, make a list of questions you might have if you were the child. Depending on the ages of your children, you may decide to have separate conversations, and that's okay. You'll want to conduct the discussion in a place that allows for privacy, but is familiar to the child. Pick a place that has little or no distractions. If possible, try to sit next to or near the child. Do not stand or pace at any time during the conversation. The child may have a favorite place or chair to sit. That's okay too. We want the kids to be comfortable during this discussion. However, if you have a favorite chair, you know the one, the place of authority, the throne no one else is allowed to sit on, avoid it. The reasoning here is, you want to be at your child's level and you want your child to be at your level.

Be sure to let your children know they have done nothing wrong. Assure them that they have done nothing wrong. When you have something very important to discuss with your entire family, you should communicate this with your children. Let them know that their presence is very important in family discussions. You may want to label important meetings involving the entire family "Family Discussions" or something like that. Be sure to let your children know that these meetings labeled "Family Discussions" never involve them having done something wrong. Always make sure these discussions are important family matters that involve them and that you are interested in their opinions. An example might be planning the family vacation, or God forbid, an illness in the family etc.

Next, be direct and honest with your child. Remember, these are new times, and depending on your children's ages, it may surprise you as to what they already know. So don't dance around or mislead them, be accurate and to the point. If you are not honest with your kids and they know it, **it will be hell trying to get them to take you seriously again**. That is, if you can ever get them to have important conversations again. Be honest and up front with your kids. They're not stupid and if you don't have an answer to one of their questions, tell them that you will get the answer. Don't forget, because if you do, you will loose credibility and they will turn to other sources for the answers. Be prepared to clarify words and terms that your children may have picked up from other kids, or may not understand. Putting the shoe on the other foot is being prepared to ask your children to clarify words or terms that you do not understand.

Do not push or press your child into answering questions, or for that matter into the conversation. All children are different. One child may jump in with both feet, while another sits silently listening. You can probably toss a coin as to which one will absorb the most information. Of course, you need to be prepared, because depending on their ages there might be a lot of giggling, and that too is okay. It is extremely important during your discussions that you do not display horror, anger, or disapproval. Remember that these "Family Discussions" are kind of like neutral territory. As children become omfortable with situations, they tend to open up. If you show disapproval during a discussion, when it comes time for the next one, your child will show you what disappearance is. A common mistake made by many parents is thinking that because a kid is so young, he or she has nothing important to say. How could they, since they haven't lived long enough to really know anything about anything? On the contrary, if a parent will take the time to listen, kids have many important things to say. Sure, maybe some of it's not too important to you, but you have to stop and think, it might be important to them and probably is. I'm going to quote somebody here, but be damned if I can remember who, "Kids are people too."... Wonder if it was anybody important? I know one thing that's important and that is that we have to remember, just because we live in the grown-up world, full of important things, doesn't mean that a kid's world isn't full of important things also. Some grown-ups have been lucky enough to find out that some of the kid's stuff is more important than the grown-up stuff.

Well I guess it's time we get deeper into it. During these discussions <u>never</u> suggest answers to your children. They're smart. Although they may not know how to form an answer at the moment, give them time and ask them to think about it. Ninety percent of the time they'll come up with something. Don't push them for an answer or an opinion they're not willing or ready to offer. Do not ask any of your children to remove clothing for the purpose of demonstration. Be sure to let your children know why this discussion is necessary. Try to help them understand. Remember, almost all of the terrible things happening to children today are coming at them from the adult world, not from their world. <u>Help them understand</u>. Reassure your children that you are there for them.

I always find it funny and disturbing at the same time that parents will teach their children to cross the street safely and fire safety is taught in our schools and at home etc, so you would think that it would make sense for parents to prepare their children against sexual abuse. **"Not Happening."**

We should begin teaching our children as soon as they are old enough to learn simple safety instructions. Remember, do not become disappointed or frustrated. Each child is different. Some children are capable of learning about safety as early as age two. Incorporate the information about sexual assault into general teaching regarding personal safety. Repeat the information often. They should be periodically reminded throughout their growing years, continuously reinforcing what you have taught them. Do not perpetuate the myth of the "Dangerous stranger." While it is very important to teach your children about the "Dangerous stranger", it is extremely important for children to understand that people they know, trust, and even love, may also try to take advantage and hurt them. Sad to say, most children are sexually abused by someone they know, and too often that pitiful excuse for a human being is a family member.

It is important for your children to learn the correct terms for their body parts. This will enable them if necessary to tell you or someone else that they have been sexually abused or if someone tried to abuse them. It will also enable them to better express themselves and not be afraid to do so. Even very little children can tell you something is wrong if they have learned the proper words to do so. If children do not know how to express themselves properly, they are left at a real disadvantage. The bad guys, "Pedophiliacs," are counting on parents who have not properly instructed their children. Many sexual offenders have walked free due to a lack of quality parenting. Don't complain about slow arrests due to poor police work, when possibly the entire tragedy could've been avoided with quality parenting. If everyone does his or her job, there is no finger pointing!

Your children must also learn that because an individual is an adult or an older child, possibly in a position of authority, such as a babysitter, that authority doesn't give them the right to do bad things. For example, no one has the right to put his or her hand down your pants. **No one**, not an adult, not a babysitter, no one should touch your body unless you want them to, nor should they force you to kiss them. **No one** has the right to force you to do anything that you know is wrong, nor does anyone have the right to do anything that makes you feel uncomfortable.

Teach your children they have the right to say "no" and then help them to learn how to say it assertively **"NO!"**. When a child wants something bad enough, they know how to be assertive, so it's your job to direct their ability to be assertive. It is your job to teach your children about the power and control they have over their own bodies. "My Body Is My Own" is not simply the name of this book, it is a fact that all children have to learn. There should be no limitation on their right to decide who should touch them, who they should hug, who they should kiss. For instance, when strangers and friends or a relative makes a fuss over a child, and the child is uncomfortable, doesn't want to be hugged, doesn't want to smile, and definitely doesn't want to be kissed, the child is often thought of as cranky, unfriendly, or a brat. The honesty that children possess is often an embarrassment to parents. Be honest yourself, who in the hell wants to give a stranger a hug, much less a kiss. I often wonder what children are thinking in these situations. Your children's thoughts might go something like this. "Oh jeez, he's your friend, you kiss him", or "If uncle Burt would put his teeth in, I might consider shaking his hand." Just one more, my favorite, "Oh no, Aunt Bertha squeezed me un-constipated the last time I let her hug me." I know, I know, un-constipated isn't a word, but it describes the situation so well that it should be.

Children should be allowed and even taught to rely on their instincts.

Be careful. You may destroy those "Protective instincts" when you force your children to respond in certain ways, especially in ways that they don't want to respond. Part of doing your job is supporting your children and their decisions not to get up close and personal when they choose not to. When we force our children to respond in certain ways, we confuse them and cause damage to their "Protective instincts."

You must teach your children that there are no secrets with adults, only surprises. Sexual offenders almost always tell children, "This is our secret, don't tell anyone." Help your children to understand a surprise you can tell while a secret you don't tell. Teach your children that if an adult says, "This is our secret, don't tell anyone", they must tell you the secret. Teach your children that there are no secrets from the family. Let them know that they can tell you anything. Assure your children that you want to hear what they have to say, and that you will listen and believe them. **It is most important that your children have confidence in you.** They must have confidence in you! Your children need to know what to expect from you, and they need to know that you will believe them. The best way to do this is by opening those lines of communication as soon as possible. This is where "Family Discussions" come into play and are most valuable. If a child suspects that he or she is going to be yelled at, embarrassed, talked down to, or not believed, you can believe this, that child will not be talking to you. This is why neutral territory "Family Discussions" are so important. Part of the growing experiences toward maturity is to be included and accepted into important "Family Discussions."

Children should not be taught to automatically assume adults, and people in general, including those individuals in positions of authority, are right or able to do anything they please. This leaves children extremely vulnerable to exploitation by people who have legitimate power and authority over them, such as brothers, sisters, teachers, babysitters, etc. Let your children know they have the right to act verbally: "Leave me alone" and "I'll tell." Also, let your children know they have the right to act nonverbal by pushing someone's hand off them or running away.

Now we're going to enter an area a little tougher for the little ones, but not impossible. This may take a little more patience on your part.

Stick with it. The responsibility of how your children answer the telephone and the door is on you! It is up to you to teach your children
how to answer the telephone and the door safely. Again, even very
small children can be taught these skills. I have witnessed children as
young as two years old answering the telephone and the door properly
and safely. The key is for them not to let anyone know they are alone.
Which by the way, I know I don't have to tell you that a two-year-old
should not be left alone, nor should any child in my opinion until at
least fourteen years of age. In many states fourteen is the law.

Teach your children to say that their father or mother is busy and
cannot come to the telephone or door if someone asks for them. Have
them answer the telephone or door, calling out, (in a loud voice) "I'll
get it, Dad / Mom" and teach them to take a message or have the person call or come back later. They must know <u>never</u> to open the door
for someone they don't know. Your children must be taught to <u>never</u>
open a door unless you say so, making it okay. Your children need to
learn the difference between being familiar with someone, such as the
ice cream truck driver or the paperboy and someone they really know.
Another important subject you need to get across to your kids is that
very bad and evil people do not always look bad or evil, as I mentioned before. A great way to do this is for Mom, Dad and possibly an
older sibling to create short skits or miniature plays. I believe that this
technique is nothing short of genius, especially, when a little humor is
added. When children witness their parents portraying children, they
seem to find it extremely humorous and definitely pay particular attention. The twist is, someone portraying the obvious villain looking
type, who turns out in the end to be the good guy. This approach
works and makes it easy for your children to learn the dos and don'ts.
It is also important that you teach your children not to offer information about himself or herself or anyone else in the family, and this too
can be incorporated into a skit. If someone wants to use the telephone
to call for help, tell your child to say, "**No**, but I will make the call for
you" and under no circumstances are they to let them in. People can
be persistent and assertive when they want something. They can also
be intimidating, especially when dealing with children. Teach your
children to be persistent and assertive right back. Here is the "Command Presence" that I spoke to you about earlier in the book. Arm
your children with the courage and the knowledge to recognize danger

and the confidence to make intelligent decisions about their own safety. Remember to teach your children to be <u>proactive,</u> not reactive. To some parents, all of this can seem a bit overwhelming. Keep in mind that you're going to incorporate all of the above into teaching your children personal safety. You know, crossing streets, running on a pool deck, etc. If you will remember, we talked about the use of games, songs and music. Again, (depending on the individual ages of your children) you may wish to have separate discussions. You may also wish to consider adding a quiz to your discussions. If this sounds good to you, here are a few sample questions for them:

1. Do you know your telephone number, including the area code?

2. Do you know how to make a telephone call from a phone booth?

3. Do you know your full address, including the state?

4. Do you and your parents have a set plan in case you become lost or separated?

5. Would you go with an adult who isn't a relative if he told you your parents had sent him?

6. Would you take a present from a stranger?

7. If you were afraid, would you ask a police officer for help?

8. Would you ask another adult for help if you were afraid?

9. Do you know what to do when your usual ride after school does not show up?

10. Do you know that you have the right to say "**No**" if someone tries to touch your private parts?

11. Do you know that you should tell your parents or a trusted adult if someone tries to touch you in an uncomfortable way?

12. Do you know that you can trust your parents, that you can tell them anything, and that they will help you?

These are some sample questions that you may consider using. However, with a little forethought, I have confidence in your ability to develop many more questions pertaining specifically to your children and their particular needs.

During your "Family Discussions", your children may have some ideas of their own regarding their safety. Listen to them and give them real consideration. If the idea your child comes up with is not a good one... all right, I'll say it, and if the idea your child comes up with stinks and is really ridiculous, handle it carefully. You may want to try letting them down easily by saying something like, you might be right, but what if the "Stranger" does this...maybe you should do this... Then, praise the confidence you have in the child's ability to follow your instructions. Also, there is the possibility that your child will actually have a good idea, or an idea that would not compromise their security. Praise the child and somehow try to incorporate their idea into what needs to be done. It is extremely important that your children feel that they are contributing to the "Family discussions", and nothing satisfies a child more than knowing that they are accepted and that they are contributing.

Now comes what I consider the tough part, teaching your children the proper time and correct situations to exercise their newfound assertiveness. Because one has achieved the level of "black belt" in karate, does not mean he or she gets to beat up people whenever they choose. Rather, it is nice to know you have the power when needed. The beauty of possessing their newfound knowledge is that it endows them with "Command Presence." Assure your children that when they use their assertiveness at the proper time, you'll back them up one hundred percent. Some children may find this to be a whole new experience. Consequently, they may experiment on friends, teachers or what could be worse yet, they may try experimenting on you. At first you will be alarmed, and question yourself, "What kind of a monster have I turned loose?" Then when you gather your senses... you'll blame me. Once the dust settles, and you put things in their place, namely your kid, things will then balance. You will discover great satisfaction in knowing beyond a shadow of any doubt, your child is prepared to take part in his or her own safety... with assertiveness!

Teach your children

Without constant open and honest communications between parents and their children, all is lost. Somehow, through events and time the home has become a battleground and the family divided has turned into the armies. At least that's the way the children see it. Parents are the enemy! Generally, it is an unspoken, but definitely exists. Some parents have to come to the realization that their prized possessions are not the beautiful home on top of the hill or the shiny new automobile, that's right, even if the shiny new is a Rolls Royce. Your prized possessions, above all, are your children. All else is simply stuff! If some

124

parents would give their children the attention they give their stuff, not only would the house become a home, but also, America would be an even better, safer place to live. Let's face it folks, you sure as to hell wouldn't let your beautiful car sit at a dark corner unattended, until the wee hours of morning. Yet, some of you will let your beautiful child sit at that same dark corner unattended, until the wee hours of morning. **<u>Go figure!</u>** Again, if it is not safe or wise to leave your stuff at that corner, please tell me, how can you allow your child to stay at an unsafe place like that corner, until the wee hours? Maybe they're right, maybe some children should consider their parents the enemy!

In today's society, too many parents consider parenting simply providing food in their kid's tummies and a roof over their heads. Oh yeah, and Nikes on their feet. Which, by the way, makes me wonder, are you supplying your children with such expensive tennies to provide positive traction, aiding them to escape the clutches of strangers, or are they for quick getaways from the cops? Now, before you get angry with me, I will be the first to admit, I could be totally off base with my question. You may have innocently purchased those shoes for the sake of quality. The fact that your kid will now look really, really cool or hot, or whatever word is in by the time you read this, standing on that corner at 100:AM has nothing to do with it. You probably argued against buying the shoes until you were blue in the face, citing failing in school when you bother to show up, and you have done nothing to earn such an expensive pair of shoes. Finally, you succumb to the constant barrage of pleading and promises. Stick with me, I'm making a point here. The point is I have witnessed children milling around on corners and worse places in the middle of the night and early morning hours, but looking really cool...or whatever. They're all dressed up in their favorite team's jerseys, expensive jackets, and of course those can't live without em, my folks had to mortgage the house to get em, tennis shoes. What in God's name are we teaching our children? In the first place, you are obliged to teach your children to be individuals, not followers. Granted, some kids are not meant to be leaders, but this does not mean they have to be followers, they can be individualists. Followers generally end up milling around in the middle of the night and followers generally end up being losers! Teach your children about the demons out there in the real world, watching, waiting to pounce on the losers. Oh, and for Pete's sake, stop trying to buy your children's love with stuff they haven't earned and don't deserve.

If a child has <u>earned</u> something very special such as a pair of expensive tennis shoes, he or she obviously isn't wasting time in a mall or on some corner in the middle of the night, putting them self at risk. They have been taught correctly and learned wisely!

It is very important to teach your children the difference between what looks good and what is good. As long as your child believes that being cool depends on what he or she has to wear, you're in trouble, and so is your child. If you're trying to win your children over by buying them nice things, **stop it**. If your children were putting their well being at risk by exhibiting a lack of interest in their own safety and future, why would you reward them with nice things? Please tell me, do you think you're teaching your children good traits? Do you think you're teaching your children self-esteem, scruples, and ethics? How about duty, honor, good work ethics and principles? Do you believe you are teaching your children any quality values? If your answer is yes to any or all of the last three questions, I am obligated to inform you that you're probably suffering from being under the influence of cheap dope.

The reasoning behind my conversation with you about what your kids are wearing and why you keep buying is that it's human nature to continue negative activities if you are rewarded for them. It should be obvious to you as concerned and caring parents that if your child is not doing the right things such as, if your child is hanging out spending late nights with friends, if your child is barely passing with poor grades, or completely failing in school, and if your child is worrying more about what to wear, he or she won't be interested in you, much less, quality communication with you. This is a child that will continue putting himself/herself at risk. This child should not be rewarded with anything, including special clothing. What this means is, your kids' head is in the wrong place and more than likely, bad things are heading his/her and your way.

The child I am referring to is the child that does absolutely nothing around the house to help out, yet expects money and the nice things. This is a child that will not take part in "Family Discussions" even when present. This is a child that will go out of his or her way to do the opposite of what you ask or advise. This is a child that needs his or her head screwed back on straight. The problem is you may have to use a real screwdriver. (Juuust kidding.) Allow me to re-phrase that, this is a child who needs his or her head put back on properly and pointed in the right direction. The problem is you may have to hold it there for a while. My point is, if you have a child that fits into the do nothing, handout group, there will be no "Family Discussions" working in your home. He or she may even influence other younger siblings. For the best results, avoid this all to familiar family scenario and begin teaching your children the skill of family communication as early as possible. Along with teaching your children the art of communication, they need to have the desire to communicate with you. For a child to have the desire to truly communicate with adults it is totally up to you the parents. The answer to instilling desire in your children's willingness to communicate with you is simple, it is as simple as one two three.

1. Create an atmosphere (neutral ground) conducive to open honest communication similar or identical if you wish, to what we described as "Family Discussions."

2. Listen to what your children have to say, giving genuine consideration to their concerns and ideas.

3. Believe what your children have to say, letting them know that you trust their word and will always be there for them.

If it sounds like I'm repeating these three things too much, that's good, maybe it means it is really sinking in. These are positively must-do things if you want to be successful with your children. Although, to be honest with you, your chances of succeeding in developing strong family ties through communication have proven most successful with parents who began teaching their children early in life. I'm talking real early in life, as early as the child's second birthday. However, I have borne witness to amazing turnarounds involving teenagers, so one never knows.

"Family Discussions" should become a regular, anticipated family function. One that your children truly look forward to, and you'll know your children look forward to them when they choose to remind you of it. These discussions, when handled properly, will build character and self-confidence in your children. Too often, parents make a mistake by not setting guidelines or parameters to the conversations they have with their children. For example, a child wishing to have a serious conversation doesn't always choose the very best of times. Mom might be in the middle of doing something as important as the dishes, not willing to devote her full attention to the child's conversation. Possibly, it's Dad, deeply absorbed in the relaxation of watching a football game, passing out those zombie like nods and mumbled acknowledgments. In all fairness to parents, Mom may work outside of the home and is also doing that never-ending job at home, which makes it very hard work, and Dad is totally submerged in what I hope is much deserved relaxation away from his daily grind.

We should, as tired as we might be, drop what we are doing and give the little ones the attention they deserve. We don't always, you'll have to admit. That's why it makes sense to me and should make sense to you, to set aside some special time for "Family discussions." If you have them often enough, maybe you could have the kids hold off the important stuff for the discussions. Well, would you look at that, with one sentence, I have probably completely destroyed my credibility. Okay, okay, I know it's impossible to make kids wait, especially when they feel they have something important to ask or say. However, what you can do is teach them to learn to separate what can wait and what cannot. You can also teach them to take notes and save them for the discussions. Teaching your children this will help them to structure their organizational skills. Who knows, with a little luck, they may pick up some patience along the way. If you are too busy to give your child full attention at a particular moment, then tell the child to wait. Explaining, "I want to hear what you have to say, I'll be done in a minute and we will talk." Fair warning, if you forget to talk to your children after asking them to wait, don't expect future cooperation from them. **Don't drop the ball!**

Through all of this, your most important and main goal is to instill in your children two things:

- **<u>Command presence, being proactive not reactive.</u>**

In order to accomplish these two objectives, it is important for you to arm your children with the courage and knowledge to recognize danger and the confidence to make intelligent decisions regarding their own safety. That's right, you've heard this before too, and you'll probably hear it again, that's how important it is. Think about it, if you teach your child command presence, he or she will be less likely to be targeted by child molesters or kidnappers. Your child will stand straight, head high, appearing to exude self-confidence. He or she will look to have obvious purpose and direction. Your child is going to be the exact opposite of what child molesters and kidnappers look for in a victim. If you follow my guidance, teaching your child correctly, he or she will not only appear to have these qualities, but will truly possess them. Now, add a proactive, rather than a reactive attitude to his or her command presence and you have created an unbeatable combination. Did I mention that these attributes would also assist them in adulthood? Yep that's right, they'll be the ones landing the better jobs because of their self-confidence and general attitude. If you understand the make up of most child predators, what gives them the courage to do the things they do, then you will understand why learning those two things are so important. Actually, there isn't much to understand about child predators and their courage. It's really pretty simple. Kidnappers and molesters of children are opportunists that are really quite cowardly at heart. When child predators observe confidence in the form of command presence in a child, an alarm goes off inside their heads that says unknown commodity and unfamiliar action or reaction. It frightens and discourages them and they avoid that child, because as I said, they are cowards attempting to commit a cowardly act.

Listen to your children

Déjà vu, that's right, I have previously talked with you about listening to your children. However, since communication is the key, the absolute key to a genuine relationship with your children and listening is the most important part of communication, I thought I would talk with you about it some more.

Children have always had something to say, even before any of us could understand them. First, with other children, cooing and babbling, yet their siblings and playmates seem to understand every syllable. Then eventually, Mom becomes the official family interpreter, because she has learned the language, or as us Dads put it, cracked the code. Although, if Dads will be honest, we would admit that we're taking Mom's word for it. C'mon Dads, admit it, the best we can figure out is this kid's speaking some kind of a mix between Latin, Aramaic and bubbles. By the way, many experts believe as I do, that babies often cry due to frustration stemming from the inability to communicate. I have witnessed what I consider a minor miracle. What miracle you ask? Glad you asked, I have observed babies at the early age of one using sign language their parents have taught them and using it well. I also bear witness that the children using sign language seem more content and cry much less. Which helps me confirm my belief in allowing for the exceptional child as early two years when teaching them about danger and strangers.

It's truly funny when you think about it. In the beginning, we struggle to understand their words, and swear up and down that they said Momma or Dadda first. Then, sooner or later, the time comes when we can understand what they have to say and nobody wants to listen. So what happens when nobody wants to listen? Some children invent invisible friends and some children make up stories, while others create mischief, simply to get attention. When children are starved for attention, they gladly accept punishment and even spankings for negative attention. We as human beings tend to seek out what we lack. As a child, I didn't get enough vegetables (greens) so I sought out what I needed. Among the other critters at the Ritter Ranch were rabbits, so obviously, there was rabbit food, those little green pellets. No, no, not the round black ones, I'm talking about the other end of the rabbit, rabbit food, which is heaped with chlorophyll and maybe some other good stuff. I would fill my pockets and snack on those pellets all day long. I'm sure you have heard similar stories, a kid dragging a magnet in the dirt, and then eating the metal attached to the magnet, or stories of children eating mud pies. I am told these are children lacking iron, and seeking it out instinctively. How about the stories of children eating ants and other bugs? The experts tell me that those children are lacking potassium. You see it's only natural to seek out what we lack. So why should a child's need for attention differ? **That's the key!** Pedophiles are looking for young children naturally seeking what they are lacking, attention. Remember earlier in the book, I spoke to you of the child that just won't go away? Unintentionally, some parents are sending their children into the open arms of pedophiliacs, willing to listen and eager to shower your children with attention.

It is important to talk with your children as frequently as possible. It is equally important to listen to them, always. Teach them not to lie, so you can believe them and have confidence in everything they say.

Explain how lies create doubt. Also explain how important the truth is to you and to the child and why. Let your children know about the damage a lie can cause. Explain to them how long it takes to completely believe and trust in them after they have lied. Your children must know and understand that if they lie, they will have to rebuild your trust and that will take time. Explain that it wouldn't be fair for them to expect you to automatically believe what they say after they've lied to you. Teach your children, who they are is judged by what they do and what they say. It may appear to you that I am getting off track here, but I'm not! I'm staying on track by explaining to you how everything comes full circle. Somehow you need to get it across to your children that the truth is the glue that binds you, holding the family together. While a lie is an insatiable demon that must nourish itself with lie after lie. How can you count on a child looking out for his or her own safety, if the child is heading down the wrong track? Do you believe your child will listen to you about kidnap prevention if he or she won't listen to you about anything else, and on top of that is lying to you? Do any of you believe that parents who reward their children for those types of actions in an attempt to win them over stand a chance? I cannot, in good conscience, point parents in a direction knowing that some of you, through your own actions, haven't got a chance, no matter how closely you follow my advice. This is why I feel it is my obligation to you to supply you with as much information as possible and repeat the really important stuff.

It is extremely important that some less fortunate parents are made aware of some hard-to- swallow facts. If your child fits into the do nothing, expects hand outs, and are rewarded for it category, you are probably wasting your time. Any attempts at securing your children's safety will probably be in vain. It is imperative for you to start teaching your child at an early age and re-educate an older child that possesses poor values. It is called redirection and you may wish to seek professional help. Here's a bit of good news: it's never too late to redirect a child. Children that know they are loved want to please their parents! Children want their parents to be proud of them. However some get lost along the way by making what they feel are unforgivable mistakes. Some children fall into the "Not worthy" of forgiveness or love from their parents syndrome. I'm not going to say always, but generally it is the parents' fault. So folks, it's up to you. If your child is headed in the wrong direction, turn them around. One of the best ways to start is by listening to your children. Help stop them from putting themselves at risk.

Mothers, you are a dichotomy! Half of you would plunge a butcher knife deep into the chest of <u>anyone</u> you found that was sexually assaulting your child. While the other half refuses to believe and will do nothing, knowing, yet pretending, that your boyfriend or husband isn't molesting your child. You try to convince yourself that it isn't happening, hoping it will just go away. Another thing I find disturbing is that it is fathers who go totally ballistic, wanting to kill upon learning of their child's molestation, yet it is the mothers who lead the crusade against child molestation and abuse. Go figure. Get involved, you dads. Don't huff and puff after the fact, listen to your children **now!** Get involved with your children's security **now!** There are wonderful people out there, working thanklessly to protect your children. They need your help **now!** You're supposed to be the "Great protector" though it seems you can't be bothered with the security of your own children, not to mention anyone else's child.

Great relationships between parents and children are rapidly becoming extinct today, more than ever before in our history. We could all throw our hands up in the air and say, "Kids today, whataya gonna do?" I'll tell you what we could do. We could acknowledge our faults, shortcomings and responsibilities to our children, and then we could change. Start today by opening that line of communication with your children, and don't forget to keep in mind that kids aren't stupid. If you try to hit them with all this information at one time, they're going to think you've gone nuts, especially if you've been neglectful parents in the past. If this is the case, you may consider beginning with a well-deserved apology. If your child is anything like ours, you'll find that he or she will be eager to accept your apology, but a little short on handing them out, and that's okay. Once you get through that, begin implementing your well-thought-out family plan. Don't forget to include your children in the setting up of your "Family Discussions." Getting your children involved in this project from the very beginning will not be difficult: it's called listening.

I have a special favor to ask of a particular group of mothers out there. I want you to take a trip with me, a trip back into your childhood...

132

You are six-years-old, or there about, and it's bedtime. You said all of your good nights, and now you're warm and cozy. Now that you're all tucked away in your bed, thoughts of the day go racing by as you pass into sleep. It seems that not much time has passed by when you are awakened by an uncomfortable touch. As your head clears and the blurring fades, you see your father's face looking down on you.

"Ouch, that hurts Daddy."

"What's wrong Daddy?"

"Shhh, quiet, Daddy loves you."

"But it hurts Daddy."

"Shhh... Daddy needs you."

Moments later you're crying, scared and confused and you are all wet, as if you had an accident. You are frightened and you don't know what to do. Next, you feel trembling hands trying to wipe the wetness away.

"Don't you tell your Mommy or anyone about this. It's "Our Secret" and if you do, you'll be in big trouble." "Remember, Daddy loves you."

In the morning, you stay in your bedroom as long as you can, not coming out until you know for sure your Daddy is gone. After having given it a great deal of thought, you know Mommy will know what to do. Mommy will help.

"Mommy, Daddy scared me and hurt me last night."

"What? What are you talking about?"

"Daddy hurt me, here."

"Don't be silly, your Father wouldn't hurt you, don't you know your Father loves you?"

"Yes he did, he hurt my pee pee."

"Don't talk like that, do you want to get in trouble? Your Father didn't hurt you, you had a bad dream."

"He did Mommy, Daddy hurt me."

"Don't you ever say that again. I'll slap your face. Do you understand me? I'll slap your face if you ever say that again."

Can you imagine the confusion and sheer terror if this happened to you? How would you feel if your father hurt you as I have described and then you were turned away by your mother? If no one would listen, if no one would make it stop. What would you do? **What did you do?**

Listen to your children. For the sake of all things right, don't turn

133

your back on your child and may God forgive you if you do, because I sure won't.

What kids can do

Believe it or not, your children are the best weapon you have to combat child sexual abuse and the possibility of kidnapping. Remember, earlier in our conversation, I told you that children catch pedophiles best. Children, who have been taught what to do, and actually do what they've learned, catch pedophiles best. If your children are properly prepared, the average pedophile does not stand a very good chance of successfully harming them. My contact with pedophiles has taught me that the average predator does not use force. He prefers to use trickery. Now, I don't want to lead you to believe that your children will be beyond harm by following my directions, because it would definitely be a false sense of security. As in all things, there are the exceptions to the rule. I am referring to the average pedophile and statistics. There are those pedophiles that will savagely force a child. These pedophiliacs will not and do not consider trickery in their crimes. Because there are pedophiles that are capable of force and will not hesitate to use it, you must warn your children of the trickery employed by some and the brutal force employed by others. Of course, I want you to teach your children about the tricks pedophiles will use, but how do you protect your children against savage force? There's only one positive way. Your children must learn to **"Be alert and stay away from strangers."** Now, that sounds like a simple thing to teach your children. **"Wrong."**

The problem has always been, simply warning children to stay away from strangers does not work. Children do not understand the concept or image of a "Stranger." We constantly strive to raise our children to be polite and friendly. Teaching fear is not conducive to this goal. Not to mention, statistics have shown us in many cases the abductor or exploiter of children is often someone known to the child and not a "Stranger" at all. No I'm not telling you not to warn your children to stay away from strangers. I am telling you not to be angry or surprised when it doesn't work, because often it is not the child's carelessness or anyone's fault but the perpetrator's. I want to encourage you to try to teach your children the difference between strangers and others, as I spoke of earlier in the book. The key to what your children can do regarding their own safety is getting them interested in their own safety, which is up to you and I. I am supplying you with the weapons for this battle. You have to teach your children how to use them. Below is a list of things your children can do in order to help keep themselves safe:

- I know my full name (first, middle and last).
- I know my complete address including street, city, state and zip code.
- I know my telephone number including area code.
- I know how to dial "911" and "0" for emergencies.
- I know how to use a pay telephone without using money.
- I know my family's "Secret Code Word" and I know not to go with anyone, for any reason, who does not use the family "Secret Code Word."
- I know not to put my name on anything that's mine, including jewelry, hats, caps, jackets, t-shirts, bikes, baseball glove etc. If I have no choice, I will put it where people cannot see it.
- I know not to play in isolated areas or take short cuts through dangerous or deserted areas such as creeks, vacant lots and vacant houses or buildings.
- I know to always walk and play with friends, because it is safer to be in a group or at least with one other person.
- I always practice the "Buddy System" when away from home.
- I know there is safety in numbers, no matter where I am, so I always stay with my friends, "It's safer."
- I know not to go door-to-door selling something, or for any other reason, without an adult with me.
- Before I go anywhere, I always check with my parents, or the person in charge, to make sure that they know where I am going and who I am with and that it's okay.
- I tell my parents where I want to go and who will be going with me. I also let them know how I will get there and when I'll be back. I'll always let my parents know if there's a change in plans.
- I know to always let my parents or babysitter (guardian) know where I'm going and whom I am going with.
- I know to walk on the left side of the street, facing traffic,

135

so that I can see if a car stops near me.

- I know to keep all doors and windows locked when I am home alone.
- If I am home alone and someone knocks on the door, I know to yell out, "I'll get it dad/mom" and I never unlock or open the door. I yell out, "Who is it?" If it is not some-one I am expecting, I know to say, "My mom or dad, etc. is busy and can't come to the door right now." I know to talk through the door and ask the person to come back later. If the person refuses to leave or pretends to leave but doesn't, I know to call the police by dialing "911." I know to never let a person inside my house for any reason.
- If I arrive home and see that any window or door is open or broken, I should not go in. I know to go to a trusted neighbor and call "911" or "0" for the operator if "911" is busy.
- If I am home alone and the telephone rings, I know to never let a stranger know I'm home alone. I know to say, "My mom/dad can't come to the phone right now."
- I know that it is okay to hang up the telephone if I don't like what I hear,
- such as strange noises, scary or nasty talk, or even nothing at all.
- I know that there are emergency numbers to call if I'm home alone and get scared, including the telephone num-bers to reach my parents and trusted neighbors.
- I know that a stranger is anyone, a man or woman, who is not known by me.
- I know not to go with strangers and to run away from them when one approaches me.
- I know never to accept candy, food, money, or anything else from a stranger. I always ask my parents before I ac-cept gifts from anyone, even money.
- I know to never take drugs, not even from a doctor, unless my parents say it's okay.
- If someone I know, a friend or neighbor, asks me to come into his or her house or go somewhere with them, I know to ask my mom or dad first.

- I know never to approach a car with strangers in it. If a stranger says something to me, I know not to go near the car to answer or to have them repeat the question.
- I know never to help a stranger with directions, or help them find their lost pet.
- I know never to let a stranger take my picture.
- I know never to hitchhike.
- If a stranger is following me, instead of hiding in bushes, or behind/in a building, I know to go to a place where there are people and ask for help. I know it is safest to ask a man or a woman with children for help.
- I know to keep a distance away from strangers when I'm walking somewhere or standing in a line, at least two arms distance, if possible.
- I know never to go with a person who says they are a police officer if they are not in uniform and don't have a police car.
- I know not to go with a stranger even if they show a badge.
- I know to tell my mom/dad of any strange or unusual events.
- I understand that I need help from grown-ups with the problems involving my safety.
- I know most grown-ups will listen to me and care and I know most grown-ups will help me.
- I know that some problems are too big for me to handle by myself.
- I am not afraid to talk to my parents or trusted grown-ups about problems that are too big for me.
- I know never to accept a ride from a stranger, even if he or she tells me that my Mom or Dad sent them to get me.
- I know that even though I may see and recognize certain people like the mailman, ice cream truck man, newspaper person, etc., these people are considered strangers to me. I should never go with them without permission from my Mom or Dad.
- I know it is not my fault if someone touches me in a way that is not okay.
- I know I do not have to keep secrets about people who

touch me.

- I know the difference between a "Good touch" and a "Bad touch" and that certain areas of my body are very private, like my swimsuit areas.
- I know to report any "Bad touches" to my Mom or Dad and if they are not around, I will tell a trusted adult or the police.
- I have the right not to be touched in ways that I don't like, or that make me feel uncomfortable.
- I will tell my parents or a trusted grown-up, even if the person who touched me says, "He will hurt me or my parents or anyone else, if I tell."
- When I tell a grown-up and I don't get help, I'll tell another grown-up. I will keep telling grown-ups until I get help.
- I have the right to yell "NO" really, really loud and I have the right to run away and get help if an adult or anyone else tries to touch me or take me away.
- I know that if I'm approached by an adult, and feel that I'm in a dangerous situation, it is all right to run away screaming as loud as I can. "This is not my mother or father, I don't know this person, I'm being kidnapped."
- I know that if an adult tells me to keep a secret, I know that it is okay to tell my mom and dad or a trusted adult.
- I know to call home when I get to my friend's house, the mall or anywhere I am going. I know not to forget to call again when I'm on my way home and to always come home before it gets dark, if that's the rule.
- I know if I get lost in a store or shopping mall, I will go to a cashier that is wearing a nametag or a uniformed security person for help.
- I know that I am never to go alone to movie theaters, arcades, game stores, parks, public restrooms, public swimming pools, or even schoolyards, especially after school hours.
- I know that running away from home is no fun and dangerous. I know it will not solve my problems.
- When I am having problems, I know that I can talk to my

family or a trusted adult for advice.
- I know that people who seem "Nice" sometimes do mean and terrible things to children.
- I know my three rules if I find myself in a danger situation:

1) YELL "NO!"

2) RUN AWAY WHILE SCREAMING "HELP!"

3) TELL A TRUSTED ADULT!

- I know to always tell my Mom or Dad if I'm away from them and something happens that hurts me or makes me feel uncomfortable.
- I know that I have the right to feel safe, and I know who I can trust to talk to when I am not feeling safe.
- I know that if I learn to do all of these safe things, my parents will feel better about letting me do more things.

I am a very special person. No one should hurt me. I deserve to feel and to be safe.

Chapter 4

PARENTAL ABDUCTION

Parental abduction prevention

If you and your separated spouse are having serious difficulties and you are concerned that your ex may abduct your child, you must obtain a **legal custody order**. This is extremely important because without a custody order, if your ex-spouse takes your child, no law has been broken. The order must be obtained from the court or jurisdiction of the child's home state. Take a certified copy of your custody order to your child's school administrator. Give the school administrator a certified copy of your custody order. Make certain the school staff knows who is permitted to pick up your child and who is not. You should also put this in writing to the school administrator. The second thing you need to do, since you have obtained legal custody, is get a passport for your child and notify the passport office in person and in writing that your child is not to be taken out of the country without your expressed written permission. If your ex-spouse has molested your child and you have proven this to be the case, you will need documented papers issued by the courts with you at all times.

This should be in the form of court findings or a warrant for your ex-spouse arrest. If your ex-spouse is a citizen of a foreign country and does manage to abduct your child and leave the United States, it is extremely difficult and only in rare cases possible, to recover your child through normal channels. Do not expect help of any consequence from United States officials. Nor will you receive assistance from officials of the country the child was taken to. Your best hope in this scenario would be to hire a qualified <u>professional group</u> to recover your child.

As for us, we rarely get involved in a child recovery unless child sexual abuse is <u>proven</u>.

If your spouse or ex-spouse is threatening to abduct your child, do your best to get a witness. This can help to establish the placement of safeguards into the custody or visitation orders. The court may order a sizable bond and several safeguards can also be added to orders for the parent with visitation rights. A court appointed monitor can be required. Restrictions may be placed on when and where visits may take place, and on supervision of visits, including the possibility of police supervision. Make certain your custody order <u>specifies police procedure</u>. Then, if the order is violated, the police have explicit authorization by the court to recover your child. This specification also makes it clear that the police are legally required to help you. If the threat of abduction persists, you may also wish to consult with your attorney regarding the possibility of a restraining order. They aren't always worth a lot, but it is one more piece of legal paper in your favor, which is always nice to have.

It is essential that you keep as much up-to-date information as possible on your current or ex-spouse, including date of birth, Social Security number, current residency, workplace address, automobile identification tag and license numbers. You must also be able to supply authorities with any and all credit information possible, including financial information such as bank accounts and loans. You need to be able to supply law enforcement with relatives' and friends addresses, telephone numbers and include club memberships and favorite hangouts. You have got to be prepared to supply the authorities with anything that could possibly assist them in locating your child.

Talk with your children often about how much you love them and that how you will always want them with you. It makes me sad to report to you that often parents who abduct their children tell them that the other parent doesn't want them anymore. Quite often, they will tell the child or children that the other parent has died.

A child living under these circumstances must be taught how to search for you, if the need arises. Be sure your children know how to use the telephone and especially know how to place long distance calls. Make sure your children understand that they have a right to find a way to get in touch with you.

I would like you parents involved in separation or divorce to remember two things: First, when you have children and you're in the middle of a separation or divorce, especially an ugly situation, **it's not just about you**. Second, often children are abducted because of frustration brought about by one parent withholding visitation rights. Do not unfairly use or change visitation rights with your ex-spouse. Children should be cherished, loved and protected, not used as a tool for leverage in a divorce.

What to do if your child is abducted by an ex-spouse

If your child is abducted by an ex-spouse you must immediately contact the State Attorney or the District Attorney in your county. If child kidnapping is a felony in your state, a felony warrant should be issued. Insist on it. If the District Attorney or State Attorney agrees to extradite and prosecute, the FBI can become involved. The FBI can issue a federal felony warrant for "Unlawful Flight to Avoid Prosecution" if there is reason to believe the subject has fled the state. In addition, you need to make a report to your local law enforcement agency, providing all the necessary information about your child and ex-spouse. I hope you know the drill by now, but just in case, you need to supply authorities with physical characteristics of both your child and your ex-spouse, including the most recent photographs, fingerprint card and all the other pertinent information I have discussed with you.

If your ex-spouse is working within the confines of the United States, he can be located through his social security number. One of the ways this can be done is by checking through Social Security services. This should be handled through the Federal Parent Locator Service. Access to this service can be made through all FBI agents and United States Attorneys working on parental kidnapping cases. Ask questions. Make sure this is being done. Access to these records should include, but not be limited to, Social Security, IRS, the Department of Defense and other federal agencies records as well.

If you feel your child has been taken out of the United States, check with the State Department in Washington, D.C. for passport data. Immediately notify your local passport office and any other passport office you feel your ex-spouse may consider using. The object is to prevent your child from being issued a passport and removed from the country. Also, check with your in-laws and other relatives, including friends you think your ex-spouse may have been in contact with. Check with the Motor Vehicle

Registration Department for information on the vehicle your ex-spouse is known to drive. If you believe the abducting parent may be in a particular state, you may be able to verify it through the Department of Motor Vehicles. You may also be able to locate your ex-spouse by checking with the Post Office, utility companies, banks, employers, insurance companies, subscription lists, credit cards, or any other place where an address change may be requested by your ex-spouse. Don't forget to check past telephone bills for out-of-town numbers, which may supply you with a possible destination.

If your ex-spouse is employed in a profession that requires special licensing by the state or possibly a union registration, check with the appropriate agencies and in other states. If possible, investigate old credit card bills, which may show out-of-town purchases. Keep an eye out for new bills arriving. If your child is of school age, check previous schools to determine if another school has made a request for school records. Advise the school not to transfer records without first notifying you. Contact your family doctor and dentist to see if medical or dental records have been requested and by whom. Again, advise them to not release or transfer any records to anyone without notifying you first.

Quite often abductors will have the child's name changed, or simply begin calling the child by another name. You must notify the Department of Vital Statistics in the county where your child was born. The purpose of this is to put a flag on the birth certificate to prevent the child's name from being changed. Also, request that you be notified if a copy of the birth certificate is requested by anyone. It's most important to maintain regular contact with the law enforcement agencies handling your case. Stay on it; don't allow them to put your case on a back burner. In other words, become the pain in the ass that you will undoubtedly be referred to as. All law-enforcement agencies are restricted by budget; therefore they constantly have to move on to other cases. Consequently, your case and many other cases end up on a back burner, sometimes within weeks, or sooner, after the initial report is made. One of the best ways to keep full attention on your case is to involve the media whenever possible. Your number one job is to keep the pressure on, any way you can.

If you intend to hire or involve a private investigator to assist you in locating your child, be warned. Be extremely cautious. Check them out with your local police department for any accusations, claims, lawsuits, or charges. Also, check them out through the Bureau of Consumer Affairs, which is the governing agency for private investigators. There are many qualified, honest, professional private investigators available. The problem is there are as many that are not, maybe more.

It is important that you know that if your ex-spouse flees with your child to a foreign country, many new factors come into play. For example, does your ex-spouse have family in that country and if so, how powerful are they? What are the laws of that country regarding child custody? In many countries the father rules supreme, no matter what the circumstances. You may think that because you have documentation including court orders from the United States and possibly, a warrant for the arrest of your ex-spouse, that you will receive cooperation. **Forget it!** As I mentioned earlier, your best bet is, involve a <u>qualified professional group</u> to recover your child. Of course, you'll be officially advised not to take that sort of action by all United States government agencies involved, or they may say nothing, pretending they heard nothing. There is only one agency in the world that I am aware of that will advise you honestly, and that agency is Interpol. While United States agencies will try to discourage you, Interpol's stock advice is "Your best chance of getting your child back is to get a qualified professional recovery team together, and go get your child." Having dealt with Interpol on many occasions, I have witnessed this advice being given to parents and have been advised myself, without hesitation, I might add. Never attempt to retrieve your child from a foreign country without qualified professional help.

If you do attempt a recovery without professional help, you may at minimum find yourself imprisoned. In some countries, the status of your relationship to the child means nothing and your actions will be considered kidnapping. Be warned, kidnapping a child in many countries calls for and often demands the death penalty. This will help you understand the price tag attached to the recovery of your child by the <u>qualified professional group</u> you consider hiring. By now I'm sure you have taken notice that when referring to a recovery group, I stress professional and underline. This is because there are groups that claim to be and groups that are. Problem is they're all expensive and the results will differ greatly. I have witnessed some of the most ridiculous attempts at recovering children that you can possibly imagine. There are supposed professional groups that are willing to take your money knowing they don't have the wherewithal to bring back your child. What can be worse is if they make an attempt to actually recover your child. They run the risk of, and probably will, place the child in real danger. Check out any prospective recovery group. One of the best ways is to speak to previous clients. If the group you are considering chooses not to supply references, find another group.

My recovery people refer to those recovery people as "Asshalves" due to the fact that they are not worthy of the full rank of "Assholes." I'd ask you to pardon my French... but that was perfectly good English.

If your decision is to involve a <u>qualified professional group</u>, I am going to repeat that you must investigate them. Ask for proof of their claims. Ask to speak to previous clients (Parents) of a child they claim to have recovered. Check every reference possible before making your final decision, for you are about to launch a very expensive operation. If the group you're interested in is the **"Real McCoy"**, having made successful recoveries in the past, many will know of them, including some authorities. You also need to be aware not to put full stock in everything the FBI tells you. My experience and the experience of other experts has led us to this conclusion. For what seems to be a legion of reasons, the FBI chooses not to be entirely honest with the general public. Adding to that, the FBI in some cases has been downright misleading.

I want you to also beware of any group that guarantees you the recovery of your child. The reality of it is, <u>there are no guarantees</u>!

Chapter 5

KIDNAPPED

What to do if your child is missing or Kidnapped

First, you must realize that most of the time when children are missing, they have not been kidnapped, and they are not in any danger. Generally the child has forgotten or neglected his or her responsibility to ask or inform the parents of their intention to relocate to a friend's house or their favorite play spot. First, here is a bit of good news, the technology is now available allowing you to know where your child is at all times. Through your child's cell phone, actually up to four children and anywhere in the United States. Check it out. Now, if you sincerely believe your child is missing, you should take action immediately. If your child is missing from your home, search the house, first checking the danger places, the swimming pool or Jacuzzi and any old freezers or refrigerators around. Then check the laundry dryer, kitchen oven and the fireplace and chimney. Look in crawl spaces, the attic and in all closets, through any piles of laundry and under every bed. You must search whatever a child could crawl into or wherever a child might hide. Your child might possibly be asleep or stuck somewhere, unable to get free. Check with your neighbors and the friends of your child. Ask them to diligently search their house, starting with the danger places. Now of course, the order of these procedures changes if anyone saw anything suspicious, such as a stranger near your home or child. If a stranger was witnessed nearby, immediately notify authorities, and then began your search.

146

*Be prepared in advance of notifying authorities or any other group for assistance. Have all pertinent information at hand.

If you are unable to locate your child after a complete and extensive search, call your local police department immediately and file a missing persons report.

*Allow nothing and no one to interfere with this course of action.

You need to give the authorities all pertinent information regarding your child immediately. You should have everything prepared in advance and easy to locate. In case you have not prepared in advance, you will need to supply the authorities with your child's name, clothing, date of birth, height, weight, and any unique identifiers. For example, eye glasses, pierced ears, scars, or braces on the teeth. You must not forget to inform authorities of any identifying disfigurement or abnormalities. Along with all of that, the police need to be made aware of any needed life-saving medication. Obviously, authorities will need an up-to-date photograph and a fingerprint card. Tell authorities when you last saw your child. Don't forget to tell them what he or she was wearing and what he or she was doing at the time, in case they forget to ask. Report any significant change in your child's daily routine. Request (insist) that your child be entered immediately into the National Crime Information Center (NCIC) Missing Persons File. Your child's fingerprint classification can also be entered into the (NCIC) computer file. This is the FBI's computer system and insures that any and all law enforcement agency in the country will be able to identify your child if he or she is found in another community or state. Next, call the National Center for Missing and Exploited Children for assistance. Their telephone number again is **1-800-843-5678**.

Ask your police department if your state has a Missing Children's Clearinghouse. If so, contact them and make certain that your child is registered with them, and request that this information be shared with all other state clearinghouses. Now, you need to have at least one hundred (100) duplicate copies made of your child's photograph, get them out to the news media as fast as possible. We're not talking days here, we're talking hours. I repeat, as fast as possible. Solicit the aid of your relatives, friends and neighbors. Do whatever it takes to get everything done fast. At the same time that you're having your child's pictures duplicated, have reward posters made up. The design of an effective poster is crucial. Contact the National Center for Missing and Exploited Children for assistance in your poster design. Throughout this entire ordeal, you must stay in constant contact with the authorities, insisting that they follow up on any and all leads.

Request that a community search be made. Many missing children have eventually turned up within a few blocks of their homes. Check with the FBI after 24 hours has passed to make certain your child has been entered into the NCIC. You may have to go through your local police department to check with the State Bureau of Investigation. Make sure they are working on your child's case and are totally up-to-date with their information. If you believe you know who took your child, have the police check to determine if this person is wanted for any other crimes. If your missing child is an older child, have the police check to determine if he or she is being detained for a crime anywhere. (Cover all of the bases.)

You should also search for an in-depth list of advocacy groups, which can be located in this book under **Advocacy Groups**. Each group possesses individual expertise. If your child is missing or kidnapped, it is imperative that you contact these special people who coordinate and run these dedicated advocacy groups. They can and will help you.

Fire up your computer, get on the Internet, and put out a complete description including an up-to-date photograph of the missing child. Contact all pertinent advocacy groups and ask for their help.

There are three, very important web sites that need to be contacted immediately, they are:

A.L.I.E. Foundation; http://www.alie.com

Established in the memory of an abducted and murdered Colorado child, this organization supplies bloodhounds to law enforcement for the purpose of sniffing out missing children.

Find Missing Children; http://www.rinokids.com

Dedication is the name of their game, diligent work done by these folks in creating free web pages for missing children as well as adults.

Registered sex offenders; http://www.sexoffenders.net/sgv.html

Run off copies of every registered sex offender in your community. Make sure that local and federal authorities are investigating each sexual offender in your in your area, starting with and especially the ones residing in your neighborhood. Usually, this is the first thing law enforcement does. However, I bear witness to the fact that it has not been done in some cases. You may consider having the offenders in your neighborhood monitored by whatever means possible. If investigative authorities tell you that a particular offender has an alibi and they seem satisfied, it doesn't mean that you have to be satisfied. However, the authorities in general do a very good job recovering missing children. Remember that law enforcement is trying to cover as much ground as possible and as quickly as possible. Police officers and FBI agents are human, therefore susceptible to human error. Things sometimes take, or seem to take, longer with them. The fact is that generally they are taking longer because they are trying to narrow the possibility of human error and that does take a little more time. Be patient, but not too patient.

Do you remember the case of Polly Klass? She was kidnapped from her bedroom in the middle of the night in California, 1993 and eventually found. She had been raped and murdered. Police officers, while searching for Polly, stopped to investigate what appeared to be an individual having problems with his vehicle. It was at nighttime, the same night of the abduction and on a secluded road in the search area. To paraphrase, the motorist said his vehicle was stuck, but that he had the situation under control and didn't need their help, so the officers left without investigating further. Had the officers taken the time to run a check on the individual, they would have found he had multiple convictions of sex offences. Had the officers thoroughly checked out the situation, they may have and probably would have found Polly, lying in the brush just feet away, still alive. Let's throw in a... "Nobody's perfect" here, or should it be "not everyone does their job to the best of their ability?" However, trying to be fair, I wasn't there and don't have all of the particulars. Sometimes, local law enforcement use reserve officers, cadets and in some cases enlist the aid of civilians for canvassing neighborhoods and rural areas. This generally means oversights and mistakes are inevitable. I do not wish to be demeaning to any group or individuals assisting in the search for missing children, however, in some areas of this country, reserve officers do not receive academy training and most cadets are young and inexperienced. Many civilian volunteers fit into both of those categories.

In missing children cases it can be, and often is, difficult to keep track of everything that is being done. It is important to start a file, to keep track of what law enforcement agencies are doing, and a scrapbook that will help keep you posted on what everyone else has done and is doing.

*Have a tape recorder connected to your telephone, one that automatically begins recording, preferably when the telephone rings.

*For further reference, my use of words such as preferably, consider, recommend, suggest, should etc., really means "Do It."

As I mentioned before, in order to keep your case on the front burners, you must seek out as much media publicity as possible. Many children have been identified as a result of excellent media coverage, and if the missing child sees the publicity, it may provide hope and encouragement. Contact your local throwaway newspapers and ask them to donate space to run pertinent information and a photograph of the missing child for as many editions as possible. Approach local merchants and businesses, seeking donated space in their advertising and coupon sheets. In most cases, I have found community business people are eager to help. Also, ask for donated printing from your local printing shops. Try not to put the total burden of cost on one business, involve as many printers in your community as possible. You'll need a relative or a trusted friend, possibly your pastor, to set up a donation fund. The cost of the search for a missing or kidnapped child can be astronomical, especially if the child has been taken out of the country and a professional recovery group is necessary.

Now comes what I call the checklist. Check with as many runaway shelters as you are able to locate. Check with "Religious Cults." You will find them scattered across the nation. Check out and follow through on any and all ideas and suspicions. While interviewing individuals, pay particular attention to their initial reaction. Watch their body language. If you have a gut feeling, report it to authorities. I have also found it wise to pay particular attention to women's intuition. One of God's gifts to women is their intuition. Quite often women's intuition is dead on, so pay attention to it! Honestly, if I had paid more attention to my wife Christine's intuition in the past, I may have fewer scars and bullet holes in my body today. Do not rule out anything. Even if it appears out of character or out of the question, check it out.

Have someone who is familiar with your child checking on the local hospitals and morgues, for any unidentified, injured or dead children. If you decide to hire a private detective (investigator), be very careful to obtain a reputable one.

*Get references and then double-check the references.

If financially able, and it does not go against their departmental policy, you may wish to consider hiring off-duty police officers to aid in the search for your missing child. Some police officers may be willing to donate their off-duty time. You may also consider enlisting the aid of your local chapters of such organizations as the Kiwanis, Veterans, Masons, Elks and American Legion, etc. Do not hesitate to solicit their help. Take any and all help you can get. However, there is one exception: do not solicit the help of any young persons' organizations, such as the Boy Scouts, Cub scouts, Girl Scouts, Brownies and so on. I believe the reasons should be obvious to everyone. In case it isn't obvious to all, we do not wish to expose children to the risks involved in the search for a missing child. I am aware of past cases where exceptions were made and Scouts were used in the search of fields and hillsides. I am also aware of one such search that turned disastrous. Enough said?

Your next step is to gather all of your relatives, friends, neighbors and as many volunteers as possible from your community and beyond. It's time to hit the pavement with pictured reward posters in hand.

*I advise everyone to canvas areas in teams. No one should conduct searches or have interviews with anyone, or investigate anything, alone, especially females. Always alert other members of your search party as to what you are doing, where you are, and how long you will be.

Contact and investigate every home, school, shopping mall, park, campground, playground, vacant field, vacant lot, vacant or abandoned houses, vacant or abandoned buildings, any beaches and Mom-and-Pop stores including back rooms. Don't stop there. Believe me, you have only just begun. Check out all strip mall stores, convenience stores, liquor stores, churches, gas stations, halls, college campuses, outhouses, warehouses, doghouses, firehouses, and whorehouses within a 200-mile radius from where the child was last seen.

I realize that there are some that might be offended by my addition of whorehouses to the list of places and people to be contacted and investigated. When it comes to searching for a missing or kidnapped child, it is most important not to leave any stone unturned. Personally, I have found that prostitutes are genuinely concerned and extremely helpful when it comes to missing or kidnapped children. A few years ago, while we were searching for a kidnapped child in Rio de Janeiro, Brazil, I solicited the aid of an organized group of prostitutes. Within two weeks the prostitutes had tacked up and passed out over two hundred and fifty thousand (250,000) flyers and reward posters. You should also keep in mind that the perpetrator of such a horrific crime would possibly be known or recognized by prostitutes. So it's up to you. Take offense or take action, the choice is yours. Funny, prostitutes don't seem to mind men and women of the clergy assisting in the search for a missing child.

*Immediately report any uncooperative or negligent law enforcement officers or assigned special agents to a higher authority.

Medical evaluations after recovery
Normally, at the time of the child's recovery, authorities will automatically have the child examined by a medical doctor or possibly a team of medical specialist doctors. The examination will determine if the child has suffered physical injury, including if the child was sexually molested. However, as strange and unbelievable as it may seem in this day and age, I have witnessed that some recovered children receive little, and in some cases, no medical attention. Albeit most often, recovered children do receive a complete professional medical evaluation. In any case, it is up to you, the parents, to see to it that a qualified medical specialist gives your child a complete physical examination. It is important to establish, as early as possible the extent of physical damage and the possibility of peripheral damage suffered by the child. This damage may not show itself for years. You must determine, if possible, whether the extent of physical damage to the child will be long-term or even permanent. For example, will a female victim be able to conceive (become pregnant) as an adult? Will a male victim suffer from a permanent rectal disorder?

I understand, as you must, that the initial doctor examining the recovered child, in some cases, and I have to underline some cases, is examining the child to determine injuries for the sake of prosecution. The first physical examination is not always the most thorough. Consequently, it may not be an examination completely in the best interest of the child. Again, this is not true in all cases, nor is it true of all examining doctors, just <u>some cases and some doctors</u>. It never fails to amaze and frustrate me that the examining medical doctors rarely prescribe, or even suggest for consideration, psychiatric evaluation and/or therapeutic treatment of a sexually molested child victim. The importance of psychiatric help for a sexually molested child cannot be measured.

Allow me to share with you two examples from my case histories. The first is a little girl we'll call Precious, because she was the prettiest little girl you have ever seen. Precious was kidnapped and sexually molested simultaneously by both a man and a woman. After we recovered Precious, it was discovered that the kidnappers (child rapists), while sexually forcing themselves on Precious, kept her drugged and did severe damage to the vaginal vault and rectum. Did I mention Precious was two years old? Her abductors referred to the penis as "Snake" and the vagina as "Snoopy." I've decided to use this case as an example for what I believe to be the obvious reason. Parents of kidnapped and/or sexually abused children should incorporate psychiatric treatment in the child's healing process. If Precious had not received both physical and mental assistance, she may have never completely healed. I am thrilled to report that Precious did heal, completely.

You see, if Precious didn't get all the help she required, she may have been haunted for the rest of her life. Every time she heard the words snake and Snoopy, she most likely would have suffered traumatic regression. Where in this world does a child go to escape words like, snake and Snoopy? Due to expert mental treatment, Precious does not suffer from psychological problems.

The second case involves another little girl who will remain nameless for obvious reasons. While in captivity she was kept locked in a tool shed with a dirt floor. Due to her young age, the length of time spent locked in the shed has never been determined. I do know that implements of torture were employed on her before, and during sexual attacks, to the point of disfigurement. The perpetrator also kept her constantly overly drugged, so much so that our experts all agreed **"Only a miracle kept her alive."** By the time I was able to recover her, she was in full-blown addiction. Today she is totally recovered, physically and mentally, including corrective surgeries for the disfigurations she suffered. Today she is healed and a most beautiful young lady. With expert help from professional people who specialize in these areas, **a child will heal!**

Now comes the time to address a problem head-on, a real problem that rears its ugly head, much too often. The problem is men. Husbands, fiancées, boyfriends and sometimes even fathers, who cannot seem to deal with the **"tainted ones."** By tainted ones, I am referring to women and children, most often female children, who are the victims of rape and/or sexual molestation. You've heard the stories, or maybe it's happened to you. The suffering from having been raped seems never ending. Boyfriends kinda drift away, fiancées find a multitude of excuses to call off the wedding, husbands seek divorces and fathers simply keep their distance.

In the past, I have heard the most shocking statements from fathers. It appears to me that some fathers of kidnapped and sexually assaulted children wish to pretend that the child doesn't exist. Their beautiful child is no longer **"perfect."**

During a specific conversation with the parents of a kidnapped child regarding the possibility of the child's recovery, the wife and mother excused herself to use the restroom. During his wife's absence, the husband and father of the missing child made this statement. **"I hope we aren't wasting your time, but a rescue is out of the question, it's been too long. If she's still alive, she's ruined."** The child in question had been missing for two years and two months. Judging from his wife's conversation and attitude toward the possibility of her child's recovery, she was unaware of her husband's position. This poor excuse for a human being wasn't interested in getting his "tainted child" back. In his mind, his little girl was no longer perfect. As he put it, **"She's ruined."** This man came right out and said it and he used all the words. However, I have heard the same things said by fathers of kidnapped girls, in many different ways. Like, **"It's probably too late"** or **"She will be different now"** and **"She'll never be the same."** Oh, and one of my least favorites, **"It will be all right, if she hasn't been raped."** I call this phenomenon the **"Tainted ones scarred syndrome"** the acronym is **(TOSS).** One of the definitions in Webster's dictionary for toss is, "dispose of readily or easily [without regard]."

It is impossible for us to understand this mentality, especially considering the healing I have witnessed. Of all of God's creatures, men are perhaps the least perfect, especially when you consider most atrocities committed are done so at the hands of men.

Without going into much detail, the experts have informed me that this attitude stems back to the time when one of the prerequisites to marriage was the prospective bride, without exception, must be an "untainted virgin." This attitude would be more easily understood if the reasoning behind the virgin bride were to ensure fidelity. A more likely reason is, men want (prefer) to be the first and only. The official reason was for the paternity insurance of the child's lineage, especially important to fathers. Even if the first example were the truth, to ensure fidelity, I fail to see a correlation. To compare the assurance of faithfulness or being the first and only to rescuing a loved one and quite possibly saving the child's life... well, if there is something to that, I just don't get it. Unfortunately, I come across it much too often. However, it cannot go unsaid, most that fathers do not feel that way. To the contrary, most fathers would forfeit their own lives to have their child back safely. For the fathers that feel their kidnapped child is now tainted, they need to take a good long look at their own "perfectly and untainted lives."

When a child is injured during the growing years they mend rapidly and quite often without showing any signs of the injury by the time they reach adulthood. The same is true of their minds.

Imagine if you can, a child alone in a room, frightened beyond belief, waiting for her father to come and get her. She hears someone at the door, her heart pounds with excitement. She knows it's her daddy to come and save her, but it isn't, and she is sexually assaulted again.

There are many advocacy groups you can turn to for quality help and advice. I do not know of one group that will not advise you to seek psychiatric counseling for your recovered child. I do not wish to harp on this subject, although experts have advised me that less than seventeen percent of sexually molested children receive psychiatric counseling. Acknowledged statistics tell us that at least one out of every three women have been sexually molested in one way or another before adulthood. This means that there are a lot of men and women out there shouldering the burden of molestation and probably a lost childhood, without ever having had the benefits of professional counseling. Is it possible that this is the cause of unexplainable and unreasonable out burse of anger in relationships? Might this explain some frustrating and inexplicable actions, including confrontations between couples, ignited by both male and female partners? Confusing and sometimes hurtful attacks made by both sexes for little or no reason. Is there a burden many men and women carry that their partners are unaware of? A burden so heavy it causes them to lash out at loved ones, saying regretful things, maybe things meant for another. Possibly, even they themselves do not understand why they said it. How much do you know about your partner's past? Or possibly a better question, how much do they know about their own past? Mental blocks often automatically trigger as a protective mechanism for abused children. Many men and women are haunted by unknown and unclear feelings later in life. Sadly, women are most victimized, consequently, the most haunted. Particularly those victims that did not receive professional psychological guidance when it was most needed. Maybe... just maybe.

If you are haunted by unexplainable feelings, especially ones of a sexual nature, seek guidance from an expert. Talk to a psychiatrist or psychologist that specializes in protective mind blockage. It's never too late for understanding and peace of mind.

CHAPTER 6

APARTMENT LIVING [SAFELY]

While apartment living offers many advantages, parents should be aware of the potential security problems involved in apartment living. It is unwise for parents to only consider cost, location, status and convenience when selecting a new residence. You should always keep in mind that our children are at greater risk today than any other time in our country's history. **Remember, when one child's life is dimmed, the life of every American is diminished.**

When you're trying to evaluate the safety of your child at the place you are planning to rent, or you are already living in, you should take the following elements into consideration.

1] When your children are home alone, it is important to know that they can safely lock themselves in. I am going to presume that you already know it is up to you to insure that all locks on apartment doors offer good security, and of course, that the cores of the locks will have been changed when you move in. This action eliminates the possibility of outstanding keys. Find out if the company you are considering renting from practices an essential and effective key control system. (How are the keys duplicated and handled?) Are all apartment doors re-keyed between tenancies automatically? Are you notified in advance of a superintendent or maintenance person's intent to enter the premises? Does the property owner or management have any objections to you preferring to be present during a visit by management or any other agent, including maintenance?

Always address your concerns in writing to management. If the landlord does not respond to your safety concerns, you should contact the Crime Prevention Officer of the Police Department in your area.

Remember our earlier conversation regarding pedophiles living in your community? Well, when you live in an apartment building, a pedophile may live just a few feet away.

2] The door of the apartment must have a peephole viewer with a 180 degree viewing capability. The front door should be solid core or metal with a quality dead bolt lock and the door support frame should also be of quality and tight-fitting. Exterior door hinges must be mounted on the interior side of the door.

3] The hallways should be well lit, and no bulbs left missing or burned-out. Outdoor lighting should be more than simply adequate. Streets, driveways, carports, garages, buildings and general landscape should be very well lit, with no exceptions.

4] There should be mirrors placed at the corners and bends in the hallways and corridors to prevent someone (predators) from waiting unseen.

5] All storage, maintenance and utility rooms must be kept locked at all times.

6] Security cameras should monitor all elevators and enclosed stairwells. The doors to these should have viewing windows, so you do not have to enter an enclosed area blindly.

7] Laundry rooms, basements and furnace rooms should be kept locked and also be monitored by security cameras.

8] All fire escapes should be alarmed and enclosed to prevent unauthorized access, yet allowing exit. Check if fire extinguishers are readily available and properly maintained in hallways etc. [Check maintenance dates]. Make sure your children are aware of the extinguishers and explain how to work them.

9] If an intercom buzzer system exists for the building entrance, make sure it works properly. In addition, by law the apartment must have quality working smoke detector alarms.

10] All windows accessible from ground level should be protected, if possible, by bars that are fastened to the masonry. Make sure the bars or grating can be opened from the inside, in the event of a fire and that you have a key in your possession, if one is required. Also, your entire family should have access to a window key. Make sure all windowpanes are intact. Check to see if there are working interior window locks on all windows. Check for any lever locks on windows and sliding doors that open in the down position. If you locate lever locks that lock in the up position on doors or windows, test each lock individually. This is done by shaking and rattling the door or window continuously while in the locked position to determine if this action will unlock the door or window due to the rattling vibration. If the windows or doors become unlocked during your test, request management to replace the locks with better quality devices that lock in the down position.

*Realistically, I know that most management will wet their pants in laughter at some requests, such as No. 10 instruction, so be prepared to do some upgrades yourself.

11] Landscapers and gardeners are rarely security conscious. That leaves it up to you to see to it that all trees and bushes near the buildings are not overgrown. In addition, bushes should be kept below window level.

12] It is best that garage doors are kept locked and that they are controlled by either a key or magnetic card. Electronic garage door openers are too easily purged.

13] Check apartment storage lockers, windows, doors and mailboxes for jimmy marks. Are the mailboxes prying and appropriately placed to prevent tampering by outsiders?

The quality of a neighborhood can often be determined by simple observation. However, it is always best to check with the local police department. Ask specific questions about the community, neighborhood and the apartment building you're interested in. Ask about specific crimes related to the area and apartment building you are considering. Inquire into convicted sex offenders (pedophiliacs) residing in the area. Remember that it is important to double check on the Internet for sex offenders in the community.

Once you've chosen an apartment, and have moved in:

1. Teach your children to never leave your apartment door unlocked, even if only for a moment, for instance, while taking out the trash.

2. If you are required to give the superintendent (manager) a key to your apartment for emergency use, seal it in an envelope and sign your name across the sealed flap, with your signature overlapping the flap onto the body of the envelope. This will deter against tampering. Pe-

159

riodically ask to see the envelope. (Request that janitorial and maintenance personnel do not have a copy or master key to your apartment.)
It is always best when employees can only gain entrance to apartments
through management.

3. Make an effort to meet your neighbors. Learn to look out for
each other's interest.

4. Get to know who drives what vehicles, who "belongs" and who
doesn't.

5. Teach your children never to get on an elevator with strangers.
It is always wise for children to stand beside the control panel. This
gives direct access to the alarm button. This is also good advice for
adults.

6. Never isolate yourself in a basement laundry, or any laundry
room for that matter. Nor should you ever allow your child to be in a
laundry room without adult supervision. If a situation arises that your
child must assist you by doing the laundry, arrange for a neighbor to
be there. Often sex offenders will stalk apartment recreation rooms and
Laundry facilities.

7. Instruct your child to never open the door for a stranger, even a
utility company employee or building maintenance. (This also includes
female visitors.)

8. Tell your children never to prop outside doors open for any reason. Instruct them, if they find an exterior door propped open, to close
and secure it immediately.

9. For single mothers, use only your first initial on your doorbell,
mailbox and in the telephone book. If possible, use a male's voice on
your telephone answering machine.

10. Never allow your children to be alone in the swimming pool
area or gym room. This does not mean that children should be accompanied by other children. I am talking about trusted adult supervision.

11. Immediately report any building security problems to the building manager/superintendent. Follow up to be sure the problem is
corrected.

I have found that leaving a television on with the volume set so it
can be heard from outside the closed front door to be a great deterrent.
Because a person is a criminal does not always mean that he or she is
stupid. If a predator or burglar hears sound (voices) from inside they
will most often lose confidence and beat a hasty retreat. I also leave

the television on at night (all night) with the volume turned down to zero. This allows flickering light movement to be visible through curtains from outside, and predators and burglars alike have to ask themselves, is someone home, should I take the chance? Maybe they fell asleep in front of the TV. Subconsciously, the flickering light represents movement, which will cast doubt and uncertainty in a criminal's mind. As I said before, they're not always stupid. They will generally move along looking for an easier and safer victim. (A radio is almost as good).

If you follow the guidelines for apartment living, your entire family will be safer, especially your children. The opportunity for burglary, home invasion or assault on your children will be significantly reduced. Remember that burglary is also a crime of opportunity. Statistics tell us that on an average, thirty percent plus of the reported burglaries happen without forced entry, because someone forgot to lock a door or close and lock a window. Burglary is not the only crime of opportunity. Your safe responsible behavior and a little added effort, mixed with some good old-fashioned common sense, will allow you and your children to enjoy apartment living safely.

Shopping mall [SAFETY]

These times are not only difficult for parents. Consider the do's and don'ts children have to live by in order to survive. The don'ts definitely outweigh the dos! If you stop and think about it, it's a lot of stuff, and kids are supposed to remember all of it and be a kid at the same time. So when they forget, don't come down on them as though they've just knocked their grandmother down a flight of stairs. Here's a little reminder of what they need to try to remember:

- Don't tell people when you will be home alone.
- Do say no to an adult; especially if that adult wants you to do something your parents have taught you is wrong.
- Don't hitchhike, you're asking for trouble. I hate using the phrase, "You're asking for it", so I changed it to trouble, although both do apply to kids that hitchhike.
- Do tell your parents if someone has asked you to keep a secret.
- Don't go into deserted buildings or isolated areas, even on a dare.

- Do run straight home or go to the nearest public place and ask for help if you are being followed.
- Don't let anyone take your picture without your parents' permission.
- Do carry enough money to make a telephone call home or for help, if necessary.
- Don't approach strangers in cars, even if they are asking for your help or directions.
- Do tell an adult if you see someone hanging around your house, schoolyard or park.
- Don't believe people that make promises to you like, "I'll make you a movie star or supermodel."
- Do be wary of someone who is being overly friendly. If you're feeling depressed, they may try to mislead you by showing you signs of affection.
- Don't accept jobs that seem too good to be true, or jobs that may require you to work in isolated areas. The best place to find employment is with your student job placement center, located within most schools.
- Do let your parents know where you are at all times. Keep your parents updated if you relocate.
- Don't allow yourself to be tricked or bribed into doing something stupid or wrong. **[Be smart.]**
- Do something positive if someone is bothering you in a way that makes you feel uncomfortable: tell an adult you trust.

Now, on top of all of that, add the regular day-to-day things your kids have been told to remember. You know, things like taking out the trash as soon as you get home from school. Oh yeah, and there's all that school stuff too, I think they still call it homework.

As you're well aware of by now, the list goes on and on and on. Now, try to look at it from your kid's point of view. It ain't easy, and the aforementioned is only the tip of the iceberg. Your children need to learn to practice these safety measures in order to help you to help them to keep themselves safe. They should also learn where they are safe and where they need to be observant and alert. Pedophiles are constantly on the lookout for new and easier locations to prey on children. Pedophiles and other sexual predators heavily target nudist colonies, for example. Consequently, the powers that be, are desperately trying to keep a lid on that ever so fast growing problem. So bear with me for a moment while I stray from the dangers lurking at shopping malls.

At nudist colonies, pedophiles are not only putting themselves in proximity of children, but naked children. Parents that are nudists tend to believe that club or camp security and regulations keep their children safe. Some nudist camps do not have security, while many other camps solicit volunteers or retired folks in lieu of fees. I can't help wonder if parents are aware that some of their children's pictures are secretly being taken and posted (sold) on the Internet. I believe that those parents are very lucky if that is all that is happening to their children. Nudists have told me that "It's not about sex, it's about the sun and freedom and people enjoying people, just getting together enjoying nature." I believe that most nudists believe that. However, it doesn't alter the fact that nudist colonies are ideal hunting grounds for sexual predators and profiteers and pedophiles are infiltrating many, if not all, nudist colonies.

My point should be obvious: there can be and often is sex on the minds of many that frequent colonies these days. It is only fair to inform you that nudist resorts are aware of the situation and most are taking steps to guard against the problem. One must respect and acknowledge the right of those members of nudist colonies that do partake for the simple pleasure of feeling free and any other honorable reasons. I conducted a study on this subject while employed as a bodyguard for the Miss Nude USA contestants. [One of the few fringe benefits I experienced having been a bodyguard all of my life.] My intention is to alert you to a possibility of child endangerment that may exist at nudist colonies. So please, if you are members of a nudist colony, accompany your children to different locations within the colony. Especially including enclosed areas such as bathrooms, showers and also secluded areas that are without the benefit of trusted adult supervision. Your lifestyle is just that, your lifestyle, and no one has the right to tell you how to live it. However, if you have children, you are obligated to realize that there are individuals, be they members or visitors to nudist colonies that will sexually molest your children. Your chances of tragedy striking increases tremendously if you give pedophiles the opportunity by leaving your children unattended. If you're lucky, the predators will only take your child's picture and sell it on the Internet. Go enjoy, but don't take your eyes off your children for a moment, because nudist colonies are not always safe for children.

Many parents think that their children are perfectly safe in what they believe to be secured locations such as miniature golf courses, movie theaters and shopping malls. What can happen at a shopping mall? There are parents, sales personnel and security everywhere. I am going to tell you what can happen and what is happening every day across this great nation in camera-and security-ridden shopping malls. First, I would like to share with you some true incidences regarding what children were doing and where they were when they were kidnapped.

Case histories:

Incident No. 1: In San Francisco, California, one child was kidnapped from her fenced front yard while jumping rope.

Incident No. 2: Also in San Francisco, a child disappeared off a street corner while waiting for a bus.

Incident No. 3: Another child from San Francisco vanished while walking home from school.

Incident No. 4: And yet another child in San Francisco was stuffed into a car after leaving a neighborhood store.

None of these children has ever been seen again. These examples are but from one area, one city and in a relatively short period of time. However, I can give you examples of incidents like these from across the nation. One statistic says five thousand (5,000) children are kidnapped (missing without a trace) annually nationwide. That would mean there are 10 kidnappings a week in California. Although, along with the bad news comes some good news. Most of the kidnappings are for a very short duration, generally a matter of a few hours. On the flip side of that coin is some more bad news: most of the kidnappings are for sex. I'll end this with a little mixed news, and the mixed news is most of the victims are released alive. Most is underlined because of the percentage of children that are murdered by pedophiliacs. The predators that murder our children generally do so because they do not wish to be identified. **And then there are those that simply like killing babies.**

If your child dies in an unavoidable automobile accident that is not anyone's fault, the family grieves and hurt seems to take a long time to go away. Actually it never really goes away, it becomes something else, but eventually life goes on. However, it is totally different when your child is kidnapped, so different that there are no words. Every minute of every day is spent wondering, where is my child, is she still in this state? What state is she in or is she still in this country? What country is she in? What is happening to her? Is she cold? Is she hungry? Then in time, the ultimate questions: Is she alive? Where is her body.... Is she cold?

You may think that the chance of something terrible happening to your child is slim and you might be right, but not because of the area in which you reside. Let me ask you two questions. First, what do you know about the people in the area in which you live? For that matter, what do you really know about the area? Maybe that question should be what do you think you know about the people and the area where you live? Second, are you not obligated to do everything within your power to protect your children? Remember, child kidnapping and molestation knows no economic boundaries. Wealthy does not necessarily mean safe.

It is essential to continue to remember that pedophiles are con artists who happen to specialize in children. They are also experts at recognizing opportunity. Child abductors (pedophiles) are criminals with a specialty just like burglars, bank robbers and car thieves. Before picking a victim, they generally do what amounts to research. Pedophiles are counting on parents not doing their job and on the innocence of children. Pedophiles know that children are told they are not supposed to take candy from a stranger. They also know most children don't know what a stranger is. Predators know too, the best places to find unattended children, which is why shopping malls are one of their favorite hunting grounds.

*As you have probably noticed, when referring to child abductors, kidnappers, child molesters and even predators, I often follow by (Pedophile-s). I do this as a reminder, so you have no doubt in your mind that all of these acts are committed by pedophiles and because there are those that wish to separate them.

Predators regularly roam malls in search of unattended or lost children.

Children lost in shopping centers characteristically will not ask for help. They simply wander looking for their mother or father, usually drawing attention when they begin to cry. A child in that situation is a very easy target (victim) for predators.

I truly believe most fathers are born with a natural security instinct, different from a mother's protective instinct. The problem is and always has been getting fathers to be more of a willing participant in their children's security. Maybe we should consider taking the missing children's pictures off the milk cartons and start putting them on beer cans. Maybe that would catch some father's attention. Maybe then they would become more involved in all things relevant to their children's safety. Who knows, they might even become more involved in protecting children other than their own.

It is important for all parents to realize that when you teach your children not to be coerced into anything by a potential child molester, you're also preparing a strong foundation for the child's future. They are also learning and gaining the strength to resist being talked into committing crimes, or the use of drugs, not to mention all the other dangers and influences, including peer pressures our children face in today's society.

By now, some of you are more than likely considering me some sort of an alarmist, and to a degree, you're probably right. However, some of you, hopefully most of you, have never been in the position where you had to deal with such a totally devastating tragedy as the kidnap, rape and brutal murder of a child. Fortunately, my family has never been the victim of such an inhumane and crushing tragedy. I've only had to deal with other less fortunate families. I believe my families' avoidance of victimization is due to the security precautions we have utilized on a daily basis and to our daughter's ability and willingness to learn and practice what she has been taught.

Unfortunately, I have had to deal with kidnap victims, rape victims and the families of murdered children and each time I lose a little bit of myself. It will change your life as it has changed mine. It will shake your very foundation and alter your perception of life itself. That's what it has done to me. Can you begin to imagine what it does to the surviving victims? Maybe with luck it won't happen to you, or within your family. On the other hand, if you take my advice by following my directions, you will stand a much better chance of your luck not running out. Yes, maybe I am an alarmist. I know I'm a little paranoid and I believe every parent should be a little of both, especially if they remember the FBI statistics release I mentioned earlier in the book: every 40 seconds in America a child is lost or abducted. **[FBI statis-**

tics are notoriously conservative].

Through my investigations, I have discovered that poor parenting is the number one most responsible, yet generally unintentional, act that puts children at risk. What I mean by this is that in a combination of what I can only perceive to be laziness, coupled with bad judgment, parents are using shopping malls as babysitters. My studies have born witness to literally hundreds and hundreds of children being left (dropped off) without supervision at shopping malls. I have witnessed toddlers as young as two (2) years, being led hand-in-hand by older siblings ranging in ages from five (5) years to twelve (12) years. I have observed this form of poor parenting [**child neglect**] repeatedly, children attempting to care for children, which I consider, and most state laws consider, too young to baby sit. (Many states laws describe this activity as child abandonment).

If I got a dollar every time I've seen a child left unattended in a car with the engine running while the parent ran into a store for a moment...I'd have a lot of money. Just for a moment... It only takes a moment for a pedophile to grab your child. Do you remember what George Carlin said about a moment of time? George questioned how long a moment is. Is it a couple of minutes? Is it five minutes? Just how much time is involved in a moment? Then someone asked him for a couple of moments of his time and George replied, "I don't know how long a moment is... and this guy wants two of 'em." My point to this example is exactly how long is a moment? Is a moment what you had in mind when you ran into the store for just one thing, just like the other eighty-two people ahead of you in line? Moments have a habit of turning into large chunks of time, so never leave your child unattended in your car... not even for a moment. This is particularly why pedophiles have chosen shopping malls and strip malls as one of their favorite hunting grounds, looking for a kid alone, or left in a car for just a moment. If you will remember, I have spoken to you about what pedophiles count on: they specifically look for things parents do or don't do that are wrong. Child abductors are looking for, and they are very good at finding, lost or unattended children. A young child being attended to by another older, but underage child, is an unattended child. Other children witness many kidnappings, although they rarely make good witnesses.

Shopping malls and arcades are particularly good hunting grounds for pedophiles due to the hustle and bustle of shoppers and the chaos of kids at play, which in general creates an atmosphere of confusion. Predators also rely on most of the public's attitude, which is **don't get involved**. Most shopping mall security cannot be counted on due to a lack of, or inadequate, training and staffing. Adding to that, some malls policies prohibit mall security from entering stores. This inhibits the quality of security, including communications and relations between mall security and the individual stores' security, which, by the way, in many cases is nonexistent, believe it or not. Many shopping malls do not have standing security procedures regarding missing or kidnapped children. Consequently, while shopping in a mall, the security and safety of your children is up to you, as it should be, and as conscientious parents would prefer.

Below is an itemized list of things parents should never do regarding their children and shopping malls:

- Never use a shopping mall as a night or daycare center.
- Never drop your kids off at a movie theater in a mall, leaving them unattended.
- Never allow your children to loiter or simply hang out at shopping malls.
- Never allow your children to use the public restrooms unattended.
- Never allow your children to go back to your car alone.
- Never allow your children to go outside of the mall alone.
- Never allow your children to go into or play in a toy store while you are shopping elsewhere.
- Never allow a stranger to watch your children for any amount of time for any reason.
- Always be leery of anyone volunteering to watch your children for any reason.
- Never allow your children out of your line of sight.
- Never allow your children to eat in restaurants or open areas alone.
- Never leave your children unattended at a shopping mall event. For example, waiting to see Santa Claus or listening to a band play, etc.
- Unattended means without trusted adult supervision.
- Unattended means alone and does not mean with other

children makes it okay. **With other children is alone!** Please forgive me if I sound patronizing, but too many children that are left unattended at malls are never seen again.

If your child is missing while you are shopping at a mall, you must immediately notify the nearest store employee or security officer. Preferably mall security. Let them know what has happened and demand all exits and entrances to the mall be closed and locked. After the exits and entrances are secured, or at least in the process of being secured, supply security with a complete description of your child and explain exactly what happened. Do not allow store employees or security to persuade you to give them details of what happened and a description of your child before they secure all exits and entrances. Security may wish to perform a quick search of the immediate area where the child was last seen before executing a lock-down. This procedure is followed by some security because most children are lost and not kidnapped. That's not good enough. That is not acceptable. Demand a lock-down immediately.

If you have a photograph of your child on your person, turn it over to security and ask that they make copies (color copies if possible). If the child is not located and mall personnel have no choice but to allow people to exit, make sure real police officers have been notified and are involved before exits are reopened. Make sure copies of the picture of your child are made and passed out to security and police officers posted at the exits. If possible, have as many recent photographs of the child brought to your location as quickly as possible. Remind security and police that the child may be wearing different clothing and its hair may have been cut and/or dyed. There are documented cases where the child's appearance had been radically altered before exiting the shopping mall.

Parks and playgrounds [SAFETY]

As is our custom, we regularly take our dogs for walks in different parks around our area. Klaus is a 146-pound Giant Schnauzer and Hendrix is a 22-pound Miniature Schnauzer. Both are Pepper Salts. Not that our dogs names, or their descriptions are important to you, I just like talking about my dogs. What should be of interest and importance to you is what we have witnessed while walking our dogs in parks and around playgrounds in our community. Time and time again we have observed children, literally by the scores, playing in the parks and playgrounds without supervision. Because of my business, I am always on the lookout for predators in areas that are known to be their hunting grounds and pretty much every place else I go. Through the years, I have become pretty damned efficient at spotting them. It's much like a police officer's ability to spot a robber casing a bank. Quite often, it's the middle of the day, when most men are at work or supposed to be. Here comes an individual cruising very slowly past the park or playground and paying a great deal of attention to the children as they play. I truly believe more children would be abducted from parks and playgrounds if it weren't for somebody walking their dog, or someone across the street mowing their lawn, or maybe a couple laying on a blanket a little way away. Predators seem to be more apprehensive and cautious in parks and playgrounds then they are in other targeted places like shopping malls. I believe this is due to the activity of the people in the area and the geography, which generally means open spaces. Unlike malls, in parks people are at leisure and seem to be more observant, while people in shopping malls are on a mission, moving more quickly and there is a lot of confusion. Of course, pedophiles also realize there is always the chance that they are being unknowingly observed from someone's window.

This is not the turn-of-the-century, or the 1940s, or even '50s, a time when children, for the most part, could roam neighborhoods and even further safely. It is difficult for me to comprehend parents that willingly drop off (abandon) their children at parks, playgrounds, amusement parks, beaches etc., no matter what the reason or excuse. It is not conducive to the child's safety. In addition, I know that most experts would consider it downright stupid. Oh, and by the way, in some instances, the authorities may consider this child abandonment, which can be a felony. Generally, you're safe from the wrath of law enforcement, as long as nothing serious happens, during your lapse of good parenting. Although, if something does happen, don't be too surprised when you're charged with a crime.

Unsupervised supervision, which is what I have labeled this activity, does not teach children independence, especially considering the ages of some of the children I have witnessed abandoned by their parents. What it does do, most often, is implant poor parenting into your child's mind. This lack of parental responsibility also contributes to juvenile delinquency. Some folks need to realize children will not necessarily do what their parents say, but they will, most generally, do what they see their parents do. Parents who would never consider leaving their children without a babysitter at nighttime seem to think nothing of dropping the same children off at a park or beach without supervision. Go figure! On second thought, maybe they are the same parents that leave their children alone at nighttime.

Parks and playground safety for your children is as simple as one, two, and three:

1. Don't leave your children unattended at parks or playgrounds, or any other location open to the public.

2. Don't allow your children to be approached by strangers in public places, which means you've got your eye on them constantly.

3. Don't allow your children to use park or beach restrooms without trusted adult supervision.

Being a responsible parent isn't easy, yet at the same time, it's not really too hard. You simply have to care enough. It's called love and **love is unselfish dedication**.

Sleepover [SAFETY]

The great American adolescent pastime is sometimes referred to as a pajama party or slumber party, when the participants are girls, that is. While the girls are planning the slumber parties, the boys are plotting the panty raids, but that's another story. I wonder... do kids still do panty raids, or am I really dating myself? Sorry, once again I digress. Although pajama parties are generally innocent fun and panty raids usually harmless, the problem most often occurs when parents know nothing about the people where their son or daughter is spending the night. Oh sure, they know their daughter's girlfriend, but too often parents don't take the time and the necessary steps to find out about the people. Sometimes some parents don't even take the time to find out about the sleepover supervision. I am sure many of you have heard of the incidents where a parent was not present, or the supervision was an older brother, only to be discovered days, weeks or even months after the event. That is, if it's discovered at all. Generally, that sort of discovery is found out due to an accidental slip of the tongue, not because of good parenting.

The reported cases of sexual child molestation during sleepovers are frankly overwhelming. Of the crimes reported, the perpetrator is most often an older sibling of the girl hosting the party. However, in too many cases the predator is the father of the girl hosting the party. Please do not forget that many child molesters are also parents.

Murder or disfigurement is mostly unheard of involving molested sleepover victims. So, no worries, the victim of this particular crime will make it home alive and in one piece. He or she will have only been raped, in one way or another.

Do yourself and your child a favor: learn all you can about the people you're turning your child over to and never do it blindly. Visit the home, meet the parents of your child's friends, find out about the sleeping arrangements, and gain knowledge of all who will be present the entire stay over. Determine if other people will be dropping by. Find out if any older male siblings or male relatives will be present, visiting or spending the night during the sleep over. If so, it may be wise to reconsider. It is very important for you to find out who may be dropping by. Just because you know the family and feel it is perfectly safe to entrust your child to their care does not mean you can trust their relatives or friends also. How many times have you heard folks say, "I don't understand, he seemed to be a great guy, nothing like this ever happened before, I'm shocked?"

Possibly you may know and like the older brother of your child's friend. You may even trust him explicitly and he may have nothing but the best intentions. Please allow me to describe three actual events involving separate cases. Let me tell you about the "situations" and what triggered the molestations, as they were explained to me by the perpetrators.

[The names have been changed]

First Case:

Julianne, an eleven-year old girl, had four of her girlfriends ranging in ages ten to twelve, over for the night. Jeffrey, Julianne's fourteen-year-old brother had been playing and joking around with the girls off and on all evening. Jeffrey earned mostly B's and sometimes A's in school. He also participated in sports and had never been in any trouble. According to his parents, Jeffrey had never exhibited any signs indicating he was even remotely interested in sex, much less capable

172

of molestation. However, as Jeffrey explained to me, the thought of sex didn't cross his mind until the girls sat on the living room floor with their legs crossed as they played a board game.

I asked Jeffrey,

"What was it that made you think of sex when you saw the girls playing the board game?"

His answer,

"Two of the girls were wearing pajama shorts and one, Celia, wasn't wearing any underwear, I could see everything and I guess I got excited."

"Then what happened?"

"I couldn't get what I saw out of my mind. I waited until I thought they were asleep, then I went to Julianne's bedroom where all the girls were sleeping."

"How were they sleeping?"

"On top of a blanket on the floor."

"Go on, go ahead."

"I went over to Celia and put my hand up her pajama shorts."

"Is that all you did?"

"No, I put my finger in her."

"Why did you do that?"

"I don't know, Celia started to cry and I ran back to my bedroom."

Second Case:

Arlene was celebrating her ninth birthday with a swim party and a sleepover that included six of her best friends. Also attending the party were several adult friends and members of the extended family, uncles, aunts, cousins and nephews. One of Arlene's uncles, Bill, a 22-year-old college graduate, played extensively with the children in the pool. When the sun began to set, the children were told to change into their clothes. The changing room was a poolroom approximately fifteen to twenty yards from where everyone was gathering to eat. According to Bill, he thought all of the children had finished changing and had left the poolroom. When Bill entered the pool room to change he found Jody, an eight-year-old red head still inside and just pulling her bathing suit off.

Bill continued, he said to Jody "Always the slow poke."

He said she laughed as he laughed, and then he said he realized that she didn't seem to mind his presence while she was naked.

"What happened next?"

" I offered to dry her off and before she answered, I started drying her."

He continued,

"As I was drying her I put my hand between her legs and rubbed, I remember she looked up at me and said, I have to pee-pee. I didn't want to let her go, I took her hand and put it on me, and helped pull back and forth. I think it only took two or three times before I reached orgasm. It scared her when I ejaculated and she started yelling and screaming and pulling away. I held her by the arm for a second, but I was afraid someone would come in, so I let her go. And as you already know, everyone came in, and here I am." (Bill is in prison)

Third Case:

You know what? I have decided two case incidents are enough. If there are those of you that don't get the picture yet, allow me to share what I got from each interview. The point that both Jeffrey and Bill were trying to get across to me was, it wasn't intentional, nor did the thought of child molestation cross their minds prior to the incident. It just happened. Did circumstances put things into play that normally wouldn't have happened? Was either Jeffrey or Bill predisposed to commit these crimes against children? Who knows? And when it comes to your own child being sexually molested, who cares? What you do need to care about is whom you're about to turn your children's safety and well being over to for the night or weekend. Find out. Dig if you have to and please consider yielding to second thoughts if you're not 100 percent positive that your child will be safe.

Camping and campground [SAFETY]

Some of the most notable kidnappings of children have occurred while camping with their families. Just to name one, Laura Ann Bradbury, a little blonde three-year-old, kidnapped on October 18th, 1984, while camping with her family at Joshua Tree National Monument in California.

A search for little Laura went from the immediate area to statewide and then nationwide. Searches for Laura have even been done as far away as South America, which I conducted myself in coordination with the Adam Walsh Child Resource Center, sadly to no avail. I did uncover two girls that possibly could have been Laura, but the ages weren't completely jiving and I ran out of money, which meant time. There is some controversy over a skeleton found in the desert. The experts argued, some claiming it to be Laura's remains, others say the skeletal structure is that of a much smaller child, probably that of an infant.

Our hearts and prayers go out to the Bradbury's, once a strong family now shattered and dismantled. I could tell you more about what has happened to the Bradbury's since the loss of Laura, and believe me when I tell you, it's overwhelming, but it's nobody's business. They've already suffered too much. When things aren't going so good, you might want to think about the Bradbury's, and maybe say a little prayer for them. While you're at it, you might want to thank God your own children are safe.

Remember this, every time a child is murdered our national progress is stalled and a little piece of humanity and America dies with each child's death.

There are plenty of do's and don'ts for children while camping, including a few that parents might not normally think about. It's not always easy for parents to remember that the times are changing and so are the people who are committing the crimes. Mere children themselves commit many child molestations. So one of the don'ts while camping that is seldom heeded by parents is, don't allow your children to leave your line of sight while they're playing with other children "Strangers" from the campground, especially older children. In addition to that, if you happen to be camping next to, or near, a family and the adults make you feel uncomfortable, or are just plain weird, don't allow your children to play with their children. Now, this may sound like an unfair judgment decision, however, it is important that you realize that children are often an honest reflection of their parents and the world they live in. So, if you believe the parents to be a "little weird", sad to say, there's a pretty good chance that their children are a "little weird" as well. In today's society, weird quite often translates to dangerous, so why take a chance? Speaking of which, chance is a funny thing. Everyone has the right to take his or her own chances, but no one has the right to take a chance for someone else. Especially not parents!

The list of things to do to keep your children safe while camping is pretty short and simple:

Before choosing a campground or campsite, check with the local authorities, including the U.S. Forestry Service, regarding past crimes at your chosen camp location and in the general area.

- Do not allow your children to go hiking without adult supervision.
- Do not allow your children to go to the campground community pool, lake or river without adult supervision.
- Do not allow your children to go to the local supply store without proper supervision.
- Do not allow your children to enter any other camper's dwelling, i.e., tent, cabin, trailer etc.
- Do not leave your children sleeping while you go off on a romantic moonlight walk or for any other reasons. Many campground predators are on the prowl at night, specifically looking for children left alone, or simply the right moment. Remember that predators are creatures of opportunity and they rely on parents to supply them with their opportunities [victims].
- Since strangers are everywhere in campgrounds, do not let your children out of your sight.
- Keep with you safely, a <u>reliable</u> defense weapon, which you have been trained to use safely.
- Keep an eye out for individuals cruising the campgrounds. If they look out of place [possibly without camping gear] and you see them more than once, try to get a license number and report it immediately.

If you follow these suggestions, you and your children should be safe from all manner of beasts.

Vacation and travel [SAFETY]

First and foremost, if you're planning to travel with your family to a foreign country, contact the State Department's Citizens Emergency Center, at **(202) 647-5225** for information on the countries and areas you plan to visit. Constantly be aware of events in the country you are visiting. In addition, take the time to learn some of the basic traditions and courtesies of the country or countries you are planning to visit. In other words, find out what might offend the locals and make sure your children are made aware. For example, our American traditional hand signal for O.K. is holding up our hand touching the tip of our thumb to the tip of our index finger making a circle, while the three remaining fingers point skyward. Well, in Brazil and many other parts of South America that's a big no-no. Down there, it means the same as when we raise our hand in the air, palm towards the owner, while elevating the middle finger, hence, flipping them off.

Now that that's out of the way, let's get on with things that could cause more than a black eye. Vacationing adults and children are not so different when it comes to traveling. Both have needs and desires and both endure the same risks. However, you have to admit that children traveling are at a greater risk than their parents, simply because they're children. Generally, children traveling are more vulnerable, due to their natural habits and curiosity, not to mention their obvious smaller size. Don't forget, the degree of desirability by predators must be considered. For example, the value of blonde haired blue-eyed little girl makes them extremely desirable and very valuable. This does not mean that little boys, no matter the color of their hair or eyes are safe. It only means they don't fetch as good of a price. Don't get me wrong, I'm not trying to tell you that children have to stay indoors or constantly hide out of sight. I'm telling you to take extra precautions with your children. This will include avoiding some of the seamier attractions in foreign countries that adults sometimes like to witness firsthand. For those parents a little less adventurous, it simply means being constantly on alert. Be aware of your surroundings and the people that may be paying extra attention to you.

Other vacation spots where you need to be extra careful are many of the Caribbean islands. Most islands are governed by large countries such as the Dutch Antilles or by the Netherlands. When something terrible happens such as a family member becomes missing or is the victim of foul play, you may find out quickly that you are pretty much on your own. Often the governing country will wash their hands of the matter by saying that the island has a governor and its own police force, they will handle it. Our law enforcement agencies such as the FBI have their hands tied due to a lack of jurisdiction. So guess what? You are basically on your own. [Most island police forces are under-trained and generally inadequate.]

Many foreign countries are safe unless there is political upheaval, which is obviously something all vacationers need to be aware of. However, it's a whole new ballgame in many of these countries regarding your children. For example, many countries in South America, if not most, are relatively safe vacationing choices if you stay in the tourist areas. On the other hand, these same choices may be very dangerous for teenagers and younger children. Generally, unsafe locations and bad situations that vacationers sometimes find themselves in, could have been avoided with a little forethought and research.

Oh yeah, applying some good old-fashioned common sense goes a long, long way also. For example, wouldn't it be wise to remind your children that all of the rules at home that apply to strangers and answering the door would apply during travel and in hotels as well? Because of the excitement and adventure involved in vacationing and travel, children need to be reminded about keeping themselves safe. The same safety rules that apply on the streets of America should be applied everywhere, although there are some minor exceptions. For example, in many countries, pedestrians do not have the right of way, not even in a crosswalk, and some drivers seem to take pleasure in the possibility of making you their new hood ornament. You should understand, in some countries the value of human life is not held in the highest esteem. This especially applies in poverty-stricken countries where they see death every day and have become blasé about it.

I would be remiss if I didn't warn you of the ever-growing mysteries involving cruise ships and missing vacationers. I'm sure you have heard the horror stories; they are in and out of the news with some frequency. If you're not from this planet or are someone who doesn't partake in news reports, you can easily find out about cruise ship mishaps [missing people] on the Internet.

Here are some more tips on keeping yourself and your children safe while vacationing:

- Make sure you have two copies of the identification pages of your children's passports. Keep them in separate places.

*By the way, many of my suggestions may and generally do apply to adult safety as well. [One of those common sense things we talked about.]

- Educate yourself and your children, especially teenage children, on the local dress codes and customs. Provocative dressing may attract unwanted attention and you may offend some locals. **[Offended locals in some areas respond by throwing rocks.]**

- Learn about places to avoid. This can be accomplished by questioning authorities or other "seasoned" vacationers and friendly locals.
- If possible, try to dress and even act like a local. At a minimum, always act as if you know what you are doing and where you're going.
- Again, avoid clothing that will attract unwanted attention. This is especially directed at teenage females.
- Remind your children that they have the right to say aloud "No" to an adult if they are being bothered or made to feel uncomfortable, even in a foreign country.
- **"No"** is understood in most languages.
- If you're being followed or harassed, you may not receive the help you expect, or are accustomed, to from foreign authorities. Try to stay in a public place where there are many people. Keep a close watch and depending on age, hold on to your children.

- If the locals begin touching your skin and clothing, it doesn't necessarily mean that you're being accosted or in danger. In some countries, it is a custom, a show of approval, admiration and curiosity. [So don't be too quick with the pepper spray.]
- Before leaving your hotel, place all valuables in the hotel's safe or safe deposit box. At a minimum, don't exhibit any expensive jewelry. Desperate locals may easily mistake costume jewelry for something of
- value. This goes for the kids also. Keep in mind that many people in foreign countries assume that all Americans are rich, including their children. These precautions can lessen the risk of being robbed. They also will help avoid being mistaken for wealthy Americans that can easily afford a large ransom to retrieve their kidnapped child.
- Do not rent flashy or expensive vehicles; you will only be targeting yourself and your children.

179

- Do not draw attention to yourself by displaying large amounts of cash.

*It is important for you to remember that in many countries, what you spend for a single night in a hotel, a family of three or four locals can live comfortably for a month.

- Don't needlessly display guest room keys in public or carelessly leave them on a restaurant table, at the swimming pool, or any other place where they can be easily switched or stolen.
- Never invite strangers to your room.
- When returning to your hotel in the evening, use the main entrance and be observant, look around before entering parking lots. The time you would be most vulnerable to be kidnapped is at the end of the day.
- If you see any suspicious activity, report your observations to hotel management. The best response for help will generally come from the hotel you are staying at. Normally the hotel staff will take great measures in to see to their guests' safety. They depend on tourism and will protect their reputation.
- Once back to your room, check the room, making sure there are no intruders. Close the door securely, using all locking devices provided.
- [Traveling with your own locking device is always a good idea.]
- Check any sliding glass doors and windows, including any adjoining room doors, to make sure that they are locked.
- Never answer the door in a hotel room without verifying who it is. If a person claims to be an employee and you are uncertain, call the front desk and ask if someone from their staff is supposed to be there. Also ask them if anyone has access to your room and if so, for what purpose. If you are suspicious or uncomfortable with the answers you receive, don't open the door. If it isn't an emergency, they'll go away.

*(It is better to be thought of as "Weird" by people you will probably never see again in your lifetime, or by anyone else for that matter, than it is to risk being tricked into tragedy.)

- Speaking of risk, there is no reason to allow anyone other than family and trusted friends to take pictures of your children while on vacation.

*If your child is missing, immediately contact the closest American Embassy for help.

- Have cash ready to enlist the help of locals and I don't mean just the local police. Tell them that you will pay them a preset and agreed amount <u>only for results</u>. No monies up front! Let them know that they will be rewarded with the agreed amount of cash when they have recovered your child.
- Never let anyone know you have the money. Tell them it's on the way. Assure them that you are able to pay the agreed amount, but no more, explaining that all Americans are not rich.

*If you do not get results within a day or two and you can afford a team of qualified specialists, I suggest you hire them as quickly as possible. Depending on the location, the "Real McCoy" should be able to be there and ready to work within one or two days at the most. True experts will have wheels in motion in the country in which you're vacationing <u>before they arrive</u>.

Chapter 7

PEDOPHILES ON THE INTERNET

How is it done?

First, pedophiles need a relatively safe bastion. Wittingly or unwittingly, the Internet Relay Chat (IRC) and other "Undernets" provide it to them, giving them a forum where the trading of child pornography is socially acceptable. Thousands of people worldwide join the preteen trading channels each day. The majority of these people are interested in trading and selling sexually explicit photographs and movies of young children. Many of the photographs are of children being forced to have intercourse or to perform oral sex with adults. Additionally, the individuals using these channels frequently discuss with one another their various child molestation success stories.

[Which means, we're talking about hard-core pedophiliacs again.]

IRC channels are similar to the chat rooms offered by "Online Providers" such as America Online, but are not proprietary. They are accessible to anyone with an Internet connection and the necessary free or shareware software. The users of these channels are able to communicate in "Real-time", which is similar to America Online "Instant Messaging", meaning that they are able to type messages that are seen by others instantly. They may convey their messages to all of the other users on the channel, or they may communicate privately, one on one.

Undoubtedly, the feature of greatest interest to pedophiles frequenting the Undernet portion of IRC is the ability to send and receive private files. The simplest way to accomplish this is via DCC. To send another user a file, one has only to right click on the users name and select, "DCC Send" from a drop-down menu and attach the file. It is by this method that most illicit pornographic material is transferred. Files are also exchanged via FTP, a similar transfer protocol requiring a little additional software and know-how.

With technology advancing by leaps and bounds, parent's have to keep up to date as to what's new and what is it capable of doing. The new rage with kids today is the "iPod" and it's pretty neat. The iPods capabilities are nothing less than amazing. It is small enough to fit in a pocket and it holds tons of music. The iPod can even hold games and movies. That's right, even full-length movies; it has a 2-inch by 2-inch viewing screen. The downside to the iPod is that the porn industry has made pornography available for downloading to it. Of course, you must be at least eighteen-years-old to download legally and you need a credit card. The problem is, some kids have access to their parent's credit cards. Yes I know that most children don't

have the use of their parent's credit cards, but that really doesn't matter. It doesn't matter because most porn sites offer free previews that anyone at any age can view. I hope that you are getting the message. You cannot purchase the kind of technology available today and hand it over to your child without knowing the devices capabilities. If you do decide to gift your child with one of the latest and greatest gadgets available, you must learn its capabilities and also learn how to monitor its use.

Who are they harming?

"Who are we harming?" is the question asked by the pedophiles that use the preteen channels. I believe we all agree when I say they are obviously harming the children involved and their families. They are harming all children by propagating the growth of child sexual abuse. The practice of sexually abusing children has become more socially acceptable because the pedophiles promote child erotica. The result of their actions horrifically damages the lives of the victimized children and their families.

NAMBLA is a group of boy-child lovers, which strongly and frequently objects to being labeled "child molesters." They claim that they take no part in harming children. Now keep in mind that their motto is, "After eight is too late." or some such crap. No I'm right, that's the crap! In some parts of the country, authorities suspect NAMBLA members of having attacked many children. Tell me, is there anyone out there that believes that people who truly believe in that motto and present literature supporting it, or act on it if given the opportunity, is not taking part in directly harming children? Even if NAMBLA members, or any other of the child-love organization members, were able to refrain from child sex, they may be indirectly responsible for harming children through their web sites. In fact, case histories exist that prove my point. NAMBLA web material was found in the possession of two men that were arrested for kidnapping a child. I personally choose to make no distinction between pedophiles and child molesters. I have a difficult time separating someone who would sexually abuse a child from someone who supplies information encouraging and condoning sex with children. If you are able to make a distinction between child molesters and pedophiles, then you can probably make a distinction between what some other people believe, which is, that child molesters should be executed and pedophiles should be hanged.

Links have been discovered that are generated from boy-love sites into child organization databases. They display children's complete names and personal information, including the schools the children attend. These links easily give child abductors, molesters and child predators a way in. The information held by the child organization databases can be especially harmful in the wrong hands due to the in-depth information regarding each child. To give you an idea, most child organization databases not only supply names and addresses, they also detail each child's interest, aspirations, etc. As far as I'm concerned, NAMBLA and all of the other child-adult love groups can plead innocent to harming children all they want. Their pleas are falling on deaf ears here. They should be recognized by all parents for what they are: the enemy. They should also be recognized as I do, the enemy of all children. I don't really give a damn what they call themselves, or how they try to explain their beliefs. They are pedophiles, and in some cases, they are tormented souls that often have other paraphilias, like sadism and masochistic tendencies, which makes them extremely dangerous to your children. There is a spectrum of pedophile types and their propensity is to harm children.

Rather than acting as a "harmless outlet" as pedophiles claim, the trading of child pornography and the spreading of stories of conquests and techniques employed, has for many, become a hobby and to many more a way of life. This encourages the creation and application of increasingly more child pornography. In addition, this activity that the pedophiles have referred to as a "harmless outlet" encourages and inflames the viewers, which is what honest pedophiles have in the past admitted to me during conversations. It's obvious to me and I hope a no-brainer to you that this activity is extremely harmful. Anyone trying to convince you otherwise is definitely trying to con you.

While the Internet is a tool, which can be used to educate and entertain our children, it can also be an easily accessible and dangerous window to the dark side of our world. Most teenagers are unknowingly at risk when surfing the Internet channels. Unfortunately, most children accidentally stumble onto all sorts of pornography, including preteen sex sites. It's easy to do. All you have to do is search under the words teen, adolescent, kids, or a word as innocent as child and sooner or later you will find yourself in the middle of it. Without warning, you can find yourself looking at a photograph of an eight-year-old girl performing oral sex on an adult. The webmasters use what is referred to as trigger words or "Triggers" to land you on their sites. Words like, young, toys, girl, sisters, fantasy and so on. My point is that a child could easily end up in the middle of it by simply using the word "doll." The web owners/operators often claim that no one can get on their site without filing their date of birth. That is a lie. But if it were the truth, what's to stop a child from putting down the wrong date of birth? All of this really doesn't matter, since most porn sites have in-depth and extensive previews. Something that constantly haunts me is when I first close my eyes attempting to sleep and my mind revisits the obviously tortured looks on the children's' faces in the photographs and movies that I have witnessed where they have been forced to act as a "willing participant."

Remember, pedophiles will tell you that sex with children is not abusive, like so many of them believe. Some will try to convince you that it's not their fault, they cannot help feeling attracted to children.

A studied opinion

Experts have conducted in-depth research regarding the effects of adult-child sex and they are nearly unanimous in their disagreement with the previous statement. The notion that sex with children is in reality not damaging to them is false, say most experts. Needless to say, I agree. Since countless cases of sexual child abuse related problems are diagnosed in individuals every day, it makes this another no-brainer as far as I am concerned, and you also, I hope.

Let's start off with children's feelings of guilt and betrayal when they are sexually exploited by adults and then made to feel it is their fault. As we discussed earlier, children being made to feel responsible for what has happened is a common tactic of many child molesters. Child molesters are really good at convincing molested children that they have done something terribly bad and everyone will be angry with them and not like them anymore if what they did is discovered. Their molesters frequently tell molested children that they will be taken away from their parents and punished if they tell anyone "what they did." I find it astonishing that they can actually utter the words, "who are we hurting?"

Pedophiles like to make a distinction between consensual and non-consensual sexual contact, always asserting that the former is not harmful to children. However, as the legislatures and courts of most nations have ruled, children are too young to give informed consent to such activity. Child victims are most often too young and trusting to know that they are being manipulated, or feel powerless to stop it. Often, they fear displeasing the adult. Even in cases where children feel no immediate emotional trauma at the time of the molestation, there are frequently adverse effects to their self-esteem later in their life. Sexually abused children are more prone to develop other psychological problems and generally do.

As for the second issue raised by Undernet pedophiles, it is indeed true that a large number of adults feel attracted to children. However, most do not act on those feelings.

Studies and conversations I've had with Internet pedophiles revealed that many of them were themselves victims of child abuse. One of their defenses is that they were sexually abused as children and that they cannot help their feelings. I personally do not believe that this excuses their actions. Do you? I believe it does not excuse them any

186

more than such a defense would excuse a man who knows he has Hepatitis B or the Aids virus, and sleeps with and infects an unsuspecting woman who trusted him. Sexual desire does not excuse extremely injurious actions and pedophilia is a psychological condition that does not necessitate action. Interview after interview with child molesters have convinced me, by their own admissions that rather than trying to control their desires, they involve themselves in activity like frequenting teen and preteen chat rooms that fuel their desires as they search for new victims.

Allow me to enlighten you as to the popularity and power of some of these Internet gathering spots for kids. That's right, it's no longer the burger or coffee shops, it's the chat rooms. These days it's one chat room in particular which kids view as their personal private site. "Myspace.com", as of this writing hosts forty million registered users. Keep in mind that you do not have to register in order to utilize Myspace. This particular sight enjoys an average traffic of twenty million users per month, and as many as fifty seven million profiles at any given time. Yes, there are some rules in place designed to protect the public. One rule is you must be at least fourteen years old to jump on. [Gain access.] Of course, no child would ever lie about his/her age. The average time spent on Myspace is two-and-a-half hours a day.

On the Internet, one out of every twenty-five kids is hit with obscenities of one sort or another. A child will see everything from medical, foot and pee fetishes to S&M and scatting fetishes. What is scatting? I hope you can forgive me for explaining it, but since your children may be seeing it, I guess you should know what it is. I'm sure you know that the meanings of words change over time and with each generation. Words like hot, cool, gay and so on. You know, hot means cool, cool means hot and gay still means a state of being, but with a slightly different twist. Scatting is a word used for a style of singing that some of the great entertainers such as Louis Armstrong "Satchmo", Mel Torme, Duke Ellington and Scatman Crothers were known for. Today, scatting also refers to sexual acts involving multiple usages of feces, most often human feces.

In fairness to Myspace management, they do try to police their site by adding new security and protective technology regularly. And if undesirable material is reported, it is removed immediately. However, the overwhelming amount of Myspace's traffic makes it impossible to completely secure the site, or even reasonably secure promptly. It is truly a shame that a great place for kids to gather is corrupted by a steady flow of predators in quest of their next victim. Unsuspecting children do not know whether they are communicating with another fourteen year old or a vicious human being that has already murdered two children. There are available programs that will transfer where your children have gone on their computer to your computer, including their keystrokes. If you decide to check what your kids are doing on Myspace, you need to be aware that many children post more than one profile, which makes them even more vulnerable to predators. Also, be prepared to learn a new language, really, I'm serious. Many kids have created (invented) a new language they use on the chat sites. Aren't kids amazing? Let me ask you a question, in English. Would you allow your children to play at a park that is stalked by pedophiliacs several days a month but you don't know which days? Myspace is literally a catalogue for sexual predators.

To give you an idea of how popular Myspace is, it recently sold for six hundred million dollars. [$600,000,000.] That's pretty popular, I'd say.

I am going to put you inside a pedophiliacs head for a moment by sharing with you a letter written and sent to "Pedowatch." I hope that by sharing this letter, it will give you a little more insight. I truly believe, as I've explained, that knowledge is one of your most important weapons in this war. I also feel it is most important for you to know and recognize the enemy, which is why I introduced him to you in the very beginning of this book. It is also why I am sharing this letter with you now.

*None of the wording in the letter you're about to read has been changed or altered in anyway.

01 April 1999

To: pedowatch@pedowatch.org

Subject: Child Sex

Hello,

I am a Pedophile and my daughter loves to have sex with me. She often brings her friends over for me to have sex with. I used to think I had a problem but after meeting a lot of her friends and finding out they have sex with their parents and siblings too put me at ease. I have sex with her and her friends on a constant basis. They enjoy what they do, they do well in school, and they show no psychological distress. If any of the girls have a problem we talk it out. That's something that parents who don't like child sex don't do. Talk to their kids. Last year, I made over $15,000 off selling pictures and videos of my daughter, her friends and I. Just last week my daughter told me "I know it's illegal daddy but I like having sex with you and I'll lie to keep you from going to jail."

Now you tell me, what kind of problems do we have?

[I have purposefully chosen not to include the authors name or initials.]

It is my understanding that Pedowatch is literally inundated with letters containing abusive comments and some out-and-out attacks on them from pedophiles. The letter that I chose to share with you is but one example. I personally have seen and read an abundance of them. Many defend their actions with claims that they are totally against child pornography and the sexual exploitation of children. Some even praise the good work Pedowatch and their volunteers do. However, the number of supportive letters pale in comparison to the letters like the one I shared with you. Not that it matters much, since it's extremely difficult to appreciate letters like this one that condones child exploitation and pornography and the letter's author admits to bedding a child as young as four.

On one hand, what we have here is an individual who will not hesitate to have sex with his own daughter, oh, and with anyone else's children, too. It is obvious, judging from the man's letter, that the guy is an entrepreneur in every sense of the word. I mean, if you have children that completely understand everything that is going on, including the laws that forbid it and all the reasons why, then why not make a buck or two on the side. If his child and from what I could gather from his letter, the neighborhood children as well, are as willing as he explained, why not turn a profit to boot? I mean, as they say... "Who are they hurting?" The selling of movies and pictures of his own child and other children naked and partaking in illegal and immoral sex acts, makes him one hell of a businessman in my book. I guess fifteen thousand dollars ($15,000) extra a year is enough to make any father turn on their daughter and other little girls for pleasure and profit. After all who could blame him? Sounds like it's not his fault at all. Although he didn't mention the ages of his daughter and the other girls, it sounds like they are knowledgeable children that are fully aware of what they are doing, including realizing any possible future ramifications. I'll bet it's not the father at all. I'll bet it's the children that set the whole thing up and in the process demoralized him. Yep, that's probably what happened.

On the other hand, we have an individual who wrote another letter to Pedowatch that considers the actions of the first man despicable, although he admits that he himself has had sexual intercourse with a child as young as four and has no qualms about doing it again. His letter didn't divulge whether the four-year-old is his own child or not. In my opinion, if anyone's interested, there seems to be but one way to separate these two gentlemen, put one in prison for life and execute the other one. That's a joke. Really. Okay... maybe.

The shared opinion among pedophiles is that they possess a special understanding regarding children that average parents and adults don't have. They feel it is their obligation to share their affection and love with poor unfortunate children, my words, not theirs. However, I guarantee you that no matter how pedophiles put it, the meaning will be the same and I've heard them say it in a bunch of different ways. Pedophiles consider your children to be neglected and in need of their attention. NAMBLA and groups like it are desperately seeking legitimacy, and they are turning over every rock they can to find it.

What's being done about it?

The commercial sexual exploitation of children has aroused an increasing awareness in the past years culminating with the World Congress Against Commercial Sexual Exploitation of Children located in Stockholm since 1996. However, the media has not covered the commercial sexual exploitation of children in Central and Eastern Europe with sufficient detail or hardly at all. The problem usually is pictured as one typical of South American and South Asian countries. This is far from the truth. The absolute fact of the matter is sexual exploitation of children takes place in almost every country in the world. However, this does not mean that because it is going on in Brazil that it is being done by Brazilians or Portuguese exclusively, or at all. Many nationalities are deeply involved, including guests in some countries that are simply operating from that location. The identities and positions that are held by these individuals would literally rock and shock you to your core.

Many children of post-communist countries are forced into prostitution, suffering from the production of child pornographic materials. The trafficking of children for sexual purposes is literally a thriving business in those countries and is second only to the trafficking of drugs in many countries. Most post-communist countries have no institutions or mechanisms to fight against sex crimes against children. Cases uncovered are isolated, claim authorities, and officials most often deny the existence of the problem. Sound familiar? Submerged in their complicated political and economic transformations, these countries have little to no finances available, nor do they have the ambition, to deal with these problems. Therefore, while the West has finally encouraged the defense and enforcement of human rights in the transforming countries, the breaching of the most basic rights of the children in these regions has been completely neglected.

Due to the realization of the immediate profits made from the distribution of child pornography, it is now overflowing into the United States via the Internet and other vehicles of distribution, but mostly the Internet. The Russian Mafia is responsible for some of the trafficking in child pornography, but not nearly the quantity previously believed. Those other people I have been telling you about [people in high places.] have been very busy purchasing and kidnapping children, forcing them into prostitution, and child pornography. They have also become involved in the distribution of child pornography.

The ones that would rock you and shock you to your very core know who they are. The powerful positions some of them hold are beyond belief.

I can't stand it. I've got to give you at least one example. In the recent past, the Israeli embassy in Rio de Janeiro, Brazil was raided along with the Israeli Ambassador's private residence. The raid was a joint effort involving several law enforcement agencies, led by special Delegados and regular Brazilian police. The reason behind the raid was suspicion of child abuse and possible manufacture of child pornography. What the authorities exposed is but one of many examples of what I was telling you will shock and rock you to your core regarding individuals in high places. A combination of individual interrogations and the search of both locations uncovered multiple atrocities inflicted against children.

Where to begin? I guess the home of the Ambassador is as good as any place to start. The police discovered box after box of movie films and VHS movies of many of the Ambassador's employees, friends, guests and even himself partaking in hardcore sex with children. Most of the children were locals, but many were not. The investigation revealed that the Ambassador was supplying many of the embassy's invited guests with children for sex. The sex acts took place at both the Ambassador's home and within the embassy. Many of the embassy employees were arrested. However, the Ambassador himself escaped arrest by fleeing in the middle of the night by jet aircraft. So I guess the moral of this story is that some people in high places are committing high crime. Well, let's get back to it.

As IRC is internationally accessible, national laws are difficult to implement. Among the Internet community, IRC is seen as a medium for free thought in communication on a worldwide basis. Those who do have some control, the IRC Operators and Administrators, barely regulate it. As a result, many people have found a safe place for the discourse of otherwise socially unacceptable activity and subject matter.

Ironically, some software pirates, who will remain anonymous, use the Undernet to exchange pirated software and are generally the staunchest opponents to regulation of IRC. However, they are also among the only ones inhibiting the exchange of child pornography on the "preteen" channels, using techniques considered by IRC Operators and Administrators to be more reprehensible than exchanging pictures of child molestation. Again, go figure. They are occasionally successful in driving some members off such channels as #100 % and PreTeenPics, Myspace, IRC, and sometimes even completely off the Internet.

One of their techniques employs a type of program called an "OOB Nuker," which sends the pedophiles computer data that takes advantage of a flaw in Windows and causes system instability. This interference forces the individual to reboot and log back on and in some cases give up, if the attacks are continuous. A similar tool known as SSPING, instantly freezes the remote computer, causing the loss of any unsaved data and locking the system up until the computer is rebooted.

By using techniques such as these, the self-proclaimed anti-pedophiles risk potential repercussions from the IRC Operators and their own Internet providers. To many among the Internet community, their actions are the lesser of two evils. I personally think they're wonderful, doing a great moral service to parents and children everywhere. Especially considering that government intervention is frowned on because of the potential for it to spread and lead to regulation unrelated to child pornography. Consequently, as things stand, I see nothing wrong with a little unconventional but warranted policing. Keep up the good work guys, and thank you for caring enough for our children to take such an unselfish risk.

Despite occasional antagonism, the trading of pedophilia continues largely unchecked on the IRC Undernet and elsewhere on the Internet. It remains to be seen whether increased public attention to the matter will drive the pedophiles back undercover or at least result in IRC policy changes. The information supplied by the relentlessly hard working anti-child molestation and pornography site Pedowatch, has already increased law-enforcement investigation activity regarding child pornography on IRC.

Additionally, of some concern is "Usenet," which consists of tens of thousands of Internet discussion groups, as of this date. These groups are often called "Blogs, Newsgroups and Chat Rooms." Some of the groups are organized by topic, and if you can think of interest shared by at least a few people, there is likely already a newsgroup or blog site devoted to it. Over one million messages are posted to newsgroups and blogs each day. Usenet is a great source of information on any subject, from alien life to political life. Whoops, I think they're the same. The problem is, no one organization controls Usenet. Discussion group messages are stored on many new servers around the globe. These servers pass content back and forth, ensuring that all of it is accessible to everyone who has a newsreader or is using one of the web-based services. Some individual newsgroups are moderated, meaning there is a person who decides what will be posted and what messages will not be allowed. Unfortunately, most newsgroups are not moderated. So obviously, they are also used by some as a medium for distributing images of child pornography and for advertising services involving the exploitation of children. Most pedophiles do not seem to be bothered by the fact that they are committing a serious felony by downloading sexually explicit images of children, which tells me they're getting away with it most of the time.

Surprisingly, contrary to common misconception, the individuals known as "Spammers" who post illegal material to the Usenet discussion groups can indeed be traced, arrested, and convicted. So why is it that most of the rare arrests involve much lesser crimes? Surprisingly, very few Spammers seem to be traced and arrested for such a serious crime, so serious that I consider these crimes an assault on humanity itself. Yes, I am surprised when I see so little funding dedicated to stop such horrific crimes. Yes, damned surprised when I see what appears to be endless funding used for sting operations involving many police officers, expensive homes, fancy cars, airplanes and yachts etc., to catch one man buying cocaine. This society needs to draw a line, a moral line. A line strengthened with sufficient federal funding that is reinforced by punishments that truly match the crimes. A line that unmistakably says, LEAVE OUR CHILDREN ALONE!

While Usenet does not have nearly as many people involved in uploading child pornography as are active uploading on the preteen channels of IRC, thousands download the relatively few images that are posted to newsgroups and chat rooms like Myspace. If you discover your child or children using Myspace, get them off and out of there as fast as humanly possible. Myspace is an extremely dangerous site for any child to visit. Literally thousands of images are downloaded by all ages of other people who frequent those groups and chat rooms. Additionally, some people post advertisements for services involving the exploitation and sexual victimization of children, and pedophiles use them as a valuable tool in their search for victims. These messages reach a large audience, but worse, they reach a large audience of specifically those individuals who are interested in activities detrimental to children. Did I mention that pedophiles are regularly talking with your children?

No one affiliated with the Internet or law enforcement seems to be able to answer the question, when will the pedophiles be stopped from using the Internet for illicit activity? Especially considering that there are thousands of pedophiles regularly exchanging child pornography on the networks of Internet Relay Chat, and although to a lesser extent, in the chat rooms of the online services such as America Online and others. Something needs to be done. Additionally, there are web sites devoted to child pornography, and there are organizations and clubs comprised of pedophiles who use the Internet to share, sell, and acquire collections of child pornography. There are also "Third World Resort" web sites offering to procure child prostitutes, for paying customers, of course.

Most parents don't realize that their children are at risk of sexual abuse and are opened to the possibility of abduction by simply being on the Internet unsupervised.

Welcome to cyberspace, the newest sidewalk for sexual predators. Watch out for your children…watch out for yourselves.

Internet pornography was scrambling to pass their proposals before time ran out on the 105th Congress. What in the hell is with scrambling to beat a midnight deadline on the last day of Congress all about? Don't get me wrong, I truly do appreciate any effort to detour child pornographers from their sick activities. However, I do not understand that a crime so repulsive as child pornography is being left until the last minute on any agenda. Any and all crimes against children need to be not only first, but also foremost on everyone's agenda, no exceptions. If this sort of sloth-like activity was due to the opposition's blockage tactics, please except my apology. The problem I have witnessed most are a lack of coordinating efforts and plain old feet dragging.

On a much more positive side, the House did approve, the Online Child Protection Act (HR3783), authored by Representative Michael Oxley (R-Ohio). This Act imposes criminal penalties on commercial Web sites that will allow children access to material deemed "Harmful to minors." My hats off to you, Representative Oxley! Thank you, and those who assisted you in a very worthy task. You've got my vote.

There are several major Internet players desperately trying to thwart or at least scale back, the bill and all similar bills. They are continuing to do their behind-the-scenes lobbying. Their argument is now and always is, that the bills proposals could inadvertently subject them to liability. There are some innocent companies that could theoretically be caught up in the attempt to stop pornographers on the Internet. Disney and America On Line to name a couple. They believe they should have broader exemptions because they do not engage in the sale of pornography. I guess we'll have to leave all of that to them to work out. The important thing is we have good movement in a good direction.

I believe that it is important to inform you about the good stuff that is being done by a few heroes in Washington, DC, and acknowledge the companies that are cooperating as well. All is not doom and gloom. There are lots of great people and concerned corporations doing their best, accomplishing some pretty good stuff. We're not alone and all is not lost.

Although it is fantastic to see someone making some headway in Washington DC, with this bill doing that, and that initiative is over there, with HR# _ _ _ proposal to be floored next and on and on, we cannot afford to back off or even ease up. Nor can we drop or relax our guard. Keep in mind that the creeps on the streets are still out there, and believe me when I say they aren't going anywhere soon, if ever. There will always be some monster, holding out a piece of whatever attracts children at the time. You know that the molesters of children will always be trying to lure your child, no matter what's going on in DC.

Forget for a moment the stereotypical images of a man handing out candy to lure children on our streets. Imagine instead, an unknown and unseen friend who sounds just like your child, just like another youngster, using his or her computer to strike up a friendship. This new friend agrees with everything your kid says and has all the same likes and dislikes. He or she seems to have the same problems and says that they too are misunderstood and treated unfairly by mom and dad. Your child's new friend is more than likely a male, but could possibly be a female, using chat rooms on the Internet to create relationships. Once the innocent child or teenager is hooked, their newfound friend types," Come meet me, let's get together, we can meet at a coffee shop or the mall."

Inside your computer and hidden in the anonymity of cyberspace lurks the newest form of pedophile, an electronic friend who cannot be seen, nor watched. Another scary aspect of this electronic entity is that it is almost impossible to track him down. Sexual perverts who will enter your home to prey and pounce on your unsuspecting children, via the computer. He is capable of entering your child's bedroom... and you can't see him.

There are many documented cases of children going off to meet with their new Internet friend, some even leaving town, never to be seen again. Pedophiles have been known to purchase bus and even airfare for willing victims. If for whatever reason, arranging transportation for a child does not work out, predators will often go to the child.

Case history:

*Names and places have been changed

Nina, a bright and beautiful, 13-year-old brunette from Ogden, Utah with aspirations of becoming a veterinarian, constantly surfed the superhighway, more commonly known as the Internet, free from parental hindrance. Since Nina's parents were unfamiliar with computers and their workings, they didn't interfere. Nina met new friends frequently and they would share the woes of being teenagers regularly. Eventually, Nina found a new friend who really seemed to relate to her, and even had a few good ideas about Nina's everyday situations and problems. Her name was Jackie and Nina thought Jackie sounded pretty independent for a 14-year-old, which drew Nina even closer. I know all of this because Nina kept a diary, a very detailed and well-documented diary.

Nina and Jackie talked about everything from their teachers at school to their boyfriends, and, of course, eventually sex. Jackie seemed more sexually adventurous. Nina was impressed as her writing implied. Each time they spoke, their conversations became more steeped in sex, Nina sharing her thoughts, exposing her curiosities. Jackie slowly, deliberately, delving into her fantasies. Eventually, Jackie began verbally sharing her sexual activities with Nina. Evidently, according to Nina's diary, much of the topic of conversation became Jackie encouraging Nina to masturbate often and even during their communications. Jackie seemed determined to press Nina into partaking in self-pleasure while she explicitly described to Nina her own sexual escapades. Nina's diary is unclear as to whether she completely followed Jackie's suggestions and directions. While reading Nina's diary I was able to determine that Jackie was purposely precise and exact in her timing, carefully controlling the flow of information and suggestions (directions) during their conversations.

As I read on, I definitely got the distinct feeling that Jackie was stalking Nina as cautiously as a lion would stalk an impala. The sexual conversations she initiated with Nina started innocently with simple imagining this and fantasizing about that. They talked about their own bodies and feelings. Then, gradually from one conversation to the next, Jackie became more adventurous and more explicit. She continuously encouraged Nina to experiment with herself, as Jackie claimed she did. From touching her brother's penis, which Jackie declared was nothing since "We run around the house naked all the time", to allowing her boyfriend to, and I quote, "BF me with his finger." If you don't know, trust me, you probably don't want to know.

Nina eventually decided, or to be more exact, was talked into meeting with Jackie, face-to-face. As I am sure, you have surmised by now, Jackie was a Jack, probably between the ages of 20 to 30 years. Nina did not survive her meeting with Jackie. Authorities eventually located most of Nina, approximately 80 miles from her home.

Now, right off the bat I know that some of you are thinking, even saying it out loud that would never happen to your child, your kid's smarter than that. Allow me to set you straight on something, if an adult predator sets his sights on a child and has all the time he needs without interference, no child stands a chance. We are dealing with individuals that share successful techniques. Just consider that factor. Never mind the possibility that many child molesters are highly intelligent individuals in their own right. If you really believe that it couldn't happen to your child, then you more than likely also believe that if your child were ever taken, the police would have her back safely in your arms within minutes. Yeah right, and eight track tapes are making a comeback.

The numbers involving child abductions and child sexual abuse via the Internet are mounting rapidly, and the protection afforded by cyberspace creates a frightening world where the abuse of children can hardly be tracked. Parents, law enforcement agencies, social service programs and even Congress are scrambling to formulate new systems of protection for children and prosecution for the offenders. No one knows how many children have been lost to a "new found friend" on the Internet. What they do know is, along with the cases, the number of missing children keeps going up.

Computers have changed the world as much or more than the introduction of the automobile. Try this on for size, it wasn't very long ago when kidnappers would hold a child for ransom. It was very risky business for the culprit, collecting the one-time ransom money without being caught. Today, the child abductor can remain in the security of a single location and sell millions of pornographic photos and videos of a child all over the world, at almost no risk of ever being caught.

The seriousness of the problem is compounded by the vulnerability of the victims being pursued on the computer. As I've said, child molesters traditionally prey on children with low self-esteem, a need for acceptance and awkward social skills. In today's world, but especially in America, there is also a technological gap between parents and children. Frequently, children are more technologically adept than their parents, and parents need to find ways to bridge that gap. Parents and caretakers must be the first line of defense in this new and terrible playground. Parents, I am urging you to monitor your children's usage of computers. Spend time with your children while they are online.

All it takes to lure children on the Internet or Worldwide Web is the creation of a data bank, and one hacker determined to molest children. It's a brand new world of terror, with no previous guidelines, nor are there new references for guidance. Although law enforcement agencies are increasing their surveillance on the information superhighway, we can't expect much at this time. These crimes are not easy to investigate, much less prosecute. Since person-to-person communication via computer falls under, and is protected by, privacy laws, everybody's hands seem to be tied.

The abuse of children, whether by abduction, pornography or both, is now operating on the three major online services, America Online, Prodigy and CompuServe, as well as the worldwide Internet, smaller online services and locally operated computer bulletin boards. Bulletin Boards and chat rooms are a total haven for Pedophiles. There are no names, no faces, and a forty-year-old man can easily pass himself off as a ten-year old kid. Furthermore, some Internet services unintentionally help pedophiles locate children by labeling chat rooms. An example would be, "Prexteen" x7x8x9, which indicates to pedophiles that this chat room is for children ranging from ages seven, eight, and nine years, and so on. Within these rooms comes an underworld of individuals, most of whom trade and distribute child erotica. Though it is clearly outlined in AOL's "Terms of Service" that vulgar and sexually explicit room and screen names are not allowed, these rooms seem to function. In fact, they flourish.

I wish to be fair to America Online, Prodigy, CompuServe, and the other online services that are not allowed by federal law to monitor E-mail. Consequently, I can see their point. Why should they be held responsible and accountable for what they are not allowed to control? It's a problem, a problem that offers no easy solution, although I do believe that it would be a monumental mistake to allow government to handle it.

Our privacy is one of America's greatest gifts to its people and it should be protected and preserved for its survival, without exception. However, pedophiliacs must be stopped, for a society without complete child protection laws does not deserve to survive!

Parenting the Internet

Understanding the Internet is simple. To put it simply, the Internet is a large number of computers "Networked" together. When you connect [go on line], you become part of the network.

Anyone with a computer and modem can make information available via the Internet. You may not be aware, but with a little shareware software and a couple hours of learning how to use it, anyone can do it. Any Internet user can make available to everyone else the Web pages that exist only on their hard drive, even if the individual's ISP does not allot them free Web space on their server. Likewise, the user can make any file on his hard drive available for download by everyone on the Internet who has an FTP program, which all the new Web browsers have built in. So, obviously it is impossible to prevent illicit offensive, illegal and dangerous material from being made available to everyone via the Internet. Some of the perpetrators can be punished. Eventually and hopefully, this will have an impact on others contemplating to commit similar crimes. However, at this time, it is impossible to completely prevent it. It is also possible that it will never be completely prevented.

Now, add to this situation the international use of the Internet in relation to the national of Internet crime investigating agencies. It becomes evident that many perpetrators will evade punishment, which in turn, reduces the deterrent effect and increases the amount of illegal activity. This scenario and improvements in media software have enabled illicit material to be created, reproduced and distributed en masse like never before. Additionally, the geographically unrestricted and seemingly anonymous communication afforded by the Internet has given rise to a great many people, saying things to others that they would fear speaking in person. The experts eventually hope to turn this into a false sense of security. We'll see.

While on the Internet, your child could easily encounter material inappropriate for children, as I've mentioned. This is often caused by "Key words" used by sites to direct net surfers to them, which I've also previously mentioned. To serve as a reminder, the key words will be common everyday words like child, teen, innocent, pregnant, young, blue, cherry, pure and anatomy. The list is endless. The danger, needless to say, is that children are often helplessly catapulted into unsavory sites. Unsuspecting children can, and often do, find themselves in the middle of hard-core pornography. Sometimes, kids will end up in conversations, and often involved in, correspondence with adults who mean to harm them.

Important things parents can do to shield their children while they use the Internet:

There are many things parents can do to protect their children from unwanted exposure on the Internet. Allow me to do a little name-dropping: Net Nanny, Cyber Patrol, and Cyber Sitter just to name a few pieces of software, are available to help keep your kids safe. However, no procedure, technique or software is 100 percent effective by itself. Especially when kids are as smart as they are. Many middle school kids know how to get around protective programs and they are ever so willing to share what they have figured out with others. Your two best bets are installing screening software and personally being present, supervising your children while they are on the Internet. Screening software is a parental tool designed to prevent harmful material from reaching children that are surfing the Web. Some screening software programs even limit access to chat channels and chat rooms. Although this software is designed to screen out inappropriate material, there is still a strong possibility that children will at some time encounter, illicit subject matter or activity. Don't forget what I just told you about how intelligent kids are, especially when it comes to computers. Believe me, if there is away around computer protective software, they will find it.

There is, however, positively beyond the shadow of any doubt, one certain way to insure your children are protected. Sit right there with them while they access the Internet. Stay right there the entire time they are on the Internet. If you leave your child unattended on the Internet and believe he or she will tell you everything they're seeing and doing, you're probably mistaken. How's that for a nice way of putting it? Are you nuts or what? Your kid's probably is going to lie his head off. If it is impossible to sit with your child while he or she is

201

on the Internet, then you need to locate the computer in a highly visible common area of your home. Studies have proven that seventy percent of kids (middle school ages) lie to their parents eighty to eighty-five percent of the time. Although, in all fairness to the little freeloaders, they don't lie every time they open their mouths. Much of their lying is by omission. In the case of a child innocently surfing the net and BAM, there it is, out of nowhere the kid's up to his or her neck in pornography. First, they think you're not going to believe them. First, they think your going to be mad. First, they think you're going to forbid them to be on the computer ever again. First, they're going to be embarrassed. No those aren't mistakes or typos. First is what I meant, because all of that stuff is going to jump into the innocent child's thoughts at the same time, first.

The aforementioned screening software, as I said, cannot completely insure that your children will not encounter objectionable material, nor is it likely to be able to anytime soon. Most such programs work by barring access to certain Web sites that are titled with profane and suggestive words. However, many sites are triggered by words that are not, or shouldn't be, considered suggestive, such as, art, pink, cheery, etc. Some programs also analyze words in the content text, although sites that do not contain words that ring an alarm are accessible. Another problem is not all sites that contain, say hard-core pornography or "kiddy porn" use key words. Additionally, in the process, occasionally some harmless and beneficial sites are inadvertently screened out.

I am not saying that the screening programs are completely ineffective, only that they cannot entirely take the place of parental supervision. They are, in fact, surprisingly effective and are a good secondary choice for parents. Especially those parents whose children primarily use the World Wide Web and are not active on Internet relay chat and online chat rooms such as those of America Online and the Usenet newsgroups. Only when in the company of a trusted supervising adult should children access those areas. Kids obviously aren't going to like this, and most will assume you don't trust them. You need to explain that you have no choice and that it is not a matter of not trusting them, it is a matter of protecting them, because you love them. That's right, lie to them if you have to. Just kidding. Remember, no one knows your children as well as you know them, so you determine if your needs more of an explanation. If so, be straightforward, be careful, and proceed.

For some families, a combination of screening software coupled with a little parental supervision will serve you and your children best. Again, no one knows your children better than you, which makes it your call. However, if the latter is your choice, there are ways to check to see if you made the right choice. In your computer manual, if you will take the time to thumb through it, you will discover that there are ways to find out what sites are being visited. Now you might be asking yourself, is this a little devious? Yep! Is this being a little untrusting? You bet! Is this an invasion of your child's privacy? Most likely! Is this something most parents would do? Probably not! Is this something I should be doing? Absolutely! Especially considering, a young teen, male or female, that may not be preoccupied with sex or had never considered voyeurism, is suddenly catapulted into a pornographic site. Keeping in mind, your average teenager's hormones are bouncing around faster than a Ping-Pong ball at a championship tournament. Then all of a sudden, unexpectedly, in front of them is not only the opposite sex, but naked. Probably doing something your child may have heard about, but never thought possible. Natural curiosity dictates that most preteens or teenagers will revisit that site.

Here's some things you should consider:

*Never buy your children a computer if you have zero computer knowledge and you have no intentions of learning. Or, you can consider a computer for your child's homework and games with no Internet hook-up.

*Never allow your children to be using a computer in their room with the door closed.

*Learn from an expert [Computer geek] all of the ways to keep tabs on where your children have been and what they have been doing on the computer.

*According to an evaluation of screening software published by PC World magazine (a periodical whose judgment Pedowatch endorses), two programs stood out as considerably better than their competitors [at this time]: Cybersitter by Solid Oak at (800-388-2761) and SurfWatch by SurfWatch Software at (800-458-6600).

Cyber Snoop is yet another alternative. Pedowatch does not recommend it for general use by all parents, because of the potential to

203

harm parent-child trust. Still, in some situations where parental supervision is limited or nonexistent, it may be the only option. Cyber Snoop is offered by Pearl Software and can be contacted at (800-732-7596). Cyber Snoop is an "after the fact" analysis tool that allows parents to view a record of their child's Internet activity while he or she was on the computer. On the other hand, I feel, because the stakes are so high, that Cyber Snoop is a much-needed tool (weapon) that will definitely aid parents in this war. However, this too is a personal call.

Lord knows, we wouldn't want to do anything that would get between our children and pedophiles or pornographic suppliers that could possibly cause a rift with our kids. I want to be very, very clear about this. If you know, or even suspect, that your child is involved with any of the aforementioned, do anything you can, anything humanly possible, to get between your child and the pedophiles and pornographers. If this means acquiring sub-rosa "special" tools, so be it. Think of it this way: if your child is surfing porn sites or involved in chat rooms, especially after you requested that they don't, then it is your child who is deceiving you.

The importance of some of the ten suggestions (commandments) I'm going to give you is dependent on the age of the children using the computer. Younger children should not be allowed unsupervised access to a computer, period.

1} Starting today, get more actively involved in your child's online experience and become more computer literate.

2} Know what your children are doing on the computer, at all times. If you don't know, ask them. Kids love the idea that they can teach an adult something, especially their parents. Hey, you know what, it may even bring you guys a little closer.

3}Place your computer in a high traffic location, such as a den or family room, almost anywhere except the child's bedroom.

4} Watch for children spending extended lengths of time at the computer and investigate what that is all about.

5}Set time limits for your children regarding Internet use.

6} Limit your child's access to specific online areas, e.g., use screening software and forbid unsupervised online chat, no exceptions.

7} Read your children's unfamiliar e-mail.

8} Monitor your long distance telephone bill.

9} Never allow your child to arrange a face-to-face meeting with another computer user, even if you know beyond the shadow of any doubt that the other computer user is a child, without parental supervision. Explicitly inform your children of this rule, because kids do it regularly these days, often unbeknownst to most parents. The fact is, some pedophiles use their own children to lure other young ones.

10} Encourage your children to report suggestive, obscene, or threatening e-mail and bulletin board messages.

Actually, I want you to do one more thing. I want you to teach your children, "The Internet safety pledge." The Internet safety pledge is another reminder that your children must play an active role in helping to keep themselves safe.

The Pledge:

*I will talk with my parents so we can set up rules for going online. We will decide upon a time of day and length of time I can be online and the appropriate sites I can visit. I will not access any information I have not been given permission to use.

*I will tell my parents right away if I come across information that makes me feel uncomfortable and I know is wrong.

*I will never send my picture or anything else without first checking with my parents.

*I will not respond to any messages that are mean or make me feel uncomfortable. It is not my fault if I get a message like that, and if I do, I will tell my parents immediately so they can contact our online service.

*I will never agree to get together with someone I meet online without first checking with my parents. If they agree, I will then make sure it is in a public place, and that at least one of my parents or a trusted adult is with me.

*I will not give out personal information such as my address, telephone number, parents' work number or address, or name and address of my school, without my parents' permission.

*Of all of these things, I give my word and make a promise.

Child Molester I.D. Line

I have chosen California as my sample state for two reasons. First,

205

it ranks up there at the top of the list when it comes to resident sexual offenders. Second, as I have previously mentioned, California happens to be the state in which I reside. Consequently, it is the state I personally am most familiar with regarding the sexual offender laws.

On July 3rd, 1995, the Child Protective Act of 1994 began the demising process. This action will provide the public with greater access to information about California's, and ideally, (with law enforcement co-operation) all of the other states' registered sex offenders, who have preyed on our women and children. This information can be obtained by calling the Department of Justice "900" fee-based telephone service. The cost for using the services is a flat rate of $10 for information on two subjects. Parents concerned about person's behavior in their neighborhood or around their children can call to determine if previous sex offender information exists on the individual. This service may help to block a child molester's attempt to gain access to your children. Additionally, organizations or groups that provide child related services could use this information specifically to protect children who may be at risk. In addition to the telephone service, a DOJ subdirectory of specified registered sex offenders was published and distributed in January 1996 to sheriffs and police departments nationwide.

After you dial the Child Molester Identification Line at 1-900-463-0400, you will hear a recording that will tell you about the service. Here is a sample of what you will hear:

*The charges for using the "900" telephone service.

*That your telephone number will be recorded.

*That you're required to identify yourself.

*A warning about using the information illegally.

*Information about the subject that is necessary for a database search.

*That the "900" number is not a crime hotline and that any suspected criminal activity should be reported to your local authorities.

*That you must be 18 years of age or older to use the "900" telephone service.

[Calls will be accepted Monday through Friday (except holidays) 9:30 a.m. to 6 p.m.] Next, you will be connected with a Criminal Identification Specialist. Be prepared to give any portion of the following information:

*Remember, the more descriptive information you're able to give,

the better the response will be when checking on the subject.
    *First and last name.
    *Street address, including apartment number, if applicable.
    *Exact date of birth.
    *Social Security number.
    *Driver's license or identification number.
    *Height.
    *Weight.
    *Hair color.
    *Eye color.
    *Ethnicity [race].
    *Distinct tattoos, scars, and birthmarks.
    *I am adding for your protection this little tidbit of information.
    [It is illegal to use this information to discriminate, harass or bring harm to any registrant.]
    The purpose of the Child Molester I.D. Line is to give parents another tool to help them protect their children and loved ones from harm. It is an extremely important tool when you consider that in the year 2000, in California alone, there were over sixty-three thousand (63,000) registered child molesters and adult rapists. I used the past tense, due to the fact that the numbers are rapidly climbing daily. Some of these registered sex offenders may decide to obey the law, however thousands upon thousands will strike again. Studies have shown that at least half will be rearrested, at least forty percent of them for another sexual attack. By the way, did I mention that most sexual offenders are not registered, since they haven't been caught yet? Some will call my last statement an exaggeration, although there are many independent experts that believe that the sixty-three thousand sexual offenders statistic used is "at least" only half of the sexual offenders residing in California, alone. Remember that the sixty-thee thousand are registered sex offenders and any expert worth their salt knows that most sexual predators are not registered. Most sexual offenders have not been caught.
    While California law allows you to learn who these registered sex offenders are, many states do not. California requires you to present yourself at a police station and show your identification, then give your own reasons for wanting to ID sex offenders. Your identification and answers are recorded before the police comply with your request. This is obviously a procedure implemented to protect sex offenders from a parent's revenge and/or vigilantism. Because of this procedure,

only a small number of parents throughout the state have seen the sex offender database. Tells you where most folks heads might be. Interesting, isn't it?

Sex offenders, who are profiled in the state's Sex Offender Database, sexually abuse children every day. Obviously, the widespread release of this information will remove at least some children from harm's way. I suggest if your state is not implementing the laws for the posting of complete information regarding sexual child molesters, you need to get busy right away. It is an excellent cause for you to take a vocal stand on. State and local government will look shamefully ridiculous opposing any law that protects children. This, of course, is aside from the fact that the Federal government has ordered it to be done. This is the correct opportunity to stand firm on your rights and to make your demands. This is especially true when you consider that your best weapon in this war is their sex crime statistics. And, for a change, the "Federal Machine" is backing you up.

Some of the other states that are officially online are Indiana, Florida, Alaska and Kansas. Hopefully, more will soon follow.

It is important for all people of good moral character, parents or not, to make sure your state and your local government participates in such a worthy endeavor.

Maybe this will help to motivate you: the only children spared the lifelong torment from the memory of their sexual abuse are those that are murdered.

[Added for your protection]

*This information is obtainable because, to the best of my knowledge, it has not yet been abused. According to California law, this information may only be used to protect a person at risk. Use of this information in California is disclosed pursuant to penal code 290.4. Law prohibits use for any of the following purposes:

*Credit

*Insurance, including health insurance

*Loans

*Employment

*Housing or accommodations

*Benefits, privileges, or services provided by any business establishment

*Education, scholarships, or fellowships

*Any usage not intended by law for the intended purpose of protection of people(s) at risk of attack

208

Also, any person who uses information disclosed pursuant to this section to commit a felony shall be punished, in addition and consecutive to, any other punishment, by a five-year term of imprisonment, in a state prison. It is also illegal for any person, who without authorization uses the information disclosed pursuant, to this section to commit a misdemeanor. Any person committing this act will be subject to, in addition to any other penalty or fine imposed, a fine of not less than five hundred dollars ($500), not to exceed one thousand dollars ($1000).

In addition, any person who copies, distributes, discloses, or receives this record or information from it, except as authorized by law, is guilty of a misdemeanor. This crime is punishable by imprisonment in the county jail, not to exceed six months and/or a fine, not to exceed one thousand dollars ($1000).

I believe that these laws have been put in place to protect all sexual offenders, especially child molesters, who may be harmed or treated unfairly. You know... their constitutional rights, and all that.

I personally have included this notification of the law regarding sex offenders for a couple of reasons. One is to protect myself from being accused of supplying information [bringing to the attention] to anyone intent on taking the law into their on hands.

I personally believe that any individuals who treat a child (our children) in an inhumane manner do not themselves deserve the protection of the Constitution, nor should they be treated humanely. Therefore, in spite of the reason or reasons as to why our government created these laws, which obviously they believe are necessary, they still seem to leave a bad taste. Evidently, we (society) have in our striving to be ever compassionate, even to the worst possible criminals and have enacted laws for their protection. That's correct, at a cost of millions and millions of tax dollars annually, we choose to hide and protect those that rape, mutilate and often murder our children. I, on the other hand, have added the information regarding this law, as I previously mentioned, for a couple of reasons. The other reason is, as an advisory in order to protect the victim's parents, loved ones, friends and concerned citizens. I do this for all of the victims and their survivors, including the caring concerned citizens that witness these terrible and terrifying creatures being consistently released back into society. Knowing in their hearts that it isn't right, knowing it isn't safe, knowing something must be done. I know this because of all of my years dealing with these godless creatures and the carnage they leave in their paths of destruction. I know that the survivors know what I know. However, they that have not become victims themselves are the ones that choose to believe that these subhuman creatures have changed. They don't know what we know: we know that child predators are as knowable as their repetitiveness has proven, and they will strike a child down again and again.

Where are they, how many are there?

Available to aid parents in keeping their children safe is: www.sexoffenders.net. This service lists cities by area code, supplying you with population, zip code, the number of serious sex offenders and the number of high-risk sex offenders.

Serious sex offenders have indeed committed serious crimes, like before, during, or after a sexual attack, murdering and often dismembering their victims. High-risk offenders may be guilty of the same crimes committed by the serious offender, but repeatedly commits them. Funny, I always thought repeatedly meant time after time, hence a habitual criminal. My understanding is that there are in existence now, and have been for many years, laws and punishments for individuals that choose to keep recommitting crimes, especially the same crimes. Yet time and time again, repeating sexual offenders are set free, protected by laws our government chooses to enforce, only to have society witness, after the fact, of course, the predators striking again.

Have you noticed how easy it is to get off track when your blood is boiling? Allow me to continue filling you in about sexoffenders.net. They will allow you to do a print out, if you choose. Here is a sample of their service, which by the way, is a great aid in helping families select safer places to live. This service is in addition to the information your local police department should be able to supply you with.

Area Code 818
North Hollywood
Population: N/A
Zip Code: 90601-90607
Serious Sex Offenders = 129
High Risk Sex Offenders = 9

Agoura Hills
Population: 20,950
Zip Code: 91301
Serious Sex Offenders =12
High Risk Sex Offenders = 0

Burbank
Population: 97,200
Zip Code: 91501-91506
Serious Sex Offenders =122
High Risk Sex Offenders =1

I want to take a second to say thank you to all the folks at www.sexoffenders.net for a wonderful and quite possibly life saving community service.

Chapter 8

NATIONAL REGISTRATION OF CHILD MOLESTERS

The registration of child molesters is working great in many of the areas that it has been implemented in, because it is also being enforced. Therein lies the problem. Contrary to popular belief, it has not been implemented nationwide, and in many places where it has been implemented, it is not being enforced with any kind of regularity. I don't know whether the problem stems from a lack of sufficient funding, manpower or just sheer laziness. Possibly, some local law enforcement agencies don't like to co-operate with federal rulings. Then again, it could be the "good old boy" machine in motion.

Megan's Law is the "original" and among the most restrictive. However, in the forty-seven states where Megan's law has been implemented, it has been changed into facsimile versions of the original. [Watered down in most cases.] Virginia, Michigan and New Jersey's registries are very restrictive and difficult to access, which for the most part makes them useless. New Jersey's warnings cover only about one-third of the state's paroled offenders. As of this writing, the 1,939 convicted offenders that county prosecutors have evaluated for potential risk, only 47 (2.4%) are classified as "high risk" and subject to the widest warnings, and another 585 (30.2 %) are categorized as "moderate risks." The remaining 1,307 (67.4 %) are "low risks." In New Jersey, only law enforcement officials can receive information about "low risk" offenders. Although claims have been made of change in New Jersey, experts say it is simply window dressing.

The difference between one state and another can be like the difference between day and night. For instance, Alaska posted the entire list of its paroled sex offenders on the Web. California will provide information on all sexual offenders on CD-ROM at county sheriff offices. Then there's Connecticut, where there must not be too many concerned parents or, as the opposition likes to put it, bleeding hearts. Although Connecticut enjoys some of the best policies regarding public access to sexual offenders information in the nation, they're constantly under attack. There are individuals fighting real hard to pass laws that protect the whereabouts and identities of convicted sexual offenders, citing their right to privacy. Surprisingly, they're not receiving too much opposition, as of my last reading of the situation. Connecticut does, as of this writing, permit local police stations to release the names, addresses and photographs of paroled offenders to anyone that requests that information. In my opinion that's a hell of a great service to the citizenry, so you parents had better get out there and find some "bleeding hearts" to help you protect that wonderful service!

*Let's hear it for Connecticut, where women and children's rights outweigh the rights of rapists and child molesters... at this time.

There are States that seem to be trying to get their acts together, such as New York and Michigan. The State of New York classifies (71%) of its paroled offenders (4,738 of 6,637) as "moderate" or "high risk" and subject to public warnings.

*The numbers and percentages of sexual offenders given in this book is inaccurate due to the fact that their numbers grow daily, and many experts agree that the information supplied by some states is extremely conservative at best.

The registration of child molesters is something every parent must become involved with at your State, County and City levels. If registration and notification laws are already in place, make sure they are enforced and not watered down. If the laws are obviously window dressing, join the fight to make those laws stronger. They are your laws. It is also important to take the time to find out if your protective laws are being enforced from the streets all the way to the courtrooms.

From the past to present, it has always been the few, working hard, trying to make it safe for everyone else, trying to make it safe for your children. Doing for you what you should be doing for yourselves, for your own children. When it comes to doing jobs such as caring for the handicapped, elderly, and less fortunate in general, or simply doing the

right thing, which may inconvenience our routine, we all seem to prefer to sit back and watch others do the work. Sure, we say things like,
"Thank God for people like that, or "Ya gotta hand it to them." Sadly,
that is the extent of most people's efforts. [Useless lip service.] It's
always those same other people, doing our bidding, doing what we as
parents should be doing, or at least assisting. It's true, it has always
been the same handful of people, generally the women, the mothers.
Maybe it's because they have been victimized themselves, one way or
another. Probably some do it because they were sexually molested as
children, or possibly lost a child to a kidnapper. What is it that makes
them work long thankless hours, trying to protect our children? Why
are we not doing more to help them protect our children? Why do we
leave such an overwhelming and important task to so few?

We as parents need to realize, especially us fathers that we have to
get involved. There are monsters out there stalking our children. Waiting, watching for the opportunity to kidnap, molest and possibly
murder our children. Fathers should be the first line of defense. But
you must be willing to take more control over your children's safety.
This means you are going to have to sacrifice some of your precious
time. No, I am not being facetious. Time is precious. And what better
way to spend it than protecting your children? While you're at it,
maybe you can spare a little more of your precious time and do what
you can to protect someone else's children.

Parents need to begin realizing that they not only have the ability,
but more importantly, the power, to direct politicians and the courts.
By sheer numbers, you have the power to alter policy and to change
and create new laws. In numbers, you have the power to empower
governing agencies as to the monitoring and control of convicted sexual child molesters. These agencies are in desperate need of more
funding, more manpower and more equipment. All of this is within
your power! United, parents can make it happen. And I will tell you
how you can accomplish it, by following and actually executing the
forthcoming directions.
*Pending legislation
*Committed direction
*Letters to your government

I have been in the dreadful position of trying to comfort parents of missing children. Watching the father with his face in his hands, sobbing, repeating over and over, "Why wasn't I there? I'm her father. I should've been there. I could've protected her." Well, fathers, there is a much lesser chance of this happening to you if you simply take your position as protector of your family. Start now by getting involved! Within the pages of this book is all the information, "ammunition," you need to fight this war. Don't just read it, act on it! In this chapter, I will inform you as to what others are doing in your behalf, and hopefully instill in you the willingness to do what needs to be done.

Before we go further, I want to tell you exactly why I consider this a war, without trying to sound like an over-reacting alarmist. According to percentages and statistics, and also taking into consideration where you may live, the chances of something terrible happening to your children may be a great deal less than to others. However, when I have discussed this with parents in the past, many reply with the same statement, "I don't think we have to worry, we live in a pretty safe neighborhood" or city, or community, or whatever. It seems to me that not much thought is put into their statement, and I hear it so often that I sometimes get a little sarcastic. I generally begin by retorting, "And your children never leave your neighborhood and outsiders never enter your neighborhood" or "Do you believe that successful people, living in quality neighborhoods, are not or can't be capable of child molestation?" When this happens, I generally don't make too many points or create new friendships.

It is important to me that you try to look at it from my point of view, which is, it's not going to happen to you, it might not even happen to anyone you know, but in minutes, it's happening to someone, it's happening to someone's child right now. What makes you so special? Are you thinking it will never happen to you, it will never happen to your child? What gives you the right to leave this problem to chance, leaving your child, who depends on you, totally defenseless? Because you are the father of your children does not mean you have the right to take chances with your children's lives. Because it doesn't happen to your child, what about the children it is happening to? Shouldn't men, fathers or not, be doing something about that? Something that is, besides crying and moaning about what you should've, could've done. Get out there and do it. A child is waiting. A child is waiting for you! Take it from someone who's been there, there is nothing, nothing, in this life, more rewarding than having played an important role in saving a child's life.

Now I'm going to share with you a detailed case history. Forgive me for being so graphic, however, I feel it is necessary. My reasoning is that some parents need a good jolt in order to get them to do anything regarding their children's safety. Additionally, it is important that you be alerted to what is actually happening out there in the real world. I realize that many of you would rather not hear it, much less see it in print. I understand, because I don't like hearing it, or reading about it either, and worst of all, actually seeing it first hand, as I have. However, if you will remember, I promised to deliver a book with "No candy coating or soft shoeing." Besides, how can you properly (truly) inform your children, if you are not properly and completely informed yourself?

Case History:

[The names have been changed]

At 2:30 PM on a hot summer day in Arizona, Linda was walking home from her older sister's home about six houses from her own. Linda was carrying a new purse containing a makeup bag, combs, brush, etc. that her sister had given her two days earlier, for her thirteenth birthday. By 6:00 PM, Linda's mom and sister realized that Linda was not at the other's house, as presumed. Because it was not normally Linda's habit to visit her friends without letting someone know where she was, her mom and sister got busy calling all of Linda's friends trying to locate her, to no avail.

At approximately 6:30 PM, the police were alerted to Linda's disappearance, yet it took another hour and forty-five minutes for the police to be convinced that Linda might actually be missing. Although, in the meantime, the police did have a patrol car searching the immediate area.. Between 9:30 and 10 p.m., the police department received a telephone call reporting what looked like a body lying in a vacant lot in a new housing track that was still under construction. When the police arrived at the scene, the officers were totally overcome by what they witnessed. In one officer's own words, "Only demons straight from hell could do this." Surprisingly, and to everyone's disbelief, Linda was barely alive. She was immediately rushed to

216

the hospital, where it took two surgeons three hours and forty minutes to save her life.

The following was reported by Linda while recovering in the hospital and confirmed by two separate confessions approximately five weeks later. Linda explained how she was tricked into looking at free puppies in a box, held by a man sitting in the sliding side doorway of a parked van. When asked by a police detective, "Haven't you been warned to stay away from strangers?" Linda replied, "Yes, but the box was deep, I couldn't see the puppies, unless I got up close."

Linda hadn't realized that as she was trying to get a look at the puppies, a second man, the driver, got out of the van and had come around behind her. As the two men drove Linda around for hours, they took their turns sexually assaulting her. Linda was forced at knifepoint to perform oral sex on both men and was raped and sodomized repeatedly. Each time one of the men had intercourse with Linda, he would place his thumbs on her closed eyes and press hard. She said when he did that, "It really hurt bad and everything turned white." One of the men, Linda did not know which, bit into her vagina, causing severe damage. For Linda, this was just the beginning.

Do you remember earlier, when we talked about times changing and so are the people committing the crimes? Well, the crimes are changing too. There was a time in America, if you were being robbed and cooperated, you wouldn't be hurt. Just give them what they want and they won't hurt you. There was a time when police officers could speak with authority to criminals and the criminals would listen. They didn't like it, but for the most part, they listened. Today, if a cop screws a gun in a bad guy's ear, if he's lucky, he might get the guy's attention.

Drugs seem to have changed everything. That is, when drugs arrived on the scene, all the rules of the past no longer applied, especially considering the effect of drugs like PCP on your average creep. Some drugs of popular choice today turn what is normally a noodle-armed gutless wonder into a surprisingly strong crazed idiot, creating a maniac capable of anything.

The senseless and inhumane acts that are committed by criminals today were definitely exhibited in Linda's case.

After driving around for hours, the two men decided on a location to finish the job. (Drop the body.) However, before they were going to

217

kill Linda, they elected to rape and sodomize her several more times.

Now comes the time, the time I believe it dawns on totally deranged individuals, it's as if a light comes on in their head, that they haven't been caught yet and they're getting away with it. They realize no one can stop them, or do anything about it. It is as though a realization suddenly comes over them: what they've believed all along is true, that they are superior to everyone, especially their victims. They know now that they own this person. At that moment, the truly horrifying degradation begins. In Linda's case, the proof of their superiority began with, both men simultaneously jamming the entire contents of Linda's purse, including combs, hair brush, and other things not previously mentioned into every orifice of her body. Far from being finished with Linda, they packed all of her openings with Vicks VapoRub.

Unconscious, due to the torture and lack of oxygen, Linda was carried by the two kidnappers into the vacant lot, where one of the men plunged a knife deep into her chest. Either before or after Linda was stabbed, which was never determined, one or both of the men, also not determined, used a razor blade on Linda. They cut around the areola of each of Linda's breast and completely removed the areolas, including her nipples, which were later discovered by an officer, stuck to the windshield of a nearby car parked on the street.

Although the perpetrators tried their best, Linda did not die. Consequently, their punishment was imprisonment, rather than being turned into fertilizer, as they deserved. One of the two perpetrators was a twice-convicted sex offender who lived approximately two miles from Linda's home.

It is my opinion, and I believe many share it, that when true monsters are revealed by their atrocities, age should not be of consequence and nothing short of revoking their breathing permits should be considered.

I remember Linda's Mother saying, as she choked back the tears, "I've heard of this sort of thing happening, I just didn't think it would ever happen to us." Had convicted sex offender registration laws been in place, this crime may not have taken place.

States require the registration of convicted sex offenders, but some do not enforce the registration. We need and must insist on the enforcement of registration of all sex offenders, especially convicted pedophiles. This registration must include all cities, counties and states in America. Although registration and qualification for registration vary from state to state, the procedures are uncomplicated and pretty straightforward. The enforced registration of sex offenders will greatly aid those institutions and agencies having the responsibility for children. In addition, if all prospective employees who would have any responsibility for children, or be in the proximity of children, would be required by law to submit to thorough background checks, including criminal history, we could all sleep a little better. That is, if the employers would be smart enough to wait for the results of the background check before hiring.

While I have the chance, I want to let you know the name of a little boy, a little boy that lost his life and woke up the authorities in Arkansas and a few other states. Arkansas law requiring the registration of sex offenders is called the "Jacob Wetterling Crimes Against Children and Sexual Violent Offender Registration Act." Jacob, by the way, was an 11-year-old, abducted from his hometown of St. Joseph, Minnesota, and murdered

The following persons are required to register:

*Any individual who has been found guilty of a sexually violent offense; a sex offense; where certain offenses, the victim was a minor.

*Individuals who are incarcerated, on probation or parole, or serving any other form of community supervision as the result of an adjudication of guilt for the listed offenses.

*Any person who is committed following an acquittal on the grounds of mental disease or defect for the listed offenses.

*Any person who was required to register under the Habitual Child Sex Offender Registration Act, Arkansas Code Annotated 12-12-901.

*An offender moving to, or returning to, this state from another jurisdiction shall register with the local law enforcement agency having jurisdiction no later than thirty (30) days after the effective date of this law or thirty (30) days after establishing residency, whichever is later.

Portions of this law refer to a ten (10) day notification period, mostly dedicated to notification of intent to relocate.

The way this law reads is if an individual's name is not on rental or buyer's paperwork, there may not be a way to prove date and term of residency. Also, there are those living out of motor homes and vans.

219

What about the predators who do not intend to obey the registration laws? If these individuals intend to continue raping women or molesting children, this law provides a thirty-day [plus] window.

I consider these registration laws (requirements) very lenient, especially, considering the c crimes that these "Sex propelled creeps" commit. Many lives can be lost or ruined with a thirty-day registry window. Too damned lenient! How about totally inadequate! It's those bleeding hearts again, trying to accommodate and be fair to those who prey on women and children. I see absolutely no reason why the registration time period should be more than 48 hours, with the possibility of a short extension if proven necessary and unavoidable.

In Las Vegas, Nevada, the law requires any convicted felon to register at the police department within 24 hours of their arrival, no matter what their felony conviction.

Now you tell me, have some of our lawmakers assigned a higher value to protecting our gambling industry over protecting our women and children? If the Las Vegas Police Department and the rest of the officials there feel it necessary to register felons within a 24 hour arrival period in order to protect their gambling industry, and I assume their residents, what is the problem with a 48 hour nationwide "arrival registration law" for convicted sex offenders, including pedophiles?

Maybe we shouldn't complain. At least the women and children of Las Vegas Nevada are better protected, no matter what their lawmakers intended to protect.

I've probably stepped over the line with a nationwide 48-hour registration "suggestion." You would think by now, I would have learned that in today's society, tidbits of common sense do not apply.

Have you had enough of the way things should be yet? Good, I'm glad we are in agreement, here's some more.

Any institution or agency having the responsibility of children, such as busing companies, day care centers, schools and so on, should be required by law to submit their prospective employees to thorough background checks, especially including criminal history. The background check of a potential employee should be completed before hiring. Hiring before the results of a thorough background check is complete happens all too frequently.

Here is a list of offenses covered by the 989 Act of 1997, which require registration. I hope this will give you a good idea of some, if not most of the sexual offender laws governing your state. Some of the following offenses may seem repetitious, however they are provided as a complete listing as specified by law. [Laws vary from state to state.]

1} Rape

2} Carnal abuse in the first degree

3} Carnal abuse in the second degree

4} Carnal abuse in the third degree

5} Sexual misconduct

6} Sexual misconduct in the first degree

7} Sexual misconduct in second degree

8} Sexual solicitation of a child

9} Violation of a minor in the first degree

10} Violation of a minor in the second degree

11} Incest

12} Engaging children in sexually explicit conduct for use in visual or print medium

13} Transportation of minors for prohibited sexual conduct

14} Employing or consenting to the use of a child in sexual performance

15} Producing, directing or promoting sexual performance

16} Promoting prostitution in the first degree

17} Stalking

18} An attempt, solicitation, or conspiracy to commit any of the offenses listed as #1 through #17

19} An adjudication of guilt for an offense of the law of another state, for a federal offense, or for a military offense, which is substantially equivalent to any of the offenses enumerated as #1 through #17

20} A violation of any former law of this state that is substantially equivalent to any of the offenses enumerated as #1 through #17

21} Kidnapping, when the victim is a minor and the offender is not the parent of the victim

22} False imprisonment in the first degree, when the victim is a minor and the offender is not the parent of the victim

23} Permanent detention or restraint, when the victim is a minor and the offender is not the parent of the victim

24} Any sex offense when the victim is a minor

25} An attempt, solicitation, or conspiracy to commit any of the offenses enumerated as #21 through #24

26} An adjudication of guilt for an offense of the law of another state, for a federal offense, or for a military offense, which is substantially equivalent to any of the offenses enumerate #21 through #24

27} A violation of any former law of this state that is substantially equivalent to any of the offenses enumerated as #21 through #24

Join forces with other parents in your community and learn about the laws governing your state. Make sure your state laws are more than just adequate; make sure they're being enforced. Get behind your lawmakers, whether it is to support them, or to give them a push. Lord knows they need both. Always keep in mind that this is not about Democrats or Republicans, Christians or Jews, it's about children. So, if a politician from a party other than your own is trying to do some good regarding our children, get behind him or her the best way you can. Something else that's important to do is to grab onto the tail of any politician who doesn't support laws for children's safety and start shaking it until they do the right thing. If nothing is going on in either camp, begin asking why and don't stop asking until you have embarrassed them into action.

Specialists need to be assigned to enforce strict parole supervision on released child molesters. These parole specialists should be specifically trained in pedophile activities and their lifestyles, which will enable them to better monitor and scrutinize sexual offenders' activities. Another responsibility is the monitoring of non-convicted pedophiles in their jurisdiction.

Failure to register

A person who fails to register or who fails to report changes of address as required shall be guilty of a Class D felony. Class D felonies are punishable by up to six years imprisonment and up to a $10,000 fine.

A Class D felony describes the degree or level of felony, generally denoting that the crime was victimless and/or did not involve moral turpitude, but not always.

The first paragraph is how the law reads, and it is the law. However, due to a lack of funding and in some cases, a lack of interest, this particular law is all too often not enforced. [Ignored.] Again, attempting to be fair to law enforcement, being undermanned and under funded is most often the problem, although there are those who believe that law enforcement overall is not interested, or less interested in crimes that do not involve large amounts of cash, rewarding forfeitures and big headlines. When the big shots realized sharing the booty [monies and property] confiscated under the "Rico Act" during major drug busts with each involved police agency would allow them to better outfit themselves, they jumped on it. They also hoped the possibility of these new-found riches would provide incentives [forfeitures] for bigger and more arrest.

Ultimately, there's a price to be paid for what seems too good to be true. Actually, the American people are paying at least two prices. The first, the "Rico Act", (Racketeer Influenced and Corrupt Organizations) which allows forfeitures, was originated to aid our government in the battle against organized crime such as the Mafia and the drug cartels. The "Act" worked well on its intended targets. The problem is that our federal government and some individual policing agencies with our politicians blessings have unleashed the "Act" against the public in general. For example, unbeknownst to you, your sixteen-year-old son has been growing marijuana on the side of the house you never seem to visit. Unbeknownst to your sixteen-year-old son, he has just sold a tiny portion of his harvest to an undercover narcotics officer at his school. One investigation leads to another, and before you know it, the authorities have confiscated your home and maybe your car as well, especially if you let your little rocket scientist use your car and he transported his merchandise in it.

The second price to be paid by the American people is what appears to be a slowly evolving lack of interest by authorities in crimes that do not have big paydays. Crimes such as keeping track of the registration of convicted sex offenders, like pedophiles. Which are two more reasons this book has been written in a degree of anger.

As my investigation pointed out, our sex offender registration laws are not strong enough, nor are they enforced straight across the board. I don't want to bore you with which states, counties and cities are doing what. What I will tell you is, to the best of my knowledge, nowhere in United States of America are our children being protected as well as they could and should be.

America, the most industrialized, most civilized, and the most moral country in the world, can't or won't make it safer for kids. Funny, we can't seem to get it together enough to create complete child protection laws, or even enforce what few we have, yet we have put men on the moon.

Public notification

New Jersey was the first state to pass the law requiring public notification of released sex offenders after the death of seven-year-old Megan Kanka at the hands of convicted child molesters that had been released from custody. "Megan's Law."

Megan's law provides for the implementation of a procedure that allows police and sheriffs departments to release information on registered sex offenders to the public for the purposes of public safety. This information may consist of the name and location of the offender, but will not contain any information on the identity of the victim.

The purpose of this legislation is to provide important information to the public in the hopes that it will afford families the ability to protect themselves. School districts may also release information regarding registered sex offenders. This information can be made available to students and parents when such information is released to the school district by a law enforcement agency.

The problem is that some State agencies choose not to release this information to the public for fear of protest and possible vigilante retaliation.

[Our government, protecting and ensuring the rights of the people that rape and butcher our children.]

I am sure you have seen on television, or perhaps you have personally witnessed, or even taken part in a protest regarding the government's placement of a newly released convicted sex offender. Well, here's a case, which always comes to mind, a case when the people's protest was right on target. Because this individual's crime against a child was so grotesque, I really hate having to repeat it and I refuse to put his name in print. He was found guilty of raping, sodomizing and mutilating a child. What could only be described as a miracle kept this young girl alive in the desert after having both arms chopped off with an axe. For his crime, this pedophiliac received a six-year prison sentence, but was actually released in four years. Upon his early release, the concerned and protesting public flatly refused his relocation in their communities. After multiple relocation attempts were met with public outcry, our government managed to secretly place him in a rural location for the duration of his parole. When he was finally released from his closely scrutinized parole, he was on his own. He decided to head on down to Florida, where it didn't take him long before he killed a woman. This is not an isolated case! Sex offenders repeat their crimes more than any other type of criminal. Parents are more than justified in protesting the placement of convicted sex offenders in their communities.

How can we accept or trust our government's judgment when their laws protect the criminal and leave the innocent in harm's way? [You folks just keep on protesting.]

Available information

Again, the guide for information pertaining to convicted sex offenders living in your community can be found on the wonderful world of the Internet at: http://www.sexoffenders.net/sgv.html

This information is made available to parents and concerned public: First, enter the desired search location, like the San Fernando Valley or you can be more specific by entering the city or zip code, and like magic... " Voila"

*Name of offender
* Date of birth
*State or federal code of crime or crime(s) committed
*Description of crime or crime(s) committed

Examples:
Doe, John Joseph DOB: 1/8/47- Crime 220 - Assault to commit rape.

Smith, Robert Z. DOB: 3/4/64 - Crime(s): 288 - Lewd and/or lascivious act 288 (a) – Lewd and/or lascivious act with a child under 14.

Jones, Tom E. DOB: 10/28/72- Crime(s): 261(2) - Rape by use of force or fear 261(3) - Rape with intoxication or anesthetic 288 - Lewd and/or lascivious act 647a - Solicit to engage in lewd conduct in a public place.

As I have explained earlier in the book, www.sexoffenders.net will also supply you with the various cities' information via area codes. City information includes population, zip code and number of resident sex offenders described as serious or high-risk offenders. The difference between serious and high-risk offenders is the latter of the two seems to repeat his crimes.

*Available information may vary from state to state, including the disclosure of exact address.

[Warning] It is illegal to use this information for the purpose of harassment or revenge and is punishable by fine and/or imprisonment.

Organized sex rings

Officially, our government says there are no "real" organized sex rings operating on the Internet, or anywhere in the United States, for that matter. Although they do admit to a smattering of groups throughout the United States, they won't describe them as organized. By the way, this is quite the contrary to our findings. For example, and this is but one of many examples, in September of 1995 the FBI made numerous arrests and searched 120 homes nationwide, concluding a two-year investigation. In their own words, "These arrests have concluded our investigation of America On Line's subscribers suspected of dealing in organized child pornography." Doesn't sound like a smattering to me, especially if you will consider the hundreds of other examples that I know of.

Now I'm truly confused, especially since according to the FBI there is a lack of "real" organized child pornography on the Internet, or anywhere else in the United States. So tell me, what led to the "Child Porn Prevention Act of 1996" if there's no "real" organized child pornography, Internet or otherwise? As I understand, the 1996 Act bans computer generated sexual images of children and porn featuring adults depicted as minors.

Before we go on, I'd like to fill you in on the brief history of the "United States Child Porn Prevention Act of 1996." Obviously first the Act was introduced, and then it was upheld on August 12, 1997 by the Federal Courts. So far, so good. This is a good thing…right? Well not to some, who decided to challenge the protective Act. Way up there in Portland, Maine, a US Federal Judge named Gene Carter struck down the Child Protection Act of 1996 as unconstitutional. In April of 1998

Federal Judge Carter ruled that, "The law stretches too far." Although my wish is to point out to you what has been going on and hopefully give you an idea of what we're up against, I also want to point out that someone, at some point, knew we needed that law. Good people are realizing the extent and seriousness of the child porn problem, in spite of misleading official statements to the public.

Evidently, the FBI thinks the public in general (that's us) can't handle the truth. Or maybe they're afraid the citizenry will think the FBI can't handle the situation. The conflict between their nationwide investigations and arrests and what they say publicly, tells us they think we can't handle the truth. However, the flood of child pornography and the use of adults depicted as children in pornography, often referred to as Lolita's on the Internet, leads me to believe they can't get a handle on the situation. The truth is that both the United States Postal Service and the FBI, along with other agencies and regulatory authorities have been cracking down on organized child sex rings. I'd like to add that considering what they've been up against and the lack of funding designated toward protecting our children, I am truly surprised regarding the extent of their success. Remember, child pornography is pouring into the United States in the form of magazines, videos, discs, photographs and the Internet every day from all over the world. However, it would really be neat if the agencies involved, including the FBI, would stop with the double talk and correctly (truthfully) inform the public. If the citizenry were to know exactly what is going on (how bad it really is), I can not help but believe that they would become very active in assisting officials in solving the problem. In addition, surely parents who learned the facts about what's really going on would be more attentive to their children's safety.

Federal Resources

The Federal resources that are allocated to protect America's children are, to say the least, too little, and in many cases too late. This is especially irritating when one considers the amount of monies designated for far less important projects. For example, if some of the monies (government grants) earmarked for what I can only describe as senseless, or better yet, asinine projects and studies were rerouted toward the funding of programs designed to protect our children, it would be a good thing. What senseless grants, you ask? Well since you asked, how about the millions of dollars spent researching over and over again the effect of domestic bovine flatulence on the ozone. (For you city folks, that's cow farts.) Also studied at the tune of big bucks, the amount of time one spends sitting on the toilet and its contributing factor to hemorrhoids. (For you country folks, that's piles.) I know that both city and country folks will agree with me when I say those kinds of studies and that kind of government waste of our financial resources is truly asinine. This is aggravating when you consider the financial needs of the agencies trying to protect our children. This is especially aggravating knowing that these needs are known to our politicians in Congress and to those who direct government funding from behind the scenes.

I am personally sick and tired of hearing politicians yap on and on about how our children are America's most precious resource. Especially when considering, trying to get funding from those same people to protect our most precious resource is like pulling teeth…from a tiger's mouth. I am also sick and tired of good child protection laws being overturned by the Supreme Court, citing infringement of rights. Please explain to me and to the parents of this great nation one thing. When there are numerous children, or for that matter, one child is sexually molested, or more explicitly, tricked, intimidated and forced to participate in sexual acts with adults, when does a child's rights come into play? At what point do the children's rights absolutely protect them? After the fact? Not good enough! Nothing or no one's rights should come before the rights of a child. The Constitution of the United States reads, and I paraphrase, the rights of all the people are guaranteed, as long as they do not infringe on the rights of others. Now, call me stupid, but I believe tricking, intimidating and forcing a child into participating in sexual acts is definitely infringing on their rights. We should be demanding that our government spend every dollar, down to the very last penny, if necessary, utilizing every means possible in the protection of our children.

Our government should secure our children's safety to the very best of its powerful ability before one single dime goes to anything else!

When judges make decisions regarding a law that he or she feels is too far reaching, as was done in the 1998 reversal of the Child Protection Act of 1996, due to its language addressing "Adults depicted as children", they are overlooking something very important: They are sticking to the letter of the law and overlooking (disregarding) the spirit of the law. I also believe these judges are guilty of a gross misinterpretation and/or misuse of our Constitution. Our Founding Fathers lent great credence to the spirit of the law, which is all too often overlooked these days.

As in my work, recovering kidnapped children, it is most often the almighty dollar standing between a child and their recovery. Creating new child protection laws and expanding old ones would definitely be a good thing. However, new and improved laws would be meaningless without proper funding for enforcement of those laws. Bucks... BIG BUCKS!

Law Enforcement training

Along with the need for serious funding, there is also a definite need for the special training of law enforcement personnel. By special, I literally mean specialists should be employed to train officers working the streets. Police officers need to be able to recognize subtle signs of abuse in a child and the officers should have the correct information as to the proper handling of any particular abuse situation. Officers should also be trained by these specialists to know how pedophiles manipulate their victims. A complete understanding of the pedophile's world is a tool that no police officer should be without. It is impossible to imagine how many children's lives could be saved, simply by making sure that a street cop is trained to recognize the subtle signs of child abuse.

All too often, child molesters are able to double-talk and smooth talk their way out of situations with an investigating street cop who knows something is wrong, but can't quite put his finger on it. If your average police officer on the streets were educated in the ways of the pedophile, in time, the public would realize a significant decline in sexual crimes against children. It is important for you to remember what I spoke of earlier. Pedophiles not only trade sex stories and photographs of children, they also exchange techniques and words of wisdom to elude prosecution.

Of course, the specialized training for police officers would not

229

only target pedophiles, but would educate officers in the recognizable signs of your average every day run-of-the-mill child abuse. Because of the lack of proper training, many telling signs of child abuse are missed or overlooked by police officers every day. I have no doubt that properly trained officers would more than likely end up dealing with some sort of child abuse on many of their shifts. Now, that would be helping a lot of kids.

Prosecutor's training

Now this might seem like a silly question to some of you, but I feel it deserves asking. How in the hell can anyone properly prosecute a child molester if they possess little to no knowledge of the perpetrator's thought process or lifestyle? Maybe that's why some prosecutors are willing to plea bargain with someone having no real remorse. Maybe some prosecutors are unaware of the fact that crimes of a sexual nature are the most repeated, especially the sexual crimes committed against children. Maybe that's why they are so often willing to cut them a deal.

Let me ask you another question. Do you believe that tremendous amounts of good would come from substantially increasing funding for prosecutions and the introduction of special education for prosecutors regarding pedophiliacs and their crimes? The obvious and only possible answer to that question is yes, so why hasn't it been done? Surely, I am not the only one asking this question, and positively I am not the first to make this suggestion. Common sense tells us that with proper funding prosecutors could spend more time on their cases. More funding would mean more prosecutors, which in turn, would mean lesser workloads, which would obviously allow prosecutors to do a better job. However, the pressure would still be on prosecutors faced with the overloaded situation in our jails and prisons, which will lend to the continuation of plea-bargaining. It all probably sounds like a vicious cycle to you by now, but I know there is an answer. Coupled with real funding for prosecutions is real training for prosecutors by real specialists. The same type of specialists employed to train law enforcement. It is my opinion that if prosecutors are properly educated as to who and what sexual offenders are, especially the pedophiles, they will be less apt to plea-bargain with them. If the plea-bargaining does continue due to pressures brought on prosecutors because of our overloaded penal system, I believe that the sentencing of sexual offenders will be harsher because of the human factor involved when prosecutors are educated as to the perpetrator's state of mind (possessing no real remorse), the family devastation caused by their actions and the forced redirection of a child's life. Oh, and we mustn't forget, the prosecutor will also now know that it is almost a guaranteed fact that when released, the offender will commit the same crime again… and again.

Now of course, this is all based on the hopes that it is a fallacy that attorneys are some sort of distant relative to the snake…as some jokes insinuate. Not that I would ever tell jokes like that, nor listen to jokes like that, or for that matter lend any credence to jokes of such a nature. Although, I do know it is within the capability and power of attorneys to be one of the greatest allies of abused children, or by choice, part of the problem.

Treatment for pedophiles

Judging from our previous discussions regarding the cure for pedo philes, you probably have a good idea where I stand on the subject. However, I am willing to back step to a small degree, admitting there is the exception to every rule. Therefore, attempting to keep that in mind, I will push on with treatment for pedophiles. [With argument.] There are many reasons why this subject troubles me so much. First and foremost, having dealt face to face with rapists, child slavers, pedophiles and sexual deviants of all sorts for so many years, listening to their reasoning when they're not under the gun, facing prosecution. Under those conditions I believe that I am hearing what pedophiliacs really, truly believe, and it ain't pretty.

Let's make a comparison: the comparison will be with pedophiles and smokers. Smokers these days are inundated with literally hundreds of reasons why they shouldn't smoke. They get it from medical releases, politicians, their favorite celebrities etc. For God's sake, even their children plead with them to quit. Yet, one off the wall positive remark, or what the smoker perceives as a positive remark, and they are reinforced. Nothing fazes them, not even the things they know to be true about the medical results of smoking and the damage it does to human body. Because they heard someone say, "I'm not going to quit smoking, because when you do your metabolism slows down, and that's why you gain so much weight" or "It causes unhealthy trauma to quit if you've been smoking for a long time." Worse yet, they saw it in print somewhere. That's it, it's like being hooked all over again, they got just what they needed, an excuse. Something, anything that says what they're doing's not so bad. Honest smokers will admit that what I'm saying is the truth!

It's kinda like that with pedophiles. Someone somewhere says or writes something. For example, a Temple University psychologist published a paper concluding that, "Long term effects of child sexual abuse are not as serious as many believe." BAM! There it is... the excuse, the reinforcement. Someone has come forward to say what they're doing's not so bad, and it's not just anybody saying it, but an educated person in a position of trust, which reaffirms what child molesters want to believe.

Many papers have been published on the subject of posttraumatic stress disorder (PTSD) related to child sexual abuse. The outcome of these studies is much like the scientific finding "for every action there is a reaction." This is the conclusion arrived at by many of the learned experts, for every negative of child sex, there is a positive. In other words, for the number of papers posted exploiting the ill effects of child sexual abuse, there are approximately as many papers published celebrating the positive effects that the child (victim) receives. There have even been published studies involving incest that refer to the child (victim) as "sexual partner." Study after study, has shown child sexual abuse to have devastating effects on the victims in many areas. These studies involve the research on literally thousands of victims. One study in particular queried over 25,000 victims. The findings revealed (PTSD) included depression, victim perpetrator cycles, sexual promiscuity, academic floundering and even suicide.

Evidently, past studies and obviously future studies that praised and will praise the value in child sexual abuse choose to ignore the uncountable cases ending in tragedy. Cases that have led to such severe depression that it in turn triggered sexual promiscuity, crime and even many, many suicides.

These proponents of child and adult sexual relationships have focused on the beneficial consequences of intimate experiences in a child's development. These particular researchers will argue, and continue to argue that sexual interest and behaviors of adults with children should be considered acceptable, normal, healthy expressions, which affirm a child's sense of personal worth, independence and sexual power. They have continued their argument claiming casual sexual encounters between adults and children, especially boys, "Pass by as an incident of little importance, just another variation of routine masturbation." Other experts' papers insist that it is important for children to learn that his or her "little body" can elicit strong passions in adults. Some researchers seem to spend a great deal of time pushing the idea that sex with children gives a child a special kind of companionship. This special companionship, according to them, provides the child with security and a feeling of protection that they do not receive from parents or other adults who choose not to have sex with children. Not surprising, these professors of psychology use the same old tired explanations for the negative consequences of sexual activity with children as the common child molester uses. They claim, as all pedophiles claim, that the negativity originates from the reactions of distressed parents and authority figures (society). Well, who else would speak out against such atrocities than good parents and other adults of moral character? DUH! The negativity stems from the act, not from individuals attempting to right a wrong! You'll have to excuse the sarcasm. I find it difficult containing myself when papers are published by people I am supposed to recognize as individuals possessing impeccable credentials. People, affiliated with universities releasing papers encouraging child adult sexual relationships. Researchers encouraging sex with children on the grounds, "Such diverse experiences are viewed as enablers, enabling children to construct their own sexuality from greater possibilities." Sorry, but I'm going to be a little sarcastic. Hell, it's the least I can do.

Why is it, whenever I read one of these psychology papers, I keep waiting to hear repulsive terminology like what I had to suffer through while interviewing convicted child rapists, "If she's old enough to bleed, she's old enough to butcher?"

Experts can conduct all of the research they wish. It's not complicated: When most children who are sexually abused suffer from one or more debilitating effects stemming from sexual victimization, one must realize that something is wrong. The debilitating effects I am referring to are many. Brace yourselves, here's the list.

*Numbing of general responsiveness
*Anxiety
*Sleep disruption
*Difficulty concentrating
*Avoidance
*Hyper-vigilance
*Dissociative states
*General diminished interest
*Irritability
*Feelings of worthlessness
*Decreased energy
*Psychomotor activity
*Difficulty thinking
*Touch repulsion
*Constant state of depression
*Despondent moodiness
*Loss of appetite
*Loss of weight
*A general sadness
*Feelings of guilt
*Sexual promiscuity
*Nagging thoughts of suicide, etc.

You don't have to be a rocket scientist or a psychologist to know that child sexual abuse harms children. Nevertheless, you experts keep going, complicate the hell out of it. With all of your research and experimentation, you always seem to avoid one ingredient. With your next research project, just for sh _ _ _ and giggles, try adding a little common sense. I know, I know, that wouldn't be very scientific. On the other hand, are you aware of the illogic of applying science to a situation consisting only of fragile sensitive emotions and frail innocence? Hang that on the wall beside your degrees!

The point I am trying to make with all of this is that many of the "experts claim" that no treatment is necessary, due to their findings indicating no damage has been done. When the "powers that are" go looking for direction from the experts, in order to determine whether to administer treatment or punishment, and the experts can't agree as to the right or wrong of the situation, nothing of real consequence is going to happen for a long, long time.

Don't get me wrong. I'm not trying to diminish or make light of the value of applying the art of science to society's problems. Researchers have made many important discoveries such as the discovery of links between animal abuse and child abuse. This finding is a very valuable tool, used as an early warning indicator of children who could possibly grow up to become child abusers.

There are also new drugs being tested and some are available for use now. One such drug, Gonadotropin, releases the hormone (GNRH). With monthly injections, it claims to be long- lasting and may rid sex offenders of deviant urges when combined with regular counseling. Another treatment favored by many experts and a large percentage of America's general population is chemical castration. Most, including many of the experts, believe this to be the answer. Some consider chemical castration to be the only answer to ending the crime of rape. This line of reasoning stems from the theory that rape is only about sex and having nothing to do with control and power. I, on the other hand, believe the act of rape is not just about sex nor is it just about control and power. I believe, primarily due to the fact that the act of rape almost always consists of intercourse or other sexual acts, natural or unnatural, by force that it is a combination of power, control and sex. One of Webster's dictionary definitions of rape is "sexual intercourse with a woman by a man without her consent and chiefly by force or deception." Now, once again, you can call me stupid, but that is a definite description of sex, control and power as parts contributing to the act of rape. It is obvious to me, as it should be to you, the key words here are force and deception. If rape were exclusively about control and power, sex would not almost always be a factor, yet without the power to control, whether it is by brute strength (power) or by deception (control), there is no rape.

Because I believe it is equally power, control and sex, not simply sex that factor into rape, and possibly are the major driving forces, I believe chemical castration will not curtail rape. As a matter of fact, I believe that sexual predators who fall victim to being castrated, and that's how they will see themselves, as victims, bitter victims, who will become angry and vengeful enough to begin committing even more heinous sex crimes. Since the perpetrators of sex crimes are twisted to begin with, and since they will still have their deviant

235

thoughts, with or without the desires, I fear the worst. The worst being that the evil urges that are still in them to control weaker others may come forth with a wrathful vengeance. Their crimes will become more heinous due to the lack of a sexually functioning penis. There are many documented cases of rapists, who, while committing the act of rape, were unable or incapable of erection and chose to use implements in place of their penis. When implements such as knives, gardening tools, baseball bats, fireplace pokers, etc. are chosen as their instrument of power, they use them, as has been documented. It isn't only about power, control and sex either. There is one more ingredient. It's nothing anyone can put his or her finger on, nothing tangible anyway. You would have to witness it first hand, as I have. Difficult to label, much less describe, I guess I would have to say it's evil committing evil for the sake of evil. There are those that believe there is only one way to deal with it, truly ridding society of it. No comment!

Not to be overlooked are the many treatment programs and centers geared to cure sex offenders. (Many opponents believe sex offender treatment centers are no more than safe havens for criminals.) Again, I wish to acknowledge the exception to my overall belief that there is no cure for sexual child molesters. In a nutshell, I believe the wonderfully dedicated people that work endlessly in the attempt to cure pedophiliacs are not only necessary, but important contributors to a society desperately trying to stabilize its morals. Keeping that in mind, I wish to point out that most treatments focus on denial, which I believe is real, but also a conscious diversion on behalf of the accused molester. I believe it is a conscious camouflage to what they really believe. They truly believe there's nothing wrong with adult-child sex. They also believe that trickery and intimidation are teaching methods. They believe these are teaching methods because they know that someday the child will realize he or she was intimidated and/or tricked into sexual acts, and they will be better for it. See, even I am capable of complicating things!

Here's a list of the most common denials used by child molesters:
*Outright denial "I didn't do it."
*Minimized denial "I only did it three times."
*Rationalization "I was only trying to teach her about sex."
*Pre act: Denial of planning "It just happened."
*Post act:

1) Denial of problem
2) Denial of difficulty in changing
3) Denial of possible relapse

Many programs and centers within the sex offender treatment industry do not believe denying offenders are treatable, and thus refuse to treat them. Even many of the experts argue over the possibility of successful treatment for sex offenders, especially pedophiles. Many programs will only accept offenders who openly admit their problem. Most child molesters will not admit that they have a problem, in the beginning of treatment anyway. However, there are those experts that specialize in sex offenders who deny. They are the experts who believe that some child sex offenders dissociate and truly do not remember their transgressions. They also believe that treatment (therapy) is not just about the offense, it is about the coping strategies and the emotional well being of the sex offender. They believe sex offenders who work at treatment become healthier people and therefore are less likely to repeat their crimes. These experts believe that through proper therapy, sex offenders will be able to make better choices. Treatment will enable them to recondition their arousal responses, thus altering their crime cycle, increase their self- esteem and gain a sexual understanding. It will help sex offenders get in touch with their own feelings and those of others, improving communication and developing better social skills. Sounds wonderful. The question is, are you willing to bet your child's safety and well being on it? Oh, by the way, these are many of the same people who believe alternative forms of apology from child molesters are acceptable. This acceptance also includes that child molesters do not have to admit to their crimes. Let's see if I've got this straight. Many experts won't treat pedophiles if they don't admit they have a problem, but most pedophiles won't admit to a problem at the beginning of their treatment. Alternative forms of apologies from pedophiles are accepted, even if they don't admit to having a problem. Okay, got it, that clears everything up. Personally, it sounds to me like most of those experts got their degrees from Disneyland.

I feel it necessary to again point out that quite a number of opponents and "real" experts consider many of these programs and treatment centers for sex offenders as nothing more than safe havens for pedophiles at the taxpayer's expense. I whole heartily agree. Considering the attitude and thought process of many of the psychologists affiliated with some treatment facilities, I believe we are right. I do know that pedophiles are on a never-ending search for groups, religions, cults, etc. for protection and acceptance. It looks like pedophiles not only found protection and acceptance in the form of some treatment centers, but also have highly educated and respected professionals willing to understand, and in some cases defend their twisted ways. I am going to get away from the facts for a moment because there are those good citizens among us that will depend on some group, or solely on prayer for the solution to this problem. So, lets take a quick look at the possibility of the answer to the problem coming from those folks. What is the answer? I hope you don't think that it falls into the category of who knows. Is it possible that we cannot differentiate between what is right and wrong regarding this subject because humanity itself has been twisted from nearly its beginnings? We try to be on the side of righteousness, as do all people of good moral character, no matter race, color, or creed. Some of you are still wondering and even hoping that the answer will come from scientists in the form of a pill, or from spiritual ones in the form of a prayer? Maybe it will come from cultist, though I don't think so since some cults encourage adult-child-sex, possibly atheists have the answer. Some say... probably the scientists and atheists, that the main difference between cults and religions is that "Cults tend to be suicidal and religions tend to be homicidal." I think they're joking, I hope they are joking. Although being a Christian, I don't know that I can argue it too much since our history is pretty much overwhelming in that direction. Do you think we can find the answer in religion and prayer? Possibly. However, there are many that fear the mixture of politics and religion. There is an answer and I'm going to give it to you again...soon. I've already talked about the scientist and medicine, from chemical castration to the development of a pill that may or may not work. We've also discussed the ongoing battles (total disagreement) between researchers and their opposing findings, so what's left? The atheist! It's hard to know where atheists may stand on the subject. Atheists don't believe in God, so it follows that they obviously don't believe in the reward of heaven, or the eternal damnation of hell. However, this does not mean that atheists are child molesters, or that they are not people of good moral fiber. However, it is important for you to know that when Russia fell to communism the government became God, which made a true communist a true atheist. Modern Russia and many of the countries that fell to communism have reached world-class moral lows, reporting epidemic proportions of child trafficking and sexual abuses against children, including generations of incest.

By now for sure you must be wondering where in the heck is this guy going with this? It's obvious, obvious to me anyway. We cannot continue to wait for the answers to the problem of what to do with the people among us that choose to sexually molest and heinously murder our children. We cannot continue looking for the answers to come to us, not from prayer and not from any "group", or "scientific" study. We need to pressure our own government now! We cannot afford to wait and hope and pray for the solution. We need to take action now! Our politicians need to begin applying good-old-fashion common sense when drafting laws and punishment, because neither pill nor prayer has protected our children so far. No, I'm not saying to stop praying, nor am I suggesting that scientist stop searching. Both of these things help in some ways. What I am saying is that each and every one of us need to "take action." We need to draw the line regarding those who prey on our children. A line needs to be drawn that says if you sexually abuse, or cause serious harm to a child, your own life, as you know it, will be altered forever. A line that not only says, leave our children alone, but is absolutely clear in that you will pay severely if you don't! No ifs, no ands, no buts, and for sure no plea-bargaining's! Does this mean life in prison without possibility of parole? Yes! Predator's walking-around permits should be permanently revoked! What should happen to predators that murder our children? Their breathing permits should be revoked! Also, because the crime was committed against a child, no President, Governor, Judge or bleeding heart groups should have the means, or power to overturn, or reverse, in any way, the sentencing and swift punishment.

This solution may repulse some, although I believe these individuals will be the same individuals that continuously fight for the rights of sexual offenders and child murderers. They are the same ones who will fight for a child killer's right to live, until he kills their children. I know that my solution will work, because it already works in many parts of the world. Many Third World countries do not have this problem. That's right, even countries we do not consider civilized do not have this problem. Why? Because they do not tolerate anyone doing anything to their children, not for one moment. And when it does happen, the punishment is just and swift.

Example:

The Los Angeles Times headline read, "West Bank/Colonel Sentenced to Death in Rape Case." Dated: Friday, February 26, 1999. Ahmed Abu Mustafa, a Palestinian Police Colonel, was found guilty of kidnapping and raping a five-year-old boy, on the prior Friday. The following week, the headline read, "Gaza Strip/Officer Executed for Kidnapping, Rape." Although one of the articles read that human rights activists raised concern that the punishment would be applied frequently, I could not substantiate why. I interviewed two high ranking officials and eight other residents of Khan Yunis, which is the town the boy was kidnapped from, and no one could recall a sex crime against a child in the last four decades. This is but one example from one country. However, the same attitude exists in many countries and they are not losing their children to predators in record numbers. Actually, they rarely ever lose a child to a sexual predator.

Does this mean that I am advocating the death penalty for kidnapping and/or sexual molestation of children? No. What I am advocating is life imprisonment without possibility of parole for that particular crime. However, I am advocating death to the persons that mutilate and murder our children. If the punishments do not match the crimes, the crimes will never stop. Will it be a good deterrent? I believe so, especially since it has already been proven to be in other countries, and almost as important, I believe it'll be a great punishment.

Will it really be a good deterrent? Let's put our heads together to do a little brainstorming... I've got it, I've got the answer: it's black and white, like I've always said, simple arithmetic. If sexual crimes are the most repetitive crimes and sexual predators are the most repetitive criminals, it makes perfect sense that if you execute the perpetrators, which turns them into fertilizer, you are obviously rendering them unable to recommit the same crime over and over... That's one hell of a deterrent, isn't it? Isn't it?

240

Uphill battles

Enacting new laws

This subject falls right into the lap of every parent. We cannot wait for each tragedy to strike before trying to enact new laws, as we have continually done in the past. We cannot rely on politicians to take the initiative, because most won't, as we have continually seen in the past. We cannot leave the burden of battle with Congress to a single griev- ing mother, as we have also continually done in the past. The enactment of child protection laws is not as difficult as some politi- cians would have you believe.

It is impossible for me to list all of the existing laws pertaining to the protection of children, or why and where they fall short. However, most do fail to fully accomplish their original intent. We do not neces- sarily need new laws, although it sure wouldn't hurt. It would be sufficient to simply amend, and in some cases extend, many of the old laws. Let's toss one possibility around. How about putting pressure on our politicians in congress into amending the child labor laws to en- compass child pornography? If child pornography were placed under the umbrella of the child labor laws, it would allow farther reaching federal involvement, including the broadening of punishments. An- other avenue would be parents and concerned adults insisting (Via Congress) that already enacted laws such as California's Megan's Law, be enforced nationwide.

Adding federally enforced regulations forbidding states to ignore, alter or modify child protection laws and/or to fall prey to special in- terpretation. States that have totally ignored, or gave special interpretation to child protection laws have already adapted new child protection laws after having buckled under federal pressure to do so. Included in these modified and special interpretations is the "Right to know" law regarding convicted sex offenders living in your commu- nity. The right to know law has suffered great dilution across the United States. This law falls short due to local and state authorities either watering it down or simply ignoring it. My fear is that the inter- pretation of the right to know law is left to some ill-informed officials and often falls under the implementation of the "Good old boys" club, which means, "Ain't nothin gonna happen."

Since we've entered the arena of possible change in existing laws and the enactment of new ones, let's include talking about "rights" for a moment, the possibility of changing one "right" in particular. I wish to bring it up, not so much because it's wrong or bad, but more because of how this particular "right" is viewed and abused by criminals. I am referring to criminals sentenced to death and their "right" to appeal … after appeal … after appeal. I am not saying an individual shouldn't have the "right" to an appeal. One (1) appeal. It's the thought process of criminals that should cause us to call for change. When interviewing many criminals, as I have, one makes numerous discoveries regarding their views on life in prison, including being sentenced to death. Many prefer a life in prison sentence to life on the streets, and they have a bazillion reasons (excuses) as to why they cannot make it on the outside. To some, prison is like "old home week", because many are reunited with relatives and friends. (Their words, not mine.)

"Life is good", exclaimed Hector, as he grinned.

What do you mean?

"I mean …life is good, three squares and the rent's paid man."

No worries, huh?

"Right, no worries man. Getta little smack, getta little blow…no worries."

And no rent, right?

"Right I told you, no worries."

Prisons can be a pretty rough place, what about your safety, you don't worry about that?

"No man, you got your rules."

What rules?

"My rules!" he shouted angrily, as he slammed his fist on the table and then began laughing.

What are your rules?

"Stay high and don't cry. That's my rules: stay high and don't cry."

Are you saying don't cry because you've been sentenced to death?

"No man, so they don't think you're a sissy man, you know a queer, you know what I mean?"

Yes.

"I mean, I only been here three years. I gotta long time to go before that, I can't think about that now, man."

How can you not think about that?

"Look man, it don't matter anyway. I'm forty-one. With appeals and all that shit, they ain't gonna get around to me until I'm probably sixty. That ain't death, that's just early retirement. Sixty's good enough for me."

The purpose of sharing part of this interview with you is to let you know, how many criminals think. Yes, you're right. That is only one interview, with one person. But through multiple interviews, I have discovered many convicts feel the same way. Sure, different words and different levels of intelligence, but in general, the same point of view.

You see, some people never look past tomorrow and some individuals are incapable of considering the future at all. Many criminals don't have much to look forward to on the outside anyway and some possess a mentality capable of murdering a child. When they are sentenced to death, they know, or soon learn, they usually have between ten and twenty years, and in some cases even longer, of worry-free living ahead of them. I thought that their attitudes could be due, in part anyway, to the fact that they have been caught and are incarcerated. Now realizing they have no choice but to look at the upside of their predicament. Wrong! I quickly discovered that my little theory was, almost without exception, totally incorrect. Criminals not yet caught that I've interviewed not only thought themselves too smart to be apprehended, they, in fact, possessed the same views as those captured and facing punishment. "So what if I am caught and put to sleep? I didn't want to live much past fifty anyway."

The above quote came in passing during an interview, with a thirty-three year old, after I had asked him if he was afraid of the death penalty. He had just revealed to me that he had killed two prostitutes in the past. My point here is, that he answered without a moment's thought, which makes me wonder, even if subconsciously, do they know it will be a long, long time before the actual punishment takes place, if it takes place at all. There's another consequence of our ever-changing laws pertaining to the cruelty of the death penalty. Eventually, each individual admitted fearing the death penalty, except two. I asked each, why did you kill if you're afraid of the death penalty? Some said that it was fear of the death penalty that kept them from killing sooner. Some said that they knew they needed to die, but didn't have the guts to do it themselves. Others said they didn't know. Possibly they belong in the group with no guts.

The constant advancement of a modern and morally humane society is important to its survival. However, when some less fortunate societies than our own have remained free of crimes against children due to their unwavering loyalty to the "old ways" of punishment, maybe we should reconsider, and avoid certain modern advancements. Could be a good thing!

Something I do know for sure. If being advanced, modern and morally humane means allowing people to live one moment longer than absolutely necessary, after being found guilty of raping and murdering a child, I would rather not be any of those things. It is obvious to me that any persons guilty of the crime of raping and murdering a child should be rushed in front of God for final judgment. For those respected others who don't believe in the hereafter, how's this: quickly swept into infinity, before they can harm another. That works for me as well!

I know, I know... because of statements like that and others I've made, many folks won't read my book. I understand. I understand that their child or a loved one close to them has not been savagely ravaged and brutally murdered. I understand that they are not a mother grief-stricken with the never-ending agony of her baby's senseless and appalling death. I understand that they have not been subjected to standing over a lifeless, once beautiful, little four-year-old girl in a morgue, twisted and mangled, and so heinously mutilated by torture, that she has been rendered unrecognizable, as I have.

The assisting mortician with twenty-four years experience told me that he had assumed upon receiving the little girl that she was the victim of a horrific auto accident, or even an airplane crash. No, he was mistaken. She was the victim of a pedophiliac, a child predator with two prior convictions for child molestation.

If you do not agree with my solution to the problem that's okay, but it should not stop you from reading the book that will help to keep your children safe from real harm.

Unlike many countries in this world, eventually America listens and America changes. When enough people complain and take action and keep complaining and keep taking action, truly America will change. All of our wishes and desires for change can become reality, if enough come forward, if enough speak out, if enough want change.

*I will be sharing how to make change with you, under the forth-coming headings: Responsible Parents and Your Government, Pending Legislation, Direction and Solutions and Letters to Your Government

Crime and punishment

Finally, our great nation seems to be evolving, albeit slowly, but evolving the same. It wasn't long ago that punishment for the crime of rape was all but non-existent, or so lenient it might as well have been non-existent. We are still plagued with judges passing sentences befit-ting little more than misdemeanors and shamefully, punishing some rapists and child molesters as though they had committed mere infrac-tions of the law, rather than serious crimes.

Which politicians will step forward and take the responsibility for allowing laws to exist that will sentence a man that kidnapped, raped, sodomized and ultimately mutilated a young girl, in the hopes of kill-ing her to conceal his identity, to a lousy six years in prison? Then only having to serve four of the six years before being released. Espe-cially considering, the same judge sentenced a man to ten years imprisonment for robbing a liquor store with a toy gun. When ques-tioned about the ten-year sentence, the previously avoiding and reluctant judge finally replied, "It was his second offense for robbery. Some people never learn. If you aren't tough on them, they'll just keep coming back." The convicted man did have a prior offence, the bur-glary of a Goodwill drop-off container. This puts me in mind of old stories we've always taken lightly, like the one about the man impris-oned for stealing a loaf of bread to feed his family. How about this one, a mother that stole milk for her baby and sentenced to two years in prison. Since my research, I am not so sure the old stories aren't true stories. Is this a sign of where our society truly places its values? Is it about the dollar and not the people, not the children?

Well, this may come as a big surprise to some folks, but it's been that way since long before law enforcement became big business. That's right, big business. In the past it was mostly attitude, but today it's mostly money, big money. Many law enforcement agencies have new and unspoken objectives, which seem to be accompanied with disturbing new attitudes. Their new objective is to spend less time on what they consider less important, non-profitable crimes and focus on crimes that pay, pay law enforcement that is. Which makes one wonder about another old saying, "Crime doesn't pay." It may not pay criminals, but some police agencies seem to be doing okay by it. I touched on this earlier in the book and I want to delve just a little deeper. Why, you ask? And again, I am glad you are so inquisitive. I am informing you of this law enforcement activity because those that serve and protect us are also capitalizing on us and often misusing and misdirecting their energies and our tax dollars, energy and tax dollars that would seriously help to protect our children.

I know that you and I consider child molestation and our children being murdered crimes of the century, which need desperately to be put in check. So, if the "Rico Act", or as I call it "USA" (Unfair Shakedown Act) is absolutely necessary to our policing agencies survival and ability to remain state of the art, I guess we will have to live with it. However, I believe that our politicians need to know that we would like to see a portion of the free money directed to keeping our children safe. Some of the profits from forfeitures should be used to arrest and prosecute child pornographers, instead of buying and building a sheriff's equestrian center, which I know has been done in the past." Protect and Serve," that up!

As you can see, there are many concerns to be addressed, and the best way to do it is by jumping right in, getting involved, making your presence known. How do I do that? I'm happy ya asked. It's simple. We've got to get off your butts, gather our friends and start showing up in the courtrooms across the nation. Make your presence known to the judges. You accomplish that by informing the bailiffs as to the objective of your presence. You can count on the bailiff informing the judge. You can count on the judge knowing that you are scrutinizing his or her sentencing. You can also inform your local newspaper. All else will follow, especially when you begin complaining about certain judges and their sentencing habits. The judge will know that if he or she passes a light sentence on a criminal that obviously deserves a much harsher sentence, you'll go straight to your local newspaper, complaining of his failure to serve your community. Furthermore, he knows his possibility of reelection will dwindle rapidly.

If your personal appearance is not possible, organize senior citizens to go in your place. Seniors seem to enjoy being a pain in the ass. Most judges and politicians have great respect for senior citizens, well aware of the fact that most senior citizens actually vote, they don't just talk about it. They also fear the possibility of becoming the target of a senior with nothing but time on his or her hands. Seriously, if seniors truly have something worth saying, look out! A senior citizen, when pointed in the right direction, is one hell of a weapon, not to mention relentless. So, start planning the carpooling, or organize bus scheduling, if necessary. Do whatever needs to be done to form and organize your groups. Begin contacting your politicians at every level regarding more specialized police officers and prosecutors, more attention and funding to protect our children. The sooner you get busy, the sooner you'll see change.

Keep moving, you're on a roll. You've got the idea and the knowledge now. Remember to never lose sight of your objectives: new and better laws, and the need for the punishment to fit the crime. Most of society not only agrees with you, but also cries out for it.

Chapter 9

STATISTICS

A rguably, it is one of the most boring subjects known to man
...and woman. I agree, it could be extremely boring, but I'm
not going to let that happen. How can I do that, you ask? You're just
full of questions and I'm glad you are. I am going to make this important topic interesting to you by exposing many statistics for the sham
and shame that they really are. To give you an idea of what I'm talking
about, take a gander at this stuff.

Child Protective Services (CPS), which is a public social service
organization, gathered and combined their statistics regarding child
abuse nationwide. Those statistics determined that fifteen (15) children
per one thousand (1,000) were victims of abuse. In contradiction, statistics during the same time period from the National Incidence Study
(NIS-3), which gathers their statistical data from a combined effort of
the National Child Abuse and Neglect Data System (NCANDS), found
the figure to be more like forty-two (42) abused children per one thousand (1,000). Since both figures are horrifying, but so far apart, it
would be nice to know which is correct. Here's another one. This
one's even more pitiful, or to be more accurate, outrageous. A released
Justice Department statistic claimed that four hundred sixty-eight
thousand seven hundred (468,700) children are missing in the United
States. The FBI statistics covering the same period say it was eight
hundred thousand (800,000) missing children. Will someone please
tell me how two federally funded agencies, held in such high esteem,
could release statistics regarding the same subject, during the same
time period and be so completely screwed up (far apart)? There are
those who have suggested to me that the key words here are Federally

funded agencies, which quite often translates to over-done and done-over. It would be funny if it weren't such a seriously tragic subject. My God, to think we actually depend on these folks.

What is the purpose of statistics?

A condensed explanation of the purpose of statistics is that the findings act as a barometer, letting us (the public) and our government know where we stand on particular subjects. In addition, statistics let us know what areas we may need to focus on, pointing out specific situations or problems. Along with pointing out society's strong and weak points, statistics give our government an idea of where we rank globally. When it comes to how we compare to other countries, we may be showing a ranking better then we should, due to the range (choices) of numbers our government has to choose from. This also could be funny, if it weren't for the possibility that if honest numbers were posted, we might find ourselves in the embarrassing position of trailing a third world country or two in some areas. I believe, as many other experts do, that we are trailing in some very important and inexcusable areas, which are kept hidden from the general population. [That's you and me.]

The truth behind statistics

To start with, many statistics are unreliable due to a host of contributing factors. Major factors leading to their inaccuracy, in many cases, are the original guidelines. This involves what the accepted perimeters of the particular research are expanded or narrowed to. For example, a major city commissioned a research study regarding documented cases of incest within the city's jurisdiction for that year, for the purpose of statistics. It seems the expert in charge of gathering the statistics only considered it to be incest if the relative lived in the immediate household. I have no intention of spelling out the city's name for you, because divulging the name of the city would serve no positive purpose and could possibly cause major embarrassment, which I would never do to any city intentionally. However, everyone likes to be congratulated for what is believed to be a job well done, especially politicians and cities. So won't you join with me, and give a great big "GOOD ON YOU, Los Angeles" for refusing to waste taxpayer's money and accepting the research results upon their completion. It's great to know we continue to keep real thinkers in high places! I was unable to ascertain whether those particular statistics were released or not. Maybe there is hope. Maybe someone was smart enough to bury them.

This may be the explanation as to why many politicians disregard statistics, considering most statistics to be mere opinions. Then again, it might be because a particular statistic may not support the politician's platform or point of view. On top of that, many politicians consider statistics a double-edged sword and extremely risky. Their reasoning is simple. If statistics show what appear to be major problems in delicate areas, sexually abused or missing children for example, some politicians fear the population will begin believing tax dollars are going to the wrong projects. Oh, and God forbid, politicians don't want the citizenry to think they aren't doing a good job.

Another reason making it difficult to put stock in statistics is police reports. Not all police reports. The problems are centered mainly, but not exclusively, in small town police reporting. Generally, the problem stems from areas deprived of a budget for proper training, especially in the area of report writing. For example, it is not uncommon for a child to be kidnapped from a playground, taken to a secluded area, sexually molested and then released. The reporting officer may only address the child molestation, overlooking the crime of kidnap, or visa versa. Consequently, for the purpose of statistic documentation, it is categorized as molestation only. The same is true of a kidnapping that ends with the child being murdered. Often, the final act committed during the commission of a crime is so overwhelming that it affects thorough report writing and ultimately the categorization of the total combination of the crimes involved. This, in turn, produces inaccurate, or incomplete statistics. This is particularly prevalent in areas where the residents, including the reporting police officers, are severely shocked and shaken by the crime. Quite often, this is due to the general lack of any crime in some communities, much less crimes of a particularly brutal magnitude.

A frightening accusation has been brought to my attention, although to my knowledge, it is not yet substantiated with solid proof. It involves the altering and/or deletion of statistics for self-serving purposes. It has been revealed to me by an individual who holds a position where he would have access to such knowledge, if true. At the informant's request, and my promise, they shall remain anonymous. I was informed that in some cases statistics are altered in order to cancel and/or redirect resources ($$$) allocated for certain projects. If true, this would explain many problems existing in our society, rapidly getting out of control, when in fact, adequate funding would obviously stabilize the situation. How can our politicians be willing to allocate funding for projects as ridiculous as murals on walls beneath freeway underpasses or midnight basketball? Especially when it is an obvious attempt (experiment) to appease and entertain individuals and special groups in order to avoid possible problems, when real problems are compounding daily. I'm referring to serious problems, life-altering and life-threatening problems, like American children being kidnapped and sold into sexual slavery in foreign countries. Why is this horrifying act going unchecked? Is it because it hasn't been brought to the attention of our government, or is it because funding has been redirected? Of the two choices, it would have to be the latter, because I, and many others like me have spent a great deal of time bringing it to the attention of our government. Granted, there may be other reasons for this atrocity to continue going unchecked, but whatever they are, it's a sad commentary on our very existence, isn't it? I plan to continue investigating the allegation.

Law enforcement statistics

In spite of my previous reference to law enforcement, being part of the problem when it comes to national statistics, they are also by far the most accurate reporting agencies when it comes to statistics. Figure that one out. I'm aware that this definitely sounds like a contradiction. Allow me to explain. I am now referring to all of law enforcement on an average, which of course includes the big cities, which in turn brings all agencies batting averages way up. While lesser-trained departments affect certain statistical numbers, combined they are the most accurate of all released statistics.

The main reason accounting for their accuracy is there is no need for them to alter counts to show the need for more funding. Police department problems are real and, in some cases, desperate. In addition to that, I would like to believe that they wouldn't alter counts because of little things like honor and integrity, which are both words used in every law enforcement oath I've personally observed. When law enforcement statistics are incorrect, it's most often due to mistakes rather than skullduggery. Here's an example of law enforcement's honesty in reporting according to the U.S. National Institute of Justice. Ninety four percent (94%) of sheriffs, ninety one percent (91%) of police chiefs and ninety two percent (92%) of prosecutors claim that child abuse, which includes abductions and sexual assaults, has become the cause of overwhelming workloads. Now those are some honest statistics!

An alarm should go off in our heads when government statistics don't coincide with reputable news reporting agencies like these:
- CNN Special Report
"Child molestation is a national crisis"
- Time Magazine
"One in 42 children will become a missing child."
- Newsweek Magazine
"Abduction was the number one topic among third graders."
- NBC's Crusaders
"The one thing you can count on: there is a child molester watching."

Are these news releases accurate, or mere journalistic sensationalism? You be the judge. Here are some enormously conservative findings released by the U.S. Department of Justice. These numbers are an average of any given year.

- Three hundred fifty four thousand (354,000) children are abducted by family members.

- One hundred fourteen thousand six hundred (114,600) attempted abductions of children by non-family members.

- Four thousand six hundred (4,600) actual abductions of children by non-family members that are reported to police.

- Three hundred (300) abductions of children by non-family members where the child was taken for a long period, was never found or was murdered.

- In Seventy four percent (74%) of the abductions the victims were female.

- Sixty two percent (62%) of the perpetrators were strangers to the victims and their family.

- Eighty seven percent (87%) of the cases involved the use of force.

- Eight percent (8%) of the cases involved a ransom demand.

Even if these numbers weren't way below the mark, that's too many children in trouble.

When government statistics contradict themselves and their numbers don't come close to matching independent studies, there must be a reason. Actually, there are many reasons and I'll hit on a few of them for you in this chapter. Let's take a brief look at law enforcement first one more time.

The annual problem as previously mentioned facing law enforcement today is, since the politicians have realized the lucrative business of forfeiture, they have seen to it that some, actually many, areas of funding are cut drastically. Our politicians have decided that many areas of law enforcement can support themselves. Consequently, some law enforcement agencies feel they have no choice but to enforce the "Rico Act."

Consequently, even though law enforcement statistics seem to be the most dependable, they are as some politicians have described, a double-edged sword, and it's hacking away at us. The need for more funding means the more pressure on agencies to seize private property. It should bother you as it does me, that across this great nation uncountable wealth [free money] is ending up in government coffers and there is never adequate funding for Child Protection Services. If only a small percentage of forfeiture profits were earmarked for child safety, imagine how many children could be saved.

City, County and State statistics

Quite often it is the cities and counties, and occasionally some states, which also suffer from statistics. While overall the nation looks good according to statistics, some cities, counties and even some states are in real trouble, in some areas. These troubled areas remain a problem, due in particular, to some of our politicians choosing to recognize our nation's standing, above all else and maintaining an attitude of "Overall we look pretty good, we must be doing something right." This distorted interpretation allows them the latitude to encourage the funding of their "favorite projects" which may include corporations politicians may be indebted to. This also allows them to retain what they believe is a clear conscience. A little distorted, wouldn't you agree?

During a discussion with a California senator on the subject, he

253

constantly referred to "The big picture." I wasn't seeing "The big picture." I think I got the picture. This sounds like their version of the old "Trickle down affect", because that's what the state tells the counties and the counties tell the cities, "your not seeing the big picture." It sounds a little more to me like that other old saying, something about sh _ _ rolls down hill. Something sure stinks!

The truth is, cities, counties and frequently some states are at the mercy of "THE BIG PICTURE." Funding needed for important local, and even selective national projects, often takes a back seat when statistics make the federal picture look good. It's a shame that some of our politicians take advantage of an overall good national standing by using it as an excuse not to release funds to what can only be described as truly desperate areas of concern.

Unfortunately, our politicians have not only created a situation wherein law enforcement agencies are held responsible for much of their own funding, but at the same time they have created new crimes, and sadly a new breed of gangster. Maybe the politicians are right, labeling statistics as a double-edged sword, but for the wrong reasons.

The true crime here is not just that some law enforcement agencies are running amuck, grabbing anything and everything they feel they can get away with in the name of the law. Nor is it the politicians, not realizing they've made a horrendous mistake, but rather deciding it's all okay, considering it's for the greater good. The true crime in all of this is what is happening to children around the world, including American children. They are being forced here and in foreign countries to live in terror, suffering from the daily mental and physical pains of having been kidnapped and brutalized into sexual acts with adults. The true crime here is that there is no funding for them, so while those children are hoping and waiting to be saved, the truth is, nobody's coming.

I want to share a personal statistic with you! While attempting to raise funding for our tax-deductible charity in order to recover kidnapped children, my wife Christine and I were invited by Trinity Broadcasting to speak and be interviewed by Hal Lindsey and his wife Kim, on their television show. We also spoke on several other platforms, including the Voice of Americanism radio program five times and to many other shows and special groups on numerous occasions. These appearances resulted in donations so minimal it became economically impossible to continue. Allow me to share with you one example of our success or lack of. Christine and I were invited to speak at a prominent club's breakfast in an affluent area. The name of the club escapes me at the moment, but it's just as well, I wouldn't want to embarrass them. We had high expectations due to the club's past history of generosity. The week prior to our presentation, they raised six thousand dollars in twenty minutes for a new little league team. Anyway, we gave our presentation and showed the terrifying proof, including photographs of portions of actual recoveries. We even shared a tape-recorded conversation involving a grandmother that couldn't thank us enough for returning her only grandchild safely back home to her.

The breakfast and presentation seemed to be a great success. We received a standing ovation and people hugged us. Some were in tears. Then someone asked the inevitable question, "Do you ever have to hurt anyone, in order to bring a child back?" There it was. We knew sooner or later someone would ask that question, in one form or another. They always do. No matter how we answer it, it seems to be the deal breaker. I have a stock answer for that particular question, which is, "Once we have the child in our custody, we do whatever is necessary to see to it that no more harm comes to that child." People don't like to hear that. I guess it's the possibility of someone getting hurt that frightens folks, even if it's the sex-propelled creeps that are torturing children. Consequently, even with a standing ovation, hugs and all the tears in the world, we didn't get ten cents toward a recovery. Since this has become an all too frequent response to our cause, it has become our personal statistic. I hope that the example didn't sound like I'm whining. I hope I sounded angry.

National and international statistics

Nationwide, the combined statistics of the Child Protective Service Agencies reported in 1996 that almost one million (1,000,000) children were identified as substantiated victims of child abuse. Up eighteen percent (18%) from the last reported survey taken in 1990. Since 1996, they have risen even more substantially. I am not going to share the latest numbers with you because they are so far off [Incorrect, Wrong, Low, Misguiding, Etc.] that they are shamefully embarrassing. For those who might wish to place the blame of such outrageously high numbers on minorities, guess again. The fact is, we should all be ashamed, and we should all do something about it!

Since most Third World countries don't keep child abuse statistics, it is impossible to actually know where we rank internationally. Although we do know two things. First, because of the poverty and atrocities occurring throughout the continents of Africa and South America, our numbers undoubtedly look very good. Second, due to some of our politicians' ability to produce pleasing, or what appear to be pleasing, numbers for posting, we look even better. There will never be a clear picture regarding abused and kidnapped children, nationally or internationally, as long as there are countries that don't care enough about the children to investigate. Nor will we know the truth in the United States as long as we continue the "Smells good, looks good, so it must be good" policy. There is no excuse for investigating what is happening to our children once every four years and then juggling the count so we look better than other countries than we actually are. Of course, other countries are doing the same thing. The ridiculousness of it is that everyone knows everyone is doing it. How far has civilization come, when looking good is more important than being good? At what price does doing wrong in order to look right come? Maybe our politicians can't help themselves. Maybe it's because they've lied to make themselves look good for so long. Maybe it's the game; maybe they just can't stop playing the game no matter who pays the price, even if we pay with our children's lives. Is it possible that our leaders have lost sight of what is most important? Since some politicians have proven themselves capable of abusing power under the guise of politics, losing sight of truly important objectives is entirely feasible. It's feasible because we live in a society that tolerates the release of statistics, which claim that approximately one thousand seventy seven (1,077) child maltreatment fatalities occurred in the fifty states including the District of Columbia in 1996. Based on data from a subset of states, children younger than four years accounted for seventy six percent (76%) of the fatalities. Another independent study including the same geography and time-period concluded that over two thousand children died and eighty four percent (84%) were under the age of three years. It's one thing to tolerate conflicting statistics, no matter how ridiculous. However, it is totally inconceivable that we would tolerate the attempt to hide the facts by issuing bogus statistics, in order to avoid necessary and morally obligated funding. Which means, that in some degree, our politicians are basically leaving the torture and murdering of innocent children to heal itself. Answer me this, who is most guilty, the individual that knowingly commits the crime or the individual that knowingly allows it? Sure, the politicians are going to rant and rave about how they pour millions into the prevention of child abuse. Sorry, it doesn't cut it, not when the problem not only persists, but is rapidly screaming out of control. It doesn't cut it when unbelievable amounts of money, millions on top of millions are wasted on totally ridiculous projects every day in the United States. It's not enough. It's especially not enough when you consider the murder of children in the United States is four times that of any other country in the world. And that study excludes homicides that involve firearms. Now, how's that for a statistic? And it is an accurate statistic!

Politicians will only do what they feel they can get away with! Maybe they feel they can get away with this due to our society's rapid degeneration. For example, our society is on the verge of accepting adult-child sex, choosing to call it "alternative lifestyles." When adult-child- sex becomes an "alternative lifestyle" we might as well abolish all of our child sexual abuse laws, and while we're sticking pretty labels on ugly things, let's throw in bestiality and necrophilia. Maybe the politicians can continue to get away with it.

Independent statistics attempt to get the truth and release it to the public. However, many of those studies seem to be frequently discarded in favor of Federally commissioned statistics.

I am going to wrap up this politically warped and disgraceful subject with a few very important statistics you can believe.

1) Over sixty percent (60%) of convicted sex offenders are on parole or probation. That figure may explain why, in one year, 1988, there were one hundred fourteen thousand six hundred (114,600) attempted kidnappings by non-family members reported. The key word here is reported and since studies have shown most abduction attempts go unreported, these figures are merely the tip of the iceberg.

2) It is estimated that there are over 60 million survivors of childhood sexual abuse in America today. However, many other renowned experts claim the numbers surpass 100 million. According to a Gallup Poll, in 1995 alone, one million three hundred thousand (1,300,000)

257

children were sexually assaulted. The highly respected Mr. John Walsh, co-creator and host of television's "America's Most Wanted", who lost his son Adam to a predator, testified before Congress, stating more than one million five hundred thousand (1,500,000) children are abducted annually. So, it is obvious to me that this is a national crisis of apocalyptic proportions!

3) Reported cases of child sexual abuse reached epidemic proportions, with a reported three hundred twenty two percent (322%) increase from 1980 to 1990. [Reported cases only] The latest numbers would totally freak you out.

4) The typical child sex offender will molest a reported average of one hundred seventeen (117) children. However, again most molestation victims do not report the offence.

5) Approximately ninety-five percent (95%) of the victims know their perpetrators.

6) Approximately ninety-five percent (95%) of teenage prostitutes have been victims of child sexual abuse.

7) Approximately thirty-one percent (31%) of women in prison today acknowledged having been sexually abused as children.

8) Reliable studies have shown that children often fail to report sexual abuse because of the fear that disclosure will bring consequences even worse than being victimized again. The victim may fear consequences from their own family, and may even feel guilty for the consequences to the perpetrator. The victim is inevitably in fear of subsequent retaliatory actions from the perpetrator, since most perpetrators threaten their victims with some form of punishment. It is important to remember that many, if not most, victims feel "Something is wrong with me." Their thoughts somehow being twisted into the belief that the abuse was their fault.

9) In addition to "sexual guilt" there are several other types of guilt associated with sexual abuse. These other guilt patterns include feeling different from their peers, harboring vengeful and angry feelings toward both parents. Also, added to that are feelings of responsibility for the abuse coupled with emotional feelings regarding the reporting of the sexual abuse. The fear of disruption to the family and the appearance of disloyalty are strong deterrents. Any one of these feelings of guilt could outweigh the decision on the part of the victim to report the crime, resulting in the secret remaining intact and undisclosed forever.

10) A study of over six hundred cases of sexual abuse indicated that seventy-nine percent (79%) of the children in the study initially denied sexual abuse, or were tentative in disclosing it. Of the children that did disclose, approximately three-quarters disclosed accidentally. Although, of those who disclosed, twenty-two percent (22%) later recanted their statements.

11) Studies have proven that children with disabilities are as much as ten times more likely to be sexually abused than their non-disabled peers.

12) Long-term effects of child sexual abuse include fear, anxiety, depression, anger, hostility, inappropriate sexual behavior, poor self-esteem, difficulty with close relationships and a tendency toward substance abuse. I've repeated this as to ingrain it in your memory so you will recognize the signs, if necessary.

13) Clinical findings of adult victims of child sexual abuse include problems in interpersonal relationships associated with an underlying mistrust. Generally, adult victims of incest have a severely strained relationship with one or both of their parents that is marked by feelings of mistrust, fear, ambivalence, hatred, and betrayal. These feelings may also extend to all other family members.

14) Guilt has been universally proven the weightiest factor in child victims of sexual abuse. The most difficult guilt for many victims to overcome is the "sexual guilt," which is the guilt derived from sexual pleasure experienced by the victim. These feelings of "sexual guilt", in turn, cause many victims emotional confusion, which helps explain their frequent failure to disclose their abuse and their abuser.

*Because it felt good does not mean you should feel guilty, nor does it mean that it was your fault!

Sexuality cannot simply be regarded as a part of the self, limited to the genitals and biological aspects of reproduction, nor should it be limited to discrete behaviors. Sexuality is most properly described and understood as one of a multitude of components of the total personality, which affect one's concept of self-esteem and personal identity. When that particular component is attacked, one's self-perception is altered, and sometimes even destroyed. This is especially true when the victim is an innocent child.

*I hope that I took the boredom out of boring statistics for you.

Chapter 10

ADVOCACY GROUPS

Who are they?

Undoubtedly the easiest question to answer I've had all week. Advocacy groups are created and staffed by people who care. People who care enough to actually do something that benefits all of us. They are, in my opinion, the stuff America is made of! I would like to add that totally dedicated individuals man advocacy groups, but I can't. Not that they are not totally dedicated, but that they are mostly created by and staffed by women, making it difficult for me to use the vernacular "man." It is mostly mothers, wives, grandmothers, sisters and daughters doing the lion's share. Is it simply because the men are too busy bringing home the bacon, making it impossible for them to get involved? I don't think so. That excuse may work for a few, but very few. So why is it that mainly women are doing something we should all be doing? Overseeing the security of their children many believe should be a man's job and a father's duty. Maybe men don't get involved for fear of failure. Maybe men feel if a child is lost, they've failed to do their duty as the protector of their children. Or maybe they're just tough guys, you know the ones, they're the guys that spout off about how they will tear the head off anyone that comes close to their kid. Well tough guy, they're coming close to a lot of kids, so close that some of the kids are dying. So get involved and help make sure that it doesn't happen to your kid. It's really not that hard. Just get off your ass and start doing whatever you can to help the women protect our children. All of our children. Actually do something about the child predators now, rather than spouting off about what you'll do if and when.

Besides, what makes you think you're going to be around to do whatever it is that you say you're going to do if or when a predator stalks your child? What makes you believe you're going to have the chance? Or maybe you think you're going to know who attacked your child. Maybe you believe your child will be able to point him out for you. Tell me. Please enlighten everyone, as to what makes you believe your child will be alive to point him out for you? Remember what I said earlier about how many times I have heard fathers crying out, "I should have been there, if only I had been there." You can be there. You can be there for everyone's children. There is only one way to successfully fight child kidnappers, molesters and murderers, and that is to strike first, before they get to yours or anyone else's children.

If you will remember, I talked earlier in the book about the lack of male involvement in this war. Please forgive me for my repetition. However, I want you to savor this apology, because it's probably the last one you're going to get. I feel that it is very necessary to repeat the most important issues, especially the lack of male involvement in at least attempting to thwart these crimes against humanity. It is not merely important for fathers to do their part in fulfilling their obligation to protect children, it has now become a life and death necessity. If you read this book, yet fail to act on the information and warnings in it and tragedy strikes your child, you will have failed your child. And you will have failed your family. Am I telling you that you have to do everything I say in this book? No, but don't you think you should do something? Don't you believe that your children deserve for you to do as much as you can to keep them safe? Because your reading this book, I know that you are not one of those guys that shoots off his mouth about what he would do, whenever the subject comes up, your already doing something. It's time for fathers to be the father their children think they are! It's time to add your own personal knowledge and common sense to what I've given you and make sure your children are safe. It's time to add your strength to the strong women that have taken up this fight and take control of all children's safety.

Man's desire for battle runs so deep that when there is no battle, they substitute. They substitute with sports, sometimes even dangerous sports, and if actual participation isn't possible, they immerse themselves into viewing and make believe. Well men, I've got good news for you, there is a battle out there you can participate in. Here is a real

261

battle for real men, a battle with all the ingredients. A battle for high stakes, with life and death in the balance. And you don't even have to go off and fight on foreign soil. Although, as I've said before, you do have to get off your ass and pull your head out of that make believe modern-day battlefield called sports. You are cordially invited to join us in our real war against evil individuals attempting to rip our children from our lives. [Wannabes need not apply.] As if we don't have enough to do, it would make things so much easier if we could simply focus on the bad guys and not have to deal with generating male interest, yes, interest. What would you call it: "Bringing it to their attention?" You will never be able to convince me that men don't see and hear about the tragedies involving children almost daily on the news like the rest of us. I hope no one out there is going to try to tell me that whatever it is that stirs women into action is not available to men. As in most things we try to do regarding the travesty befalling our children, there are unnecessary and often ridiculous detours that we have to spend precious time on, like attempting to enlist the aid of men. Am I the only one embarrassed by what basically has become pleading for men to get involved? Have I said enough? Yeah. Okay, I probably won't bring it up again.

In case I haven't answered the question, who are they, to your satisfaction, they are the   extremely dedicated people that want to help you. Their organizations exist to help prevent your child from being kidnapped or sexually molested and possibly murdered. They will do everything within their power to help you recover a missing child. They exist to do everything that needs to be done, in order to wipe the child molesters and kidnapping murderers of children from our society, and they need a few good men. Damn. I said I probably wasn't going to mention that again.

What do they do?

With what would be very little investigation on your part, you will quickly discover that "Child Advocacy Groups" do everything from allocating search-and-rescue funds to supplying zip codes of areas most inundated with convicted sex offenders. In case you didn't get that, they cover everything from A to Z. If you need help, or want to help, or simply want to know what's really going on, they can help you.

Many, if not most, of the child advocacy groups specialize. For example, one group may offer information only, while another may offer state-of-the-art identification, such as microchip implants. Yeah I know, chip implants do sound like "1984" and "Big Brother" watching us all over again.

Think about it for a second. We are having microchips placed in our cars and even in our pets, in order to quickly locate and recover them, if lost or stolen. The answer to this concern is obvious, especially, after having interviewed many mothers of missing children. Without exception, mothers who have suffered the loss of their child unanimously agreed, micro-chipping children is one hell of a good idea. I guess you would have to go through that particular agony to understand. My God, look at what I just said, "Maybe you would have to go through it to understand." Have I become so desensitized and callous, or have child molesters forced us into a state of mind where a statement like that is now acceptable? Please forgive me. I pray you never have to go through that agony in order to understand. To those parents that may be interested, microchips are available to those who wish to do everything possible to protect their children. Albeit another personal call. It may assist you in your thought process to know that many kidnap victims are held captive within a mile or two of their own home and sometimes they are imprisoned as close as right next door.

Aside from surgically placed implants, child advocacy groups will help you with safety and prevention tips, kids dealing with strangers, and inscribed orthodontic or dental codes. The list of aid that advocacy groups provide seems endless, including supplying you with safety manuals and child safety videos. They will help locate and assist exploited children and also locate help services for you. Advocacy groups are doing a magnificent job alerting the public as to the latest information regarding sexual predators. There are also groups, which specialize in helping families through the loss of a child to a predator. There is even an advocacy group, which furnishes bloodhounds to assist in the search for missing children. Last but not least, a group exists that specializes in developing, producing, and broadcasting television programming to help locate missing children. This advocacy group is especially important because they understand the importance of the time factor. As I have previously explained, it is often difficult to get law enforcement to act immediately or even in a reasonable amount of time. In some jurisdictions, police will not consider a person missing for twenty-four hours. However, in fairness, that policy is rapidly changing, or is set aside nowadays by many police departments, although they still make decisions based on the missing child's age and past history, which to a degree is understandable. However, as I just mentioned, that particular policy is rapidly changing nationwide due to the fact that the chance of recovering a kidnapped child dwindles severely within a couple of hours after the abduction. Here is where "Missing Kids International, Inc." comes in. They are prepared to get that child on television almost immediately. Quality stuff. These folks know what works best regarding what people will listen to and what will catch the general public's eye. But most important, what people will remember.

Aside from all I've mentioned and a lot I haven't, I want you to know that these wonderful people who have created and are staffing child advocacy groups truly care and do want to help, if the need arises.

[Because a child advocacy group is not mentioned in my book, I am not inferring any to be less worthy of your attention. All advocacy groups have something good to offer, you must decide which will serve your situation best.]

Are advocacy groups successful?

There is no possible way to measure their entire success. I can tell you about the children recovered with the help of their efforts, but how can anyone measure the success derived from a constant flow of information regarding children's safety, supplied to parents and teachers everywhere, every day? How can anyone possibly measure the good that comes from the millions of pages of child safety literature and missing children posters supplied and distributed by advocacy groups, which they insure, are distributed across this nation?

Answer me this, is it possible that a child did not put itself at risk because of what he, or she learned regarding how to stay safe from a video supplied by a child advocacy group? Possibly it was a quality video that was specifically formulated to capture the attention and curiosity of children. Maybe it was the book or video that so many children are learning from regarding the rules of safety and strangers. It is a known fact that the very best teaching and learning technique employed today, especially, when it comes to kids, is the use of audio and visual tools. Guess what I'm trying to say is, hell yes they're successful. Then again, I would consider them extremely successful if after having spent millions of dollars they saved only one child. But that's me.

Here are a couple facts you can take to the bank. Child advocacy groups will always be there for you in a time of family crisis and it is the child advocacy groups that never stop looking for a missing child. I know this from first-hand experience. One child advocacy group was physically searching for a kidnapped little California girl eight years after her abduction. I know that this group was still physically searching for the child eight years later, because I participated in the search. So the next time you're considering a donation to a charity, I want you to please consider these wonderful advocacy groups.

Without driving you crazy with numbers and statistics, which I have tried not to do, I will be even more specific regarding the successfulness of child advocacy groups. Members from these groups have personally and physically saved children's lives. I don't think you can be more successful than that!

Do advocacy groups work with law enforcement?

Since the inception of modern day law enforcement, the "Police", and especially the FBI, have been determined to do their job without any assistance from the public, including private sectors of law enforcement. This line of reasoning also included withholding as much information as possible from the general populace, which our politicians encouraged law enforcement to do. That policy turned out to be an ever-broadening wedge between the authorities and the citizenry of this great nation, but it didn't seem to matter to authorities or politicians. It didn't seem to matter that they were coming across as better than everyone else, not needing nor willing to accept help. In addition, they had even begun to apply those policies to other law enforcement agencies throughout the United States. It didn't matter that crime, along with our population, was spiraling out of control.

Finally, in many cases they begrudgingly decided that they could no longer render a complete and publicly satisfying job without the aid of the public, or at least they admitted they could be much more effective with everyone's help. So, as the "hopelessphobes" in public office, that's politicians to those of you that may respect most of them more than I do, ranted and raved, law enforcement began opening up slowly. They began by sharing information via public announcements and press releases. Then they took the next step, which was asking for a little help here, then a little help there. It was a slow-to-go process in the beginning, but it did maintain a gradual momentum. Sometimes, but rarely, law enforcement would even squeeze out some sort of acknowledgment to public assistance.

Then it happened. A television program that involved everyone's help in locating and apprehending criminals hit the airwaves and it was and still is extremely successful. "Americas Most Wanted" was created and is hosted by John Walsh, a man obviously on a mission. Audiences everywhere accepted the show, which became a monumental success. Due to the program's overwhelming acceptance and its obvious contribution to society through aiding authorities in the apprehension of criminals, law enforcement agencies were encouraged to begin openly and on a large scale, soliciting assistance from concerned Americans. However, the show's successful popularity didn't mean much when the power people demanded the show be taken off the air. The network buckled and announced the show's cancellation, which was a big mistake, I am proud to say. The American people were having none of that and proved it by flooding the network with everything from pleas to threats. Once again, the network buckled by recanting the cancellation. My point here is that law enforcement agencies realize that they need help and that they are now co-operating with us, as much as we are co-operating with them. Most law enforcement agencies today realize that they have many avenues open to them to receive quality assistance from private industry and America's private citizens.

Advocacy groups not only work with law enforcement, but quite often act as liaison between the parents of missing children and authorities. They are also involved in assisting agencies with investigations and are frequently called on to pick up the slack when extra manpower is needed. Most law enforcement agencies not only welcome working with child advocacy groups, but also repeatedly depend on them in certain areas. In addition, law enforcement agencies, in some instances, are now admitting that private industry has available state-of-the-art technology not yet applied by policing agencies.

What do they cost?

As we are all aware, everything comes with a price! However, many, if not most child advocacy groups receive funding from grants and donations. Many, will not ask you for payment. However, on the other hand, none will refuse a donation.

This is a guess on my part, but most child protection groups more than likely depend a great deal on the kindness of human nature. Meaning that after having committed every humanly possible effort and putting their entire staff and services at your disposal, after offering you every conceivable advantage toward helping you keep your child safe, or recover a missing or abducted child, you would have to be some kind of "schmuck" not to make some sort of a donation. But that's just my opinion. I am aware of several advocacy groups, which were forced to close their doors, due to a lack of funding. One that I worked in conjunction with from time to time will surely be missed, the Adam Walsh Child Resource Center. Great, hard working, dedicated people who were more interested in finding and bringing children home than they were in taking credit for it.

Where can advocacy groups be found?

A few child advocacy groups advertise in the telephone book, very few. Some make themselves known with brochures that can be found in many different locations such as libraries, churches, police stations, schools, city hall, etc. For a quick and easy way to locate exactly what you're looking for, most child help groups will be found on the Internet.

Here is a list of some important child advocacy groups, including their Internet location:

*Child Alert
A family-friendly site by all accounts, this site pinpoints numerous resources for the recovery of missing children, and accesses agencies, legislatures, counseling services etc.
Found at: http://childalert.com
*Child Rescue
Because every child counts, this site hooks you up to multiple missing children foundations and organizations.
Found at: www.childrescue.org.uk/

*A.L.I.E. Foundation

Established in the memory of an abducted and murdered Colorado child, this organization supplies bloodhounds to law enforcement, for the purpose of sniffing out missing children.

Found at: http://www.alie.com

*Lycos Missing Children Search

Lycos makes a diligent effort to assist all involved agencies and families in the recovery of missing children by offering a user-friendly searchable database of child abductors.

Found at: http://www.lycos.com/missingkids

*Operation Lookout

This site is a location agency for missing children under the age of eighteen (18) years. This organization will assist families at no cost.

Found at: http://www.premier1.net~Lookout

*National Missing Children's Locate Center Inc.

This child advocacy group was organized to combat the rise in parental and predator abductions of children and will investigate and attempt to locate victims at no cost to the families.

Found at: National Missing Children's Locate Center Inc.

*Ortho ID

This service inscribes on an orthodontic or dental apparatus a special code that can be used for the purpose of identification or provide important medical information about a child.

Found at: http://www.orthoid.com/

*Missing Children Minnesota

You don't have to live in Minnesota to find value in this site, as is the case in many out-of-state and even out-of-country sites. Besides presenting current cases of missing children, this site contains safety and prevention tips, as well as what action to take in the event your child is missing.

Found at: Missing Children Minnesota

*Sass Kids Menu Sass stands for "Stay Alert and Stay Safe" and this resource site can and will help. Kids learn how to deal with strangers and other situations that can harm them at this street-smart site, intended to teach kids how to protect themselves.

Found at: http://www.sass.ca/kmenu.htm

*Lost Child

This site is an emergency service for missing children with headquarters in the United States and in Switzerland. This is a great site, due to its European contacts and its accurate posting of statistics. This site also posts organizations, articles and much more material related to the crime of abduction.

Found at: http://www.lostchild.net

*Middle Tennessee Missing Children's Foundation

This is an important site because this organization enlists the help of families as partners in the search for missing children.

Found at: http://www.compu.net/mtmcf

*LA Missing Children

A guide to missing children in the Los Angeles California area. This site is limited to Los Angeles, but an important site due to the lure of the movie industry. This site allows visitors to search directories by name and thumbnail photographs and it also offers links to other related sites such as: Las Vegas, Nevada, Atlantic City, Georgia, and New York City, which all have similar sites.

Found at: LA Missing Children

*Kentucky Missing and Exploited Children Unit

If after reading my book, you still don't know quite where to start teaching your children about strangers and the potential danger of abduction, this site has plenty of tips. Keep in mind what I've discussed with you regarding the age of your children, and when to start teaching them about their safety. This site also outlines the correct action to take for runaway situations.

Found at: Kentucky Missing and Exploited Children Unit

*Child Connection Inc.

This group serves the United States and Canada by locating missing and exploited children. The site is full of details about what to do if your child turns up missing, also providing prevention methods. The importance here is the Canadian link, which reaches beyond geographical boundaries.

Found at: http://www.petsforum.com/childconnection

I would be remiss not to include Polly's site in this list of national services, for Polly's ephemeral life is America's loss.

*Polly Klaas Foundation

This site is dedicated to the memory of Polly Klaas who was brutally raped and murdered. The foundation's purpose is to reach parents, children and communities concerning the prevention of crimes

against all children.
Found at: www.klaaskids.org/

The names and Internet locations offered in this book are merely a fraction of what is available to you. Take the time to browse the net and while you're at it you may want to consider hanging onto a name and net address or two, just in case. I hope you will never have cause to use any of them. Even if you don't ever need them, you may still want to consider a donation or two, because they're always there for you, if you need them. If you decide to give a little donation, maybe they'll still be there when someone else needs them.

How can I get involved?

Involvement is simple. All you have to do is contact the child help organization(s) in your area and ask, "What can I do to help?" You can also support a group out of your area, or even out of your state, if you wish. Many individuals support child advocacy groups in other areas because they like what a specific group does. If for any reason you have difficulty in locating a group in your area, contact your local Chamber of Commerce or police department. You will find that some advocacy groups have paying positions, but most child help groups need volunteers, due to a general lack of funding. I hope you haven't forgotten what we talked about earlier regarding getting involved. You can get busy in your immediate community and more specifically, your own neighborhood. Working in your own community not only serves to protect children, but it also helps to pull neighbors together.

Chapter 11

PENDING LEGISLATION

Finally, help's on the way. Or is it? Help, via newly proposed legislation, is always on its way, but somehow rarely makes it all the way. When legislation does finally make it, quite often it has been altered to such a degree that it is no longer recognized as the originally drafted proposal. When these altered (watered down) pieces of political artwork finally become law, if they ever become law, they are no longer simple, straightforward, hard-hitting laws that were intended to intimidate sexual offenders. They are usually full of so many loopholes that they appear to have been written on pieces of Swiss cheese.

More often than not, "riders" are attached to what might be considered a great act. Often it is these riders, which cause good legislation to fail passage. Lawmaking has become a game and the "good old boys" have it all worked out. Politicians will take notice of a piece of legislation that looks like it has a very good chance of becoming law, generally because it is a "makes sense" proposal. These legislators will then approach the author of the proposed legislation, or a representative, and either through favoritism or intimidation do what they call "catch a ride." Catch a ride means that they simply attach to a good piece of legislation what they want passed; generally something too weak, or even too rotten to make it on its own. Sometimes legislators are stuck in the awkward position of forcing a rider on another due to favors owed, or because they are being intimidated themselves. It's a constant power play up there on the Hill, and seniority rules.

Not all riders are bad. A few, on rare occasions, will add to the popularity of a proposed bill. Often you find yourself scratching your head, trying to figure out what these two or more proposals are doing together. Especially when they are obviously dealing with two com-

271

pletely different issues. When I claim a complete understanding of politics and politicians, I am counting on at least one of you to gather forces and have me committed. On a brighter note, there are some riders that make very good sense together, even assisting in one another's passage, but they often end up as separate bills. For example, ERISA Child Abuse Accountability Act [HR1142]. In short, it is a good piece of legislation, asking that victims of child abuse be given code to allow the creation, or assignment of rights to the employee pension benefits of their molester. In retrospect, this bill should have been a rider on a bill passed earlier, which now allows a victim of child abuse to collect awards from federal pensions. HR 1142, or whatever its number will eventually end up being, rather than being a natural part of a bill with the same goal, now fighting for life after the fact. Hoping to be realized as a natural extension of the original bill. Don't hold your breath.

I do not wish to sound ungrateful for any attempts to pass quality child protective legislature, before or after the fact. This is just a tiny example of caring politicians needing to unite in their efforts to help the children. If this sounds like I'm impatient, you'd be right, but you have got to remember that there are no words that will adequately describe the ghastly things that are happening to children every day. When we lose a week, a month, or God forbid, a year, we are going to lose a hundred, or thousands of children, because we can't get our acts together. God blesses anyone and everyone attempting to help the children, including politicians, but let's get it together.

There is so much wonderfully written child protective legislature waiting to be passed that I cannot begin to go over it all. I can tell you this: if it is obviously legislation intended to help keep children safe, for God's sake endorse it. There are new child safety proposals going before Congress so regularly that by the time you read the legislation I have referenced, it will have either passed or been voted down. When the time comes (upon your reading of this book) please address the issues and legislation before Congress at that time. I hope you would consider a blanket endorsement of all child protection legislation. All the information needed regarding pending child protective legislation can be found on the Internet.

Many states have enjoyed some success with child protective legislation, like New York's amended educational law that implements specific instructions designed to help prevent abduction and abuse.

California has passed a Bill requiring the State Department of Education to identify and distribute information about programs and curricula that will train children to recognize danger and to protect them. Hopefully other states will continue to offer child protective bills in an effort to establish tougher laws and stiffer punishments for sex offenders. Such legislation is important to the future of America and it's children. Other states active in leading the way are New Jersey, Tennessee and Pennsylvania, with their introduction of bills designed to strengthen the very foundation of child protection services. All three states have floored legislature requiring abduction and abuse prevention education to be taught in their public school systems. The remaining states are up to us; it's time to get busy.

If our school systems can teach alternate lifestyles and pass out free condoms, they sure as hell can teach kids about abduction and abuse prevention.

Start contacting public officials at every level of our government and encourage them to draft educational bills. While you're at it, encourage them to begin allocating law enforcement resources to all areas of child safety and protection programs. It's time also that our government officials begin to allocate more law enforcement resources to Internet investigation regarding crimes against children. We all know we can be pleasant and simply try to encourage our politicians to increase funding in this area and better train existing investigators. However, if you run into any adversity, start demanding. Show them how tough you can get. You know what to do. Most experts agree that a single well-written letter received by a congressman is considered to be the opinion of approximately two thousand (2,000) voters in his or her district. Hand written letters are especially taken seriously. Since there are those of you who will prefer to email their government representatives, even though postal mail will be more effective and be more apt to generate a response, I am supplying you with email instructions as well. U.S. citizens can obtain the contact information for all U.S. Senators and representatives at the following web sites:

U.S. Senators
http://www.senate.gov/senator/

U.S. Representatives
http://www.house.gov/writerep/

I believe "My Body Is My Own" will be a timeless reference book.
Not because it is so brilliantly written, but rather because of its ageless
common sense. My belief is based on the fact that I do not foresee
politicians changing their ways and habits, not in the foreseeable future anyway. I'm betting ninety-five percent of all of the information
in this book will still apply, fifty years or more beyond its publishing. I
truly hope that you prove me wrong. I was wrong once before. I believe it was in 1982 or 83. Seriously, nothing would make me happier
than you making me eat my words.

Responsible parents and your government

Parenting is a status, a position of honor and a specific function. To
maintain honor as a parent these days, one must perform functions that
sometimes seem beyond what would be considered normal parental
duties. Sometimes a parent may have to buck the system in order to
protect their child. Yet there are those parents who are allowing their
children to be raised by the system, evidently believing that the system
knows what is best for their children. Many parents are allowing television and the school system to raise their children, rather then taking
their proper place and handling normal parental duties, much less duties beyond the normal. This is especially true and important to us all
now, in today's society.

Sadly, many of us seem to have evolved into something less than
honorable parents when it comes to our children. Yes, it is very difficult to give your children the attention they need in this monetary
jungle we're trying to survive in. It's easy to feel we are doing enough
or all we can for our kids by providing a beautiful home, quality food,
and the latest styles to wear. It is especially easy to feel that way when
you consider all that stuff isn't so easy to provide. As a matter of fact,
it's damn hard to provide.

Before all of you parents let go with the "damn rights", "damn
straights" and "hell yeses", consider some of these facts. Whether we
want to admit it or not, our children are learning from television. Now,
keeping that in mind, I want you to start paying particular attention to
the shows your kids are watching and then assess, evaluate, appraise,

scrutinize, analyze, inspect and dissect what you think they might be learning. Are your children watching shows that are unrealistic and may be planting seeds of impractical illusions?

How about the shoot'em ups, where a child might learn the working functions of a weapon without the benefits regarding safety training or the reality of the danger and finality in their use? Start asking your kids, "What's cool", or since kids prefer to act and speak exactly the opposite of their parents, what's hot about the show they just watched? Pay particular attention to their answers, you might learn something yourself. Television networks offer a great deal of wonderful and beneficial programs for viewing and a lot of shows that are, at best, bubble gum for the brain. They also offer shows that may send dangerous messages to some children. Also, for your consideration is some of the preferred music kids listen to today. Am I saying that a television show your kid watches is causing him or her to run away, or the music they listen to is driving them to kill people? No, not one individual thing, not just a certain television show, not just a certain performer's music or lyrics, not just a certain friend your kid hangs with. Nor is it a particular fad or desired way of dress that is dangerous. It is not one thing, but a combination of it all, and there is one ingredient that is always overlooked when people try to place blame for a child's actions. Yes, all of these things may factor into a child's mistakes, but along with the constant bombardment of possible negatives from what many label "bad influences" there is also the child's relationship with his or her parents. What is their relationship going through? What is going on between them at the time of the child's bad decision or terrible act? What part does a parent's actions, or lack of actions, play in all of this? Are parents honoring the right to a child's privacy to the degree that children are now able to plot murder and mass-produce bombs at home, unbeknownst to the parent's? Maybe some parents use a child's entitlement to privacy as an excuse not to do their job! In case you are confused or wondering how to determine how much privacy your child is entitled to, the answer is easy. A child is entitled to none. Children should never be entitled to anything. Entitlement is a privilege and privileges are earned. Giving the privilege of privacy to a child is a statement of trust and trust is also earned. Hey, stick around; I've got a lot more common sense to throw your way.

Come on, it's not all that bad. Our kids still have their heroes to look up to and model themselves after. Yeah, our athletes and movie stars. Yeah, right! I am going to begin and end this subject with: too many of the "superstars" that our children idolize today are openly involved in drug abuse and general immorality. Sure, I'm aware that many heroes in the past suffered the same maladies, but it was kept from most, especially the children. Athletes and stars alike could do no wrong. They were admired and respected. To hear someone say, "Bogart hit a woman", or "Wayne is a drunk", were fightin' words. Today, short of murder, most of the immoral or irresponsible law-breaking antics of the "superstars" are not only accepted, they are often admired and mimicked by our children and even some adults. Chemical abuse histories and present treatment are both proudly announced and equally accepted by applauding fans and our children are watching.

By now you must be asking yourself, what does any of this have to do with child abuse, kidnappings or for that matter, any of the subject matter within this book? Well, to start off, allowing your child to watch much of what's on television today is definitely child abuse. That aside, we want our children to make good choices, common sense choices. When your kid is watching a program about runaway kids and children living on the streets, they are receiving mixed signals, guaranteed. While the commentator or interviewer is speaking of the tragedy in it all, the runaways are often laughing, smoking and yuking it up. Kids on camera saying things like, "Yeah, it would be nice to have a warm bed or a hot shower, but this isn't bad. I mean, I really like the freedom and nobody telling me what to do" and "It may be eating out of a trash can, but I get a lot to eat and it's free." What kind of messages are your children getting? Are they hearing it would be nice to have a warm bed and a hot shower, or are they only hearing the part about the freedom and nobody telling them what to do? Remember that it's human nature to take what has always been there for granted, and generally not miss it or even consider it, until you no longer have it. That's true. You're right, the message your child is getting depends on whether you're a truly responsible parent or not. It's as simple as that. Of course, there is the exception to every rule. Some parents can do everything right and their child is still going to make one bad decision after another. There's always that exception. However, generally speaking, if you're a truly responsible parent, not just saying but also doing, your child will be truly responsible as well. It's a common sense thing!

Kids do what they see, not what they hear.

Now here is what we have to stop doing in order to teach our kids the right way, the right thing, the common sense thing. We cannot continue to completely allow our school system to do as it pleases regarding teaching methods applied to our children. Years ago, the school system experimented with a new method of teaching mathematics and switched to New Math. The fast food industry almost collapsed under the expense of having to replace their cash registers with machines that would add and subtract for the high school students and graduates working for them. These poor kids could not make change and most couldn't work simple addition and subtraction.

Well, the system's at it again. Only this time it's worse, much worse. They are starting on our children as soon as they enter school with yet another brilliant experiment. Maybe you're aware of this one already. Have any of you noted that recently American students placed last in international high school level competition? But wait, there's good news: the students excel in one area, "self-esteem." They all thought they did better than they actually did. I guess it's nice to know they think they achieved something after all. This is becoming a very big problem with our kids today. It seems they are being praised in school for giving the wrong answer, as well as the correct answer. It's the old win, win situation. The problem is, everyone is losing, especially the kids. Evidently, someone in a position of authority believes that it is more important than anything else to reinforce a child's self-esteem. I believe they are right, but the answer is not by rewarding underachievement. What becomes the point of doing anything right, or is that the objective, making all children equal for the sake of the self-esteem of a few? Will it eventually come to the system asking the smart kids to reduce their level of achievement for the sake of self-esteem in others, or is the system hoping [designed] it will automatically happen? Now you tell me how these kids can make good intelligent choices about their own safety. It isn't going to matter how much time you spend trying to teach your child personal safety since they've learned in school that both right or wrong is right and they're rewarded for either choice. No matter how wrong their choices are, they will be expecting praise, that is, if they care what you think at all by then.

Yes, all of this has plenty to do with child abuse and kidnapping. You see we've spent a great deal of our time trying to teach and warn kids about the dangers out there. We can always spot the ones that aren't paying attention, or not taking it seriously. Unfortunately, I was involved in the failed recovery of one such child, a child who I knew through an associate. A child some would consider spoiled, because she was praised and rewarded no matter what, a child who refused to take personal safety seriously, or heed warnings from her parents when they traveled abroad, which was frequently. She's not being praised or rewarded now... now we can't find her.

I'd like to take a moment to take a quick look at the other side of that particular coin. Although it's hard to believe, but true, child rapists and murderers have mothers and fathers too. I can't help but wonder if some of them were praised for all of their choices, good and bad.

The question is what you can personally do. In my opinion, it would be smart for you to start by monitoring what these intellectual geniuses are teaching your children. If you discover teaching techniques that you don't approve of, do something about it. By the way, did you know that many teachers do not agree with much of what and how they are forced to teach children today? Even if doing something about it means pulling your children out of school and placing them in a private school. You may also wish to consider home study, which is gaining popularity rather rapidly. Of course, while you're forced to take this action, you should be tearing strips off your school district officials, including the superintendent of schools for your district, and smothering your local politicians with your complaints and concerns.

If possible, gather as many concerned parents together who agree with you and stand united. You may find you won't have to relocate your child after all. Especially if you gather enough parents who feel the same as you. A great place to find concerned parents is your school's PTA. Although you do not have to limit your resources to your own children's school, you've got a complete district of PTA members to pull reinforcements from. The wonderful thing about PTA members is that they are almost exclusively mothers, and if you are able to convincingly point out a problem in their school system that is possibly misguiding their children, you've got your united parents. Especially if you are able to point out that the fault or problem is such that it could be limiting their children's chance to compete and/or survive in today's society. All I have to say about that is, if you can get a fire lit under them, look out. Remember that your parental obligation to monitoring your child's life in all areas is as important as any actions taken against any possible damaging entity.

Along with working on your own personal relationships with your children, begin working at uniting your neighborhood. Begin by developing and implementing programs that will instruct parents and children alike. You can do it by passing on what you've learned regarding protection against sexual predators and any other possible child dysfunctional or misguiding activity, such as the educational experimentation previously mentioned. When you have successfully completed strengthening the security of the children in your neighborhood, start on your community. It all begins with one person, why can't that one person be you?

*Do not allow yourself to be put off, patronized, detoured through manipulation, or discouraged in any way by officials or any other authorities, including lazy neighbors. Some parents and officials seem to be threatened by what they perceive to be civilians doing police-type work, while others will willingly assist you, any way possible, while truly appreciating your concern and help.

What you can get your church to do

Approach your Pastor or church leaders about implementing adult awareness and child safety programs. Recommend separating the child safety programs into specific age groups and also, you may wish to consider separate groups for boys and girls. This book will make an excellent text for instructors and students alike, providing, discretion (common sense) is applied, relating to the age of the recipients being instructed.

Discuss with the different committee chairpersons the possibility of considering fundraisers for the purpose of donating to child abuse prevention and child find organizations, in or out of your area. It sometimes helps to suggest that the church should benefit from a percentage of monies raised, as a thank you for the use of church facilities. The church should accept it as an unexpected, but welcome tithing. Be forewarned that many churches, mostly smaller ones, do not like to sponsor anything that may take donations away from them. However, there is the possibility of uniting their efforts with other churches in your area, even churches of other denominations, to create a super fundraiser, which would not diminish their own contributions as much. What could be better than many churches of different denominations uniting in a common cause, the protection of children? One suggestion for a super fundraiser, involving many congregations, is a well-advertised barbecue, with donated food, refreshments and entertainment. A function of such magnitude would be best hosted at a local park or campground, charging admission, and you may wish to consider opening it to the public. A great way to raise money at this type of a fundraiser is by sponsoring an auction of donated items from private individuals and local merchants. If you put your thinking caps on, I'm sure that you can come up with even better ideas.

What you can get your schools to do

It would be nice if it depended on which you're dealing with, public or private schools. I guess it really doesn't matter much since both can be difficult, especially when they consider it a deviation from their norm. It has been my experience that private schools are more receptive to money-generating ideas, as long as they get their cut that is. No, I'm not insinuating that they are moneygrubbers. They should get a share. It might be wise if your first step is approaching the PTA in an attempt to gather their support, generating a little power in numbers behind you. Once that is done, you have to deal with the school, hopefully gaining the support and recommendation of the school's Principal. Then it's on to the school district, and you can bet that the person you meet with first is thinking, "Dear God, I hope this person isn't too persistent." That's right, persistent. And here's a few other things you'll need to be: unrelenting, determined, importunate, relentless, tenacious and down right pushy, if necessary. This is exactly how you have to be when dealing with individuals not used to having, or not liking, their little boat rocked. By the way, you may, no scratch that, you will be especially disturbing to them if the reason you've met is to confront them regarding educational experimentation and your desire to end it. So, a word of advice, you may want to hold that for a separate meeting.

If ... when you get the school district's approval to move forward, begin organizing and coordinating the PTA and school staff. The purpose of this is the preparation of child abuse and kidnap prevention curriculum, or at a minimum, a series of school assemblies regarding child safety subjects. When your efforts begin paying off in the form of parents and children alike responding positively and when you begin receiving congratulations on having such a great idea, it's time to hit the school district up again. This time, for quality child abuse and kidnap prevention brochures and/or booklets. Don't take no for an answer. Involve merchant donations to cover the cost, or at least a large portion of the cost. If the school district continues to resist your request, have your local statistics ready and enlist the aid of your local police and politicians. During all of this, you should have started approaching local businesses for their support in the form of cash or merchandise donations for your fundraisers, using the same format and ideas you applied to churches. Consider approaching food as well as drink manufacturers and distributors, as well. Do your best to spread the burden of support, in the form of donations, to as many companies and corporations as possible. Your local Chamber of Commerce could, if they choose, be of great assistance to you in many different areas of your efforts.

*The latest available information regarding child abuse and kidnap prevention, including   statistics, which will aid you in convincing school districts officials and politicians alike to cooperate, can be obtained from your local or state child find and child help groups. You should consider them important tools, and use them.

What you can get special clubs and groups to do

Special clubs and groups are very special, in that they are usually looking for something special to do for their community. Although some clubs and groups will respond better than others, which does not mean that the same club or group that turned you down in one city will have the same reaction in a different location. Like anything else, it's the individuals associated with clubs and groups, rather than the organization itself who make the decisions, so don't allow disappointments to discourage you to the point of defeat.

Here are the names of some clubs and groups, just to give you an idea of what's out there:

Kiwanis Club	Foreign Legion
Free Masons	Lions Club
Elks Club	Rotary Club
Legionnaires	Knights of Columbus
Veterans	Veterans of Foreign Wars
Moose Club	Women's Auxiliary
Catholic Daughters of America	ETC.

The aforementioned is to name but a few. Many are particularly known for helping children's causes. Some of these organizations also have beautiful accommodations and other properties such as camps and retreats, which are ideal for fundraisers. Handled correctly, it should not be difficult to enlist the support of one or more of these organizations. It would also be beneficial to have one or more of these organizations in your corner when approaching the officials that have the power to get the job done. In addition to that, many of the members of these organizations are doctors, judges and attorneys, which could be to your advantage. By the way, many politicians belong to these organizations, as well.

Many special clubs and groups have a lot of great knowledge and experience when it comes to raising monies for special causes, especially children's causes. Your task is to convince these organizations that educating your community's parents, teachers and children is the obvious and common sense answer to making your community a safer place. And, of course, supporting child advocacy groups helps all communities.

Remember that you are going to be empowered by numbers, so you may want to consider building your army before taking on these tasks. Speaking of numbers, if you find yourself short of much-needed people for fundraisers or anything else, contact your local Volunteer Center Assistance League (VCAL). They refer volunteers to nonprofit organizations. Also, there should be a "Retired Seniors Volunteer Program" (RSVP) in your area, which you should be able to locate in your local telephone book under City Government "Senior Information Referrals." These groups are specifically set up to lend support to causes just like yours.

What you can do at:

City level

There is nothing like starting at the top, which is the Mayor's office. If you have discovered a child abuse and/or a missing children rate of occurrence in your area, you should commit yourself and all of your energy toward persuading the mayor to immediately rectify the situation. Set a meeting with your City Manager requesting that his full attention be directed at the problem. Schedule an appointment with the City or Town Council and demand; yes that's right, demand, immediate action. The individuals who take posts as our civic leaders are directly accountable for any shortcomings that involve the safety of your community's children. They should already be sensitive and attentive to child protection and safety in their city without you having to bring it to their attention. If at any time during your crusade you discover a civic leader who is unaware of the situation, you have my permission to go ballistic. There is simply no excuse for a civic leader not to be aware of such an important issue.

The mayor needs to be convinced to work with the city manager, and vice versa, regarding the initiation of programs that will educate adults and protect children in your community. The city manager should likewise work hand in hand with the city council and the chief of police. Jointly they should enforce already existing state laws, or if none exist, create and enact municipal laws targeting pedophiles and all other sexual offender public awareness and discovery laws. If such laws are already in place, yet the problem has continued, it is time to reinforce the laws and find out why they are not being enforced. You may want to reconsider some of the individuals you've given the title of civic leader to and have placed in the positions of power in your community. A great way to test the water is by going to your local Police Department to see what information the department is willing to give you, regarding sex offenders and pedophiles in your community. You will have to be specific in your request, due to the fact that some law enforcement agencies choose not to categorize pedophiles with sexual offenders. Don't ask. I have a lot of trouble with that one my-self.

Of course, it would be wise of you to already have complete knowledge regarding your state laws before approaching your local authorities. You must have knowledge of your state laws when approaching city officials, due to the fact that some, or many, in public office possess a natural ability to dodge, double talk and generally frustrate the average citizen. [Remember, knowledge is power.] Once again, it would be wise to have already enlisted support from local organizations. This is especially important when dealing with elected officials. Also regarding elected positions, don't forget about the District Attorney, who is directly responsible for properly prosecuting sexual offenders. The District Attorney must understand the importance of the quality training of prosecutors when confronted with cases involving sexual offenders, and especially pedophiles. Be sure to let them know that you do not stand-alone. Give them numbers, if necessary. However, if push-comes-to-shove, do not tell them that you are a taxpayer and that you pay their salaries, or remind the official that these are registered voters. He or she has heard it a million times before. They are aware of it. Simply be polite, to the point and dead accurate. Believe me when I say that you've got their full attention. When it comes time to vote again, get rid of the jerks that resisted you, because it never should have become a push-comes-to-shove situation. Especially considering such an important and needed project as saving children's lives and considering that you should never have been confronted by one ounce of resistance in the first place. By the way, there is an added benefit in all of this. Your quest will definitely separate the politicians who really care and are truly trying to serve the public, from the opportunists and "good old boys club" that we've all become so used to. If you've hit a brick wall and exhausted every avenue, at that point it is all right to let the imitation of public servants you've dealt with know that he, she or they is at an end of their political career in your community. Inform them that you are going to communicate; in every way possible, to as many people as humanly possible, not to vote for them ever again and then do it.

You may also find welcomed allies in your local newspapers by supplying a journalist with authentic and accurate local statistics regarding child abuse and what appears to be a lack of interest and/or effort by city government to curtail it. Do your homework and remember, being tenacious is being successful! I can see the headlines now:

LOCAL CHILD ABUSE STATISTICS FREIGHTENING ALERTED CITY OFFICIALS FAIL TO ACT

This may seem a bit much to you. However, if you are not prepared to go all the way, don't go at all. I am by no means saying this is what you're going to have to do, I'm saying be prepared to do it, if it becomes necessary. I hope that you will be pleasantly surprised by the overwhelming amount of cooperation received from your local authorities. I always keep in mind that there are some great officials out there doing a wonderful job, displaying that they do truly care through their actions. That's about as far away from cynical as I go.

County level

At county level, you will be facing a whole new and very different ball game. You will be dealing with county supervisors and you aren't going to like their favorite answers to many things put before them. "That is a city matter" or what seems to be their most favorite, "That is a state issue", which they believe relieves them of the slightest possibility of any responsibility.

Generally, more often than not, the county will refer you to the city in which you reside. Although, given a little thought, one should realize, that since the city is within the county, the county does have a responsibility and should work with you and the city. Especially, if you've explained that you have already approached the city, to no avail. I have found it is much easier working with the state than it is to deal with the county, or maybe it's that the state just puts on a better act... It's possible. Since bureaucrats have duped me on more than one occasion in the past, this becomes a distinct possibility.

In the final analysis, it doesn't matter which bureaucratic entity you are forced to deal with, you may be faced with degrees of disappointment. It is important that you do not become discouraged and most important, that you not show enmity, for if you do, all is lost. Simply be courteous, consistent and relentless, and you will prevail.

State level

Here we are again. With your army of supporters already well entrenched behind you, hit'em at the top. Included in your well-entrenched army should be a councilman or two, and maybe a senator. Believe it or not, senators are easy to get, well the use of their name is easy to get. Senators will lend their names to most any worthy projects, which will generally give a cause credibility. Point being, it's good to have corralled one or two of them before considering taking on your Governor. The Governor's office is usually, but not always, good about addressing concerns and complaints from the general population. By now, you've surely wised up enough to know not to expect results without having to do battle. Every employee at state capitols across this great nation should have coffee money; this is a fact due to your state capitol bureaucrats' ability to pass the buck. You may find that the Lieutenant Governor's office will serve you best. However, a referral can act as an introduction of sorts. So begin at the governor's office and he or she will, as is generally the norm, pass it to the lieutenant governor's office with orders to handle it, hence your introduction.

When the time comes and you get your chance to be heard, you should be armed with as many of the accurate facts and strong arguments, as possible. By accurate facts and strong arguments, I mean having the knowledge to discuss intelligently the wasted and often fruitless funding of nothing less than ridiculous projects. Exclaim your outrage while producing cold hard facts regarding the rampant child abuse and missing children epidemic in your area and in the state. If the forum allows you the time, go through the entire list of change needed. Use old clichés like, "We can put a man on the moon, but we can't protect our children." Go ahead; use them, because they apply. Let everyone you deal with know that you are not going to go away until someone does the right thing, so that our children receive the protection they are entitled to from every level of government.

What should you expect from your Governors office? Like everyone else you approach regarding the safety of children, expect nothing and hope you are surprised.

National level

How are you at letter writing? Lots of letter writing. So much letter writing that you will have to enlist the aid of all the support you can muster. If you want results, there is only one-way to get their attention in Washington DC. This needs to be a letter writing bombardment, the likes of which Washington DC has never seen. The crusade against child sexual abuse and child abduction are not Democratic nor Republican issues, nor are they any other political party's issues, for that matter. They are simply, and in the purest form, human rights. Maybe that should be humane rights. Anyway, what I'm saying is, that it should be safe to assume that your letters can be addressed to all of the politicians in Washington DC. That's right, every single Congressman, Senator and let's not exclude the President of the United States and the First Lady. And if they have children, depending on their age(s), write them as well.

This campaign will consist of three separately composed letters sent at different intervals, each referring to the last letter and each bringing up accurate statistics, adding to the numbers of the letter before. Each letter should ask why nothing innovative and substantial is being done to protect the children. Any unanswered letters need to be resent and if that doesn't earn a reply, do it again and again. During the same time as your letter writing campaign, you will need to launch a petition seeking tens of thousands of signatures. The petition must spell out your demands for our government to take a stronger position against sexual offenders and child abductors. If crimes exist that deserves a zero tolerance stand, these must be it!

Once you have accomplished your goals, all of the letters written, all the letters sent and resent, including all possible signatures gathered, prepare to do the unexpected. It's time to do what every politician fears, almost as much as losing his or her next election, especially if he or she has not responded to your letters. It's time to show up on Capitol Hill with gathered supporters and petition in hand. Go from office to office and door to door, get to the Congressional floor and demand to be heard. Does all of this seem radical to you? Damned right it does and it is, but if you want our children truly protected now, this is the way to get it done...now. Although, if a brilliant strategist were to see to it that the press discovered what you'   ve been up to and why you're up to it, well who knows? If a good journalist were to find out that your letters did little, if they were read at all, and that in your possession are tens of thousands of signatures, well again, who knows? If that same journalist found out that you are preparing to storm Congress, determined to stay until you get results, you might not have to go after all...who knows? Remember, if you aren't prepared to go all the way, don't go at all. If it turns out that you have to go, heck, seeing DC is probably one of the things on your list of things to do before you die anyway.

All of this is obviously too much to ask of any one individual, but not so much for many, and it could be fun. Flexing citizenry muscle is always fun! I have always not only found it exciting, forcing politicians to do the right thing, but rewarding and lots of fun. Just knowing you've disturbed and maybe even totally disrupted their daily routine, you know, screwing up one or more of those three-martini lunches... ahh, what a feeling. Making them do some things they should have done on their own and knowing a few of them are really pissed because you brought it to everyone's attention. It kinda takes a little bit of the sting out of paying taxes. Definitely a good feeling. Then, there is the feeling that you have saved a child's life, another good feeling...definitely.

I understand how outrageous and overwhelming much of this must sound, but it is the only way to do it and the only way to positively insure results. In Washington DC, results come when real pressure is applied, and when pressure is coupled with national attention, you've got a winner. Power is in numbers; numbers are what count on Capitol Hill, even more power than by having celebrities speaking on your behalf, much more.

How to write effective letters to politicians and the President

Many people believe that letters to their local politicians, or to the politicians in Washington DC, are simply a waste of their time and effort. Nothing could be further from the truth. Senators and Congressman alike pay particular attention to their mail. They depend on it. If a politician is attempting to fulfill his or her obligations as sworn, they must not only read, but also actually consider, the contents of the letters received from the average citizen. Politicians do this because the letter writer's views form the politician's major listening post, regarding voter sentiment toward new and/or pending legislation. Surprising amounts of letters to Congressional offices are read very carefully by the Congressmen and Senators personally. The letters that the Congressmen and Senators don't have the time to read themselves are read by essential "Key" staff personnel, who then notify the politicians of their content.

Do not involve yourself with form letters that have identical wording, or long telegrams signed by lists of people. Also, stay clear of mimeographed petitions and any other "Bulk" entreaties, which carry little to no weight in Washington DC. The legislators know from experience that sudden outpourings with suspicious similarity are almost always from disinterested individuals. In these situations the signed individuals were probably goaded into signing the petition or form letter by some lobbyist or political action group, and could care less about the content. Your letters will at first appear to be a sudden outpouring. However, if in the content of the letters is a brief reference to the children lost forever by the minutes of every day, the recipient should understand the urgency. He or she will definitely realize the genuine concern and sincerity when the letters keep coming in.

Write your own individual letters that are carefully thought out, letters that lawmakers will appreciate. Write to your Senators and Representatives just as you would write anyone else. Try to keep in mind that you're not drafting a legal document. Do not use a computer or typewriter when communicating with politicians; write your letters in long hand. Politicians seem to believe, "This is the people speaking to me, this is what the people really feel." when they see a letter that has been handwritten. Don't ask, cause I don't know. Make sure your letters are legible and remember that the influence of your communication depends upon the point you make and the clarity with which you make it. Set forth exactly what you wish the lawmaker to consider. If your business is regarding a bill, briefly explain why you believe the bill is good or bad. Then briefly explain exactly how you feel it will affect you and others in your community. Don't be lengthy, be brief and to the point.

Now I want you to pay particular attention to this. Do not even allow the slightest contemplation or the mere thought of warning or threatening anyone to cross your mind. Are we clear here? Threats can be considered a form of extortion, (Blackmail). You may be breaking the law and you could end up in jail. Even if you're not breaking the law, threats merely antagonize politicians and will get you nowhere, except out the door. Effective letters are courteous and the legislator is well aware that wrong decisions lose votes. This also means you do not have to remind them in your letter that he or she may well be your "second favorite" candidate in the next election, if you're disappointed. They already realize that. Nor should the legislator be wooed with promises of all-out support at the polls, providing he or she votes the right way, or puts forth your preferred legislature. If you and your group or organization can muster votes come election time, they know that too. If you're pleased with a legislator's position on a bill, or with their vote, write to thank and compliment the politician on their stand. This is extremely important, because letters thanking Congressman and Senators for a job well done are altogether too rare. Complimentary letters also encourage legislators to stay on track, continuing to do the right thing.

Almost all politicians answer their mail, but if your reply is just a brief acknowledgement, write again requesting more specific information. Don't be shy: ask precisely where he or she stands on an issue. Do they propose to support it or oppose it, and why. How do they feel regarding the bill's success? It is highly unlikely that a Congressman or a Senator will not acknowledge or completely ignore a follow-up request. Most politicians will appreciate your proven interest. In short, persistence pays.

In your enthusiasm to support legislation, remember to be fair. Allow your Congressmen and Senators time to research and evaluate bills. Give them any and all pertinent information that may assist in their decision. A deluge of letters sent just as a measure is about to be voted on is not effective and for that matter, downright ridiculous. If it is close to voting time, a single intelligent letter will do more good. It is often difficult to know how some politicians will react to letters; some politicians are not disturbed by a timely deluge of mail, (months before the vote) while the legislator is still formulating his or her opinion. Yet there are others who will serve you well having received but a single letter. [Flip a coin.]

Remember that politicians can be swayed, if handled correctly. Your opinion can be theirs. When the bill you are interested in is introduced, send a copy of your letter, or a newly drafted letter, to the Chairman of the committee to which it was referred. Sometimes a bill may never get out of the committee for a floor vote. You, through your letter, can influence the committee to release the bill to the floor to be voted on.

*Whenever possible, refer to the piece of legislature (Bill) under discussion by its name and number. Always sign using your full name!

Tips on addressing your letters:

: Senators

> The Honorable John S. Doe
> Senate Office Building
> Washington, D.C. 20510

Dear Senator Doe,

: Representatives

> The Honorable John R. Doe
> House Office Building
> Washington, D.C. 20515

Dear Mr. Doe,

: The President

> President John P. Doe
> The White House
> 1600 Pennsylvania Ave. N/W
> Washington, D.C. 20500

Dear President Doe,

*The telephone number to the White House from 9am to 5pm EST is: 1-202-456-7639

[To be used for legitimate purpose only.]

Letters to newspapers and/or other publications

If you have something to say and you want it printed, keep it brief. (After having read my book, you should have plenty to say, but still keep it brief.)

Most letters should be no more than three hundred (300) words. Two hundred (200) would be better, as newspaper and magazine space is limited. You will be sharing the "Letters to the Editor" column with other correspondents on a variety of subjects. Most likely your letter will have been triggered by an atrocity committed against a child or a news story, possibly an editorial, or worse yet, some sexual child molester receiving a slap on the wrist for his terrible deed. Although your blood is boiling, remember you do not have to restate the entire premise before launching your views. Of course, we all know to limit the subject to one topic. If referring to an article, name the news story or editorial heading. If for some reason the name escapes you, you may refer to a specific phrase or part that will help identify the piece, then make your points quickly and cogently.

If you do not possess a well-developed and firm opinion on the subject, don't bother writing anyone until you do. I personally do not know how that can be possible when horrific crimes against children are in the news almost daily, and especially after having read this book. Both editors and their readers will react to a letter that has fact, feeling and direction. Since you have read "My Body Is My Own", you now possess accurate and informative, not to forget useful, facts for the newspaper's audience. If you follow my suggestions, your letters will accomplish a great deal and you will find satisfaction in knowing that you are a positive contributor to your community and to society, in general. Remember, be direct, to the point and above all else, have all of your facts in place and ready.

Always sign your letters using your full name and complete address. Also use your professional title if it is pertinent. Anonymous letters lack conviction, and obvious courage, and are generally not published. They are almost always ignored, and editors will rarely print them. In addition, letters using pseudonyms are usually discarded, because editors check on the authenticity of both the content and the correspondent. However, your name may be withheld upon request if circumstances warrant, but those occasions are rare.

Do not bother asking, or expect an editor to reply to your letter. Remember, brief, to the point and state your facts.

: Address
        Letters to the Editor
        Name of Newspaper or Magazine
        City, State, Zip Code
Dear Sir,

Direction and Solutions

Child molesters ID Line

The "Child Molesters ID Line" is truly a gift from heaven to all concerned parents, especially in these times of moral indecision by our lawmakers. Finally, attempts at protecting our children are realizing moderate success without too much political interference. At last, parents have been provided with an important way to be more personally involved in their own children's safety. Although, as is true in all things good and wonderful, we must not take them for granted, or we will lose them. Individuals wanting to preserve the rights to privacy are constantly challenging the "Child Molesters ID Line."

I consider myself a Constitutionalist. However, I also believe that when criminals commit heinous crimes, such as raping and murdering our children, many, if not all of their rights should automatically be forfeited, including and especially their right to privacy.

When individuals are convicted of a felony in the United States they forfeit some of their constitutional rights, and we don't hear anybody ranting and raving about that, so what's the deal? Maybe it's because it's a man's world, and it is mostly men committing the sexual crimes against children. You know, like why has it taken so long for women to realize justice after having been raped, and why is the justice still so damned sporadic today? Why have women's needs for medical advances taken such a back seat to the medical needs, and advances of men for so long?

Maybe I'm on to something with this. Maybe, because children are not men, and things just aren't going to happen as quickly as they would if these atrocities were happening to men. Is that it? Do we presently live in a society that considers women's needs and the needs of our children not to be as important as the needs of men? Maybe, just maybe, it is as I suspect. Do you believe it possible that there is an unspoken bond of protection? Now I'm not saying that they (men) got together and created a conspiracy of protection for themselves. I'm not trying to insinuate that at all. I'm saying that maybe, "possibly", a little tiny bit of the "old ways" is kind of subconsciously lingering on and on. It's an attitude like, yeah, something needs to be done about that and we're gonna get to it...uuhh, yeah we're gonna get to it. Don't let them slough it off. Sure, if the laws are on the books, men do something, but still too often, it's too little too late. God forbid men would ever take more action on their own, regarding the safety of women and children. How about creating and enforcing laws before a grieving mother has to damn near get on her knees, begging and pleading for change before Congress? How often have we witnessed a grieving mother pleading with our politicians for consideration, so that the same tragedy that struck her child doesn't befall another's child? I do not wish to offend the men who are doing their job, and there are a lot of them. I am focusing on the men that are leaving their job to others. Living in America has given us all a strong sense of security. We have for all intensive purpose totally relied on law enforcement to keep us safe; those days are all but gone. It is impossible for law enforcement to completely protect our children from predators.

It is of the utmost importance that parents unite against any state, county or city entity that refuses to cooperate with federal law, or having altered (watered down) any sex offenders community alert program. Parents must also band together in force against any groups or individuals seeking to provide consideration, including the right to privacy, for convicted sex offenders, especially pedophiliacs. Advocacy groups like, "Pedo Watch" or "Sex Offenders Net" and the "Child Molesters ID Line" are essential tools that aid communities by protecting their women and children. The rights of the law-abiding and the innocent should obviously come before the rights of kidnappers, rapists, child molesters and murderers...talk about your no brainers, duh! Anyone attempting to place the safety of women and children after the right to privacy of these demon-propelled, amorally driven sub-humans, obviously lacks compassion, and the tiniest bit of common sense. However, since I consciously strive to be fair and try to understand another's reasoning, I do acknowledge that there are always other possibilities. Some of these individuals could be what they are trying to protect. Just a shot from the trenches that might hit a bull's eye. Individuals guilty of committing "stupid", such as lending themselves to the protection of vermin that rape and murder children, deserve any suspicious attention that their idiotic actions may draw. Parents, you must make an effort to find out about the women's and child protective services that are provided to your community, and make sure that those services are not altered and are forthcoming upon request. Make contact with the child safety and protective service of your choice, and offer assistance. Stay alert to any attempts at revoking or changing any child protective services in your state and community. Be prepared to do battle over these services, if necessary. Do not allow anyone, or any agency, to dictate to you what is best for your children, and their safety. Take control!

Sex Offenders Net

The "Sex Offenders Net" is an important Internet watchdog, in that it is ever vigilant as to the legality of Internet sites containing pornography, of any sort. Obviously, they keep special tabs on sites advertising "underage girls", including the sites claiming "barely legal girls." Now, as if this isn't enough to do, the staff of the Sex Offenders Net spends endless hours searching the Internet for child pornography on sites that choose not to advertise. As you can imagine, this is an overwhelming, and definitely bordering on an impossible, task for any one organization.

Remember what I previously discussed, regarding the daily flow of child pornography into the United States from all over the world? Well, the most popular vehicle nowadays is the Internet. I have spent countless hours myself searching the Net, and the only thing worse than the search, is the find. Guess what, folks? The finds are easy, because the Internet is awash with child pornography. Much of it is what one would consider "Black Market", and unadvertised. Special passwords and codes are necessary for admittance to most of the illegal sites, and many pedophiliacs have access. One of the problems is, "passwords" and "special codes" seem to mean nothing to many computer savvy kids with nothing but unsupervised time on their hands. You may not realize it, but if you have a child as young as eight, nine, ten years old, and possibly younger, who spends a great deal of their time on a computer, and has been doing it for an extended period of time, you may be the proud owner of a computer genius, or at minimum, a left handed authority. The truth is that a child doesn't have to be a computer genius, there is plenty of child pornography on the Internet that doesn't require special codes or passwords.

Child pornography aside, I think it's reasonable for me to assume that you don't want your children to see bestiality, necrophilia, and individuals urinating on each other, commonly referred to as "Golden Showers" or "Water Sports" and human beings [description loosely applied] having fun with their own waste. That's right, at no extra charge, it's all available for your children's viewing, and it doesn't take a password, or special code. Now the promoters of these versions of intimacy will argue with me, they will claim that identification checks and balances are in place to insure age requirements are met, and so on. They will also argue that what they do is legal ...blah, blah, blah. The fact is, as I've previously mentioned, when entering their sites, most offer a tour and show samples, so a child does not have to actually gain access to view some of the most disgusting material available... at no extra charge. This particular research is but one of the reasons this book has been so very difficult to write, and probably why I've avoided doing it for so long. I wish it were possible for someone to pick me up and turn me upside down, and begin shaking and shaking, shaking me until it all came out of my head.

Let's begin with doing your children and yourself a big favor. If your children are using a computer, it is imperative that you activate one of the many safeguards available to you. This will help insure that the users (your kids) cannot access pornographic web sites.
[Check with computer accessory stores as to the latest and greatest service available.]

You can also help keep child pornography off the Internet by reporting to "Pedo Watch", any child pornography you may discover, including site previews. This will aid in the development of their "Report List", which is currently used by both law enforcement agencies and private citizens alike. They need our help; it isn't easy protecting your children! Become an activist! Okay, okay, I know you can't throw your body and soul into this, you've got a family to take care of, a job to go to, I understand. Although, I'll bet you could set a little time aside to alert others as to what is going on. You know, inform a few people during some ridiculous conversation that you probably wish you weren't part of to begin with. Risk shocking them all by bringing up something important. Begin by telling them about the pornography that is running amuck on the Internet. Ask them if they've installed and activated a safeguard to protect their children, and end by asking, if they have read "My Body Is My Own." You need to consider circulating information to your friends regarding the illegality of child pornography, and tell them how to report their discoveries of child pornography on the Internet. I know you want to assist Pedowatch any way you can. Pedowatch also wants to assist you. They do that by offering all applicable information on their web site, written by their staff for you to use freely as an aid in your quest to help them protect your children. Their site gives information, regarding the procedures recommended for reporting any child pornography you may discover. Plus much, much more... Look'em up. They also share their material with criminal justice organizations, allowing them to print and distribute as much material as they find useful. They also allow universities to use site text. Pedowatch believes that the more easily accessible this information is, the higher frequency of reports they will receive.

Here's another way you can help out. If you come across arrest reports involving pedophiles, or any sexual offenders on the web or anywhere else, e-mail Pedowatch so they can add them to their "Arrest Section." If you are involved in a Usenet discussion group that sometimes has topics related to sex, or know someone who is, please consider posting the URL of the "Pedowatch Report" to the Usenet. This is a great way to spread the word among some of the people who most frequently encounter child pornography and child abusers. That is, if you have the time. Am I being sarcastic? Yeah. Probably. You must forgive me. My intention is not to harass or bully you into action. I like to think of it as motivational embarrassment. C'mon, what could be more important then spending a little of your time on our children's safety?

There is also much more you can do that takes little to no effort. Here are a couple of suggestions to get you started. Encourage IRC server and "Newserver" administrators, and operators, to take part in reporting illegal child exploitation, and child pornography to law enforcement. Ask your university, or ISP, what they are doing to protect children, and to bring those that harm them to justice. Ask them for specifics; they are often long on rhetoric and short on action, so go get'em.

Another possible avenue that I feel will accomplish two goals, is for criminal justice students to consider gathering up a truly comprehensive report on this subject, for their master's theses and doctoral dissertations. The two goals accomplished will be that your work will be well received by your professor, hence, a great grade. Second, donating your papers to Pedo Watch is a great community service. This idea is so good; I wish I could say it was mine.

There are literally tens of thousands of pornographic web sites, and only a few groups monitoring them for the safety of your children. Give'em a hand, helping where and when you can. As many parents count on them, they count on us. Their job is information, and your job can be helping them get it! If they should ever go out of business, God forbid, we will all suffer the loss, especially our children. They are unsung heroes, fighting a never-ending battle. Shouldn't we all pitch in? Fathers especially need to get off their proverbial asses, and take the responsibility that has been bestowed on them. So, once again, off your ass, Pop. You've got a job to do, a duty, which you should feel privileged to carry out. Remember this: Fatherhood is a position of responsibility and honor, so show us whatcha got! I know there are special circumstances, where everyone can't do it. Guess what? Everyone doesn't have to do it. Did you know that the revolution of 1776, which gained America its freedom, was mostly fought, and won by only ten percent (10%) of the population… did ya know that? All it takes is a few determined people, who truly believe and know that they are right.

Answers and solutions

The marriage of man and computer, like most marriages, has been a love/hate relationship. Most believe it to be the savior of mankind, and cannot imagine living without it, while others are convinced it will destroy us all. Imagine… this marriage applies the ingenuity of humans to an unlimited extent of time, space and quantity, including possibilities larger than any pre-assigned finite number. This marriage is bonded by a geometric magnitude that lies beyond any known reference. Welcome to the world of computers. Welcome to infinity.

What you have just read is my way of introducing you to the most powerful weapon at your disposal, which will aid you in the war against child molesters, child pornographers and pedophiles that kill children. Problem is, the bad guys have'em too. Unfortunately, child pornographers, child slave traders [Traffickers] and pedophiles have more sophisticated communication links than do either our law enforcement agencies, or child recovery institutions and groups. However, because of groups like Pedowatch and others, we have the ability to win this war, especially as we gain governmental support, albeit slow in coming.

The President signed into law a Federal measure called "Megan's Law" on May 17, 1996 [Public Law Number 104-145], which is a measure requiring all states to release information, regarding the sexual abusers of children. The President also signed the "Pam Lynchner Sexual Offender Tracking and Identification Act of 1996" [S1675], on October 3, 1996. The "Pam Lynchner Act" seems to be faring a lot better than "Megan's Law", as far as being upheld nationwide. And contrary to popular belief, the "Pam Lynchner Act" in many states is doing a whole lot better then Megan's law. Hey, we'll take what we can get! The "Pam Lynchner Act" is progress that has pleasantly surprised many, including me.

Sadly, some states are ignoring "Megan's Law" in its entirety, while others choose to implement mere portions of it. This is another one of those, don't ask, cause I don't know, or understand either. In one case, in 1995, even before "Megan's Law" became a Federal Law, our government, in the form of the United States Justice Department, jumped in to defend what was then "Megan's Law", after it was implemented as New Jersey's state law. New Jersey was requiring officials to notify a neighborhood when a child molester, or other sex offenders were released from prison and taking up residence in a community. The assignors responsible for placement and community notification, if you can believe it, were receiving resistance from authorities. Yet since then, and since "Megan's Law" was signed into Federal Law, many states continue to ignore or use portions of, or even physically alter "Megan's Law", without government intervention or, evidently, fear of repercussion.

Why do such obviously needed and well-written laws generate such resistance? This is such a difficult question to answer, especially considering the degrees of complexity with which our society has evolved. The answer can probably be found somewhere between moral righteousness, and political correctness. It seems we now live in a society that condones the killing of our unborn, calling it choices, and the killing of abortionists, calling it justifiable... Go figure. Where do we place the blame when criminal acts, that were once considered crimes of the century have become commonplace, quite often not even making it into our newspapers, much less into the front page, if they are mentioned at all.

How have we arrived at the point in America, where we have begun to ridicule and ignore the time-proven and honored values of our forefathers, choosing to call it enlightenment? Have we become so enlightened, that we are no longer able to recognize choices that endanger our children? How have we reached such a distorted and yes, even twisted version of parenting? We are so completely complacent, that we accept the direction of government, via our children's classrooms and neglect to discipline our children, calling it building their self-esteem. No wonder we all sit around scratching our heads, trying to figure out why our kids are grabbing guns, and going ballistic at school! We are evolving into a society that will allow others to raise our, children and encourages the avoidance of personal responsibility, of both parents and children. A sure sign of an empire's decline is when it is all through striving for intelligent answers, and simply begins shifting responsibility and blame from the responsible, and the guilty. How does that old saying go? "When you're all through learning, you're all through." You've heard, or seen it and maybe indulged a little yourself. This is what we are doing every time we accept excuses, rather then accepting responsibility. "Oh, it's not her fault, she didn't have an opportunity to go to college." "You can't blame him, he never had a father" or my favorite, "He's not responsible for murdering those people, he ate too many Twinkies." [San Francisco's famous "Twinkie defense."] Don't laugh. If you'll remember, it worked. If we are not going to hold individuals responsible for their actions, please tell me the point in teaching our children right from wrong. Have we become so politically correct, that we are willing to put our children in jeopardy? I truly believe, somewhere in all of this is the answer to the original question, and many of the other answers, to the mind-boggling decisions being made by our leaders these days.

Now, are we so evolved that we can't find a little truth in all of this, and maybe a tiny bit of direction, and with a little luck, a couple of answers? Cause if you can, I believe the probability of discovering a few solutions is just around the corner. On that note, enjoy some more answers with a splash of direction, and hopefully a solution or two.

First, I want you to know, and truly believe, that knowledge combined with action will easily avoid, somewhere in the neighborhood of ninety percent (90%) of dangerous situations that your children may encounter. That's a fact! Now, because it is so important, I am going to remind you to report any detrimental, illegal, or what you may perceive to be illegal, child activity you encounter on the Internet. There is an International list of great contacts on the "Report Page" of the Pedowatch web site. Adult-child sexual interaction is illegal in the United States, as it is in most other countries, so keep a lookout, and report any findings. If you're not sure as to the legality of a discovery, report it and let the experts determine its legal status. In the United States, it is a serious felony to have sexual pictures of children in your possession, without just cause and the express permission of the Justice Department. Many other nations have similar laws. Again, keep a lookout.

Here is where you have to stay on top of things, and an example of how a little bit of knowledge will come in very handy. If you were to come across child pornography within the United States, but the pornography was introduced from a foreign country, what do you do? Possibly while traveling you discover material you consider detrimental to children, and you want to report it, what do you do? If you decide to report it while still in the country you are visiting, report it to United States officials at the US Embassy there, but don't expect much in the realm of a satisfying result. They will claim that it isn't within United States' jurisdiction, which prohibits them from doing anything about it. The reality of the matter is that they do have the right to investigate, to determine if the material you discovered is entering the United States, which would give them jurisdiction. Within the confines of the United States, the officials may claim that the perpetrators are outside of the United States, consequently out of United States' jurisdiction. In addition, it is possible that the United States officials will try to set aside any evidence you may have turned over to them, or even the evidence presented by investigating law enforcement agencies. What they should do is begin coordinating with the authorities in the country, from which the pornography is being generated, instituting an investigation, hopefully followed by arrests. The fact that fiscal pornographic materials are crossing our borders, and the international nature of the Internet, requires international law enforcement cooperation. It may be left up to you, and any politician you can enlist to aid you in the pursuit of the perpetrators.

Media coverage may be the best way to deal with an international situation. The media has the ability to provide specifics, focusing public attention on any problem, which in turn, generally brings about positive action from our government. Sad isn't it? The most difficult part of media involvement is persuading them to address the situation, in a non-sensationalistic manner. Each and every one of us should immediately begin a media campaign, alerting all of them: NBC, ABC, CBS, FOX, etc. and the newspapers, to the seriousness of the problem. Remind them that they have, and are the power to save children. Simply through reporting the truth, the media could single-handedly, and easily, win this war.

APPENDIX A

Immediate and future goals

START TODAY:

1) Educating your children, regarding their own safety, including what they can do to keep themselves safe.

2) Educating friends that are parents, regarding the dangers facing their children today.

3) Educating friends that are parents, regarding instructing their children how to be, and stay safe.

4) Determine the availability, and useful content, of information provided by law enforcement, regarding convicted sex offenders and pedophiliacs, residing in your community. If your local law enforcement agency is altering, editing or refusing to supply convicted sexual offender information, take the necessary steps to force that agency to comply with Federal law.

5) Begin locating sex offenders and pedophiliacs, residing in your community.

6) Inform your community of any sex offenders residing there, especially those living in the same neighborhood.

7) Investigate anyone having charge of your children, including teachers, school officials and associated employees, such as, school bus drivers and crossing guards.

8) Thoroughly investigate the child daycare center you use, or are considering using, and its staff, including any volunteers.

9) Investigate all avenues of travel your children use, whether they are to school, or social events.

10) Investigate any individuals residing and/or visiting the residence where your children meet with their friends, to play and for sleep over.

11) Investigate parks, playgrounds and public swimming pools that your children may frequent.

12) Investigate which states ignore, or do not require, convicted sex offenders to register and initiate a campaign of letters to the politicians

of those states, demanding a registration program. Let them know that it is of no consequence that you live in another state. Remind him or her that their sexual offenders can become your sexual offenders.

13) Encourage politicians, via letters, to step up Federal resources for national and international crimes, involving child slavery, trafficking, child pornography, and any other form of crime involving the abuse of children.

[Make them aware of the fact that children are being kidnapped from the United States, and sold into sexual slavery in foreign countries.]

14) Encourage our government to assist all child find organizations, in the linking of their computers, allowing them to share in the trading of accurate information, as quickly as the pedophiles do. Some good work has been accomplished in this area, but much more is needed.

15) Contact your Congressman and representatives, expressing your wishes that regulation be passed, which will bring child prostitution and child pornography within the scope (under the umbrella) of the currently existing child labor laws. The child labor laws already protect children from being forced to work under unsafe conditions, so it makes perfect sense to encompass child pornography and child prostitution. This will allow federal authorities immediate access to child exploitation industries, and organizations. The passage of revised child labor laws will mean that our federal government agencies will no longer be forced to wait for child pornographers to cross state lines, before they can act.

16) Write your politicians, requesting increased financial support and specialized training for law enforcement agencies. Aside from existing police training, there is a need for specific training in the areas of child molestation, child pornography, and the sexual behavior of sex offenders and pedophiliacs in general.

17) Write your politicians, requesting specialized training for prosecutors, which will aid those responsible for convicting sex offenders in understanding that pedophiliacs only show remorse at the time of their arrest, just before sentencing, and when attempting to obtain parole.

18) Write your politicians and representatives, demanding that when organized child slavery and child sex abuse rings are apprehended, they be prosecuted under the racketeer influenced and corrupt

organizations law "RICO." Prosecuting under this law will allow authorities to pursue perpetrators not actually caught in the physical commission of the crime, who are still a participant in the crime. This will allow law enforcement to arrest and prosecute the ringleaders of these crimes against our children and humanity.

19) Contact by mail, the politicians, representatives, Attorney General and the district attorney in your area, demanding the end to any, and all plea-bargaining, in all cases involving child sexual assault and/or child abuse, of any nature. [No more deals.]

20) Demand that anyone found guilty of organizing child slavery or child sex rings, including the trafficking of child pornography, by use of telephone, computer, mail, or any other mode of delivery system, and receive a sentence of no less than life imprisonment, without possibility of parole.

21) Write letters to the appropriate officials, demanding that anyone convicted of child molestation, wherein the act did not cause further injury to the child, other than the injury of common rape, be sentenced to life imprisonment

22) Contact the same officials, demanding that anyone convicted of child molestation for the second time (offence), wherein the act did not cause further injury to the child, other than the injury of common rape, be sentenced to a minimum imprisonment for life, without the possibility of parole.

23) Write a similar letter to the same officials, again demanding that anyone convicted of a child molestation wherein, during or after the assault, the child suffered life-threatening or disfiguring injuries, other than and beyond the injury of common rape, and wherein the child survives, be sentenced to a minimum of life imprisonment, without possibility of parole.

24) Write politicians, representatives and appropriate government officials, demanding that anyone convicted of child molestation, resulting in the death of a child, be summarily put to death. [Summarily: done without delay or formality: quickly executed.]

*Not decades, or longer, after their horrifying crime!

Let your representatives know that you have no objections, if those desiring to attempt medical and psychological treatment of convicted sex offenders and pedophiliacs do so. However, also let them know, that you wish such treatment to be practiced, while the twisted individuals are still incarcerated. It is very important that politicians know that you do not want anyone who has been convicted of sexual assault on a child, or a woman, released, until the sex offender is, if possible, pronounced cured.

It is also imperative to let your representatives know that you want anyone, whether it be medical doctors or parole board officials responsible for an individual's release, held accountable in civil court, if the released or paroled sex offender attacks again. It is my opinion, that the individuals in the position of power, who approve the releases of sexual offenders, are committing a crime themselves, by the mere fact that they do not have a real understanding of their charges. Many medically credentialed experts, who assist parole board officials with their decisions, hold this opinion.

What to do if you have been falsely accused of sexual child molestation

If you have been falsely accused of child sexual molestation, including incest, get an attorney. Get a damned good attorney. Fast!
The exclusion of this topic from this book would be, in my opinion, an act of grave injustice, because I can name no other false accusation as vile.

Because of the work I do, fathers wrapped up in the throws of a divorce, contact me from time to time, claiming that they have been falsely accused of sexually molesting their child. This happens all too frequently these days, especially during custody battles. Although I am not an expert in these areas, I do know a few things. To start with, I know that you are in serious trouble! Never take an accusation of child molestation lightly, as many men, and fathers do. You need an attorney, a really good attorney, one that specializes in such cases, and one that has experience and knows how to defuse false accusations of this type, quickly. You must be prepared to sell possessions, and borrow from family and friends, if necessary. As I discussed with you earlier in the book, attorneys, like most professionals, specialize, and you really do need a specialist. The average civil attorney who specializes in divorce is not a criminal defense attorney, and you have been accused of a serious criminal act. Your average divorce attorney has probably never had to deal with the tenacity of your average social worker. The traditional civil divorce attorney, generally has no knowledge (savvy) of the criminal or juvenile system, and may fail to recognize the risk you face.

Be prepared to take a polygraph examination, by an independent examiner, and possibly by, law enforcement. If the examination is conducted by law enforcement, make sure your attorney is present, and has pre-read any questions you are to respond to during the examination. It is important for you to know that law enforcement often entertains a thought process that goes something like this: if you fail to pass their polygraph examination they say, "I knew you were guilty, and this proves it." However, when you pass their polygraph examination, often they say, "This means nothing, I've never had faith In polygraph machines." This is one reason why you do not submit to a polygraph examination, without your attorney present. It is also important to know that polygraph is not the only method available, to help clear your name. If the charges are not pursued by law enforcement, or are eventually dropped, make sure your attorney has the charge expunged from law enforcement records. If you are truly innocent, my heart goes out to you, and good luck. If you are guilty, well...burn In hell.

With the combined information provided in "Answers and Solutions" and "Immediate and Future Goals", not to mention all of the other dynamite stuff in the rest of this book, you should have no doubts or hesitation, regarding an out-and-out confrontation with anyone, holding any position, who is not doing the right thing. If you feel the way my wife, Christine, and I feel, please write your senators, congressman, representatives, and all pertinent officials, demanding changes.

If you truly feel as I do, come stand beside me, against any and all refusing complete protection for children, and those intending to harm our children, for each is the enemy, steeped in betrayal, residing on opposite sides of the same sin.

Remember that evil flourishes when good men do nothing.

Appendix B

Emergency assistance:

[Telephone numbers and Internet addresses may change, or no longer
exist in time, through no fault of my own.]
How's that for a disclaimer?

National Center for missing and Exploited Children
(800) 843-5678 or 24 hour hot line (800) THE-LOST

State Department's Citizens Emergency Center
(202) 647-5225

Child Molester Identification Line
(900) 463-0400

A.L.I.E. Foundation   (Bloodhounds)
http://www.alie.com

Ortho ID   (Dental Code)
http://www.orthoid.com/

Sex Offenders Net   (Information)
http://www.sexoffenders.net/sgv.html
Missing Kids International, Inc.
Missing Kids International, Inc.
National Missing Children's Locate Center

National Missing Children's Locate Center

Operation Lookout
http://www.premier1.net~lookout

Lycos Missing Children Search
http://www.lycos.com/missingkids

Lost Child
http://www.lostchild.net

LA Missing Children
LA Missing Children
Child Connection. Inc.
http://www.petsforum.com/childconnection

Polly Klaas Foundation
www.klaaskids.org/

Child Alert
http://www.childalert.com

Child Rescue
www.childrescue.org.uk/

Missing Children Minnesota
Missing Children Minnesota
Sass Kids Menu
http://www.sass.ca/kmenu.htm

Middle Tennessee Missing Children's foundation
http://www.compu.net/mtmcf

Kentucky Missing and Exploited Children's Unit
Kentucky Missing and Exploited Children's Unit
U.S. Senators
http://www.senate.gov/senator/

U.S. Representatives
http://www.house.gov/writerep/

* Cybersitter
(800) 388-2761
* CyberSnoop
(800) 732-7596
* Some helpful net blocks   (Deterrents only)

Watch for my series of books "PROOF OF LIFE" which will be actual accounts of the recoveries of children held in sexual slavery and adults held for ransom.

INDEX

http://www.tyritterprotection.com
http://www.projectchildsave.org

Photography by Robert Daggs
http://www.impressivephotos.net

Notes: